PREDATOR CALLING

with Gerry Blair

2nd Edition

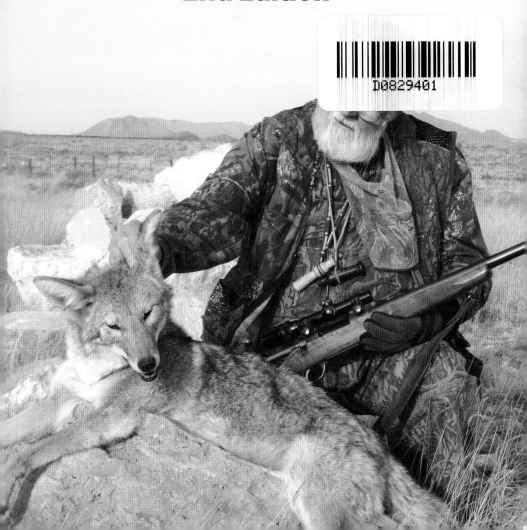

©2007 Gerry Blair

Published by

krause publications

An Imprint of F+W Publications

700 East State Street • Iola, WI 54990-0001
715-445-2214 • 888-457-2873
www.krausebooks.com

Our toll-free number to place an order or obtain
a free catalog is (800) 258-0929.

Library of Congress Control Number: 2006933683

ISBN-13: 978-0-89689-476-1
ISBN-10: 0-89689-476-2

Designed by Donna Mummery
Edited by Derrek Sigler

Printed in China

Dedication

I mainly dedicate to those who have read my writing for the past half a hundred years. Some of you have hunted with me literally and others who have hunted symbolically by reading my writing, all dozen or so of you. You are appreciated.

I also dedicate to the gang I call the Motley Crew, a cadre composed of hard hunters and others of the camo persuasion. I speak (actually write) of Danny Batastini, Mike Blair, Major Boddicker, Fred Cronk, Rich Higgins, Tyler Higgins, Gordy Krahn, Ralph and Lauren Lermeyer, Derrek Sigler, Jay Nistetter and Bill Rice. Each and all are good-uns. I be proud to call all friend.

I send a special thank you to Mark Vincent Seby, MD, who brought me back from beyond at a time when all others were convinced further effort was futile. Dr Mark was assisted by two fine young men who happen to be my sons. Gerry Jr and Michael. Thanks guys, I owe you big.

Finally, I dedicate to my wife Beverly Josephine "B.jo" Blair, a woman who loves and is loved (even though she is smarter than me). Thanks Sweetie for causing my life to be better.

Table of Contents

chapter 1

Biological Justification for Calling

I shrugged my big body into the stingy shade of a scrawny string bark juniper and pulled on the camo-colored facemask. Through the netting and through sun-squinted eyes, I looked out on the massive mesa the Apaches call Big Prairie; a crowded and over-munched community-summer-graze filled with barely alive Herefords. The terminally ill cattle, and the freshly dead, acted as a magnet to draw in gangs of hungry coyote. I was there at the invitation of the San Carlos Apaches. I was there to scream to the carrion-eaters and to the coyotes that supplemented their beef diet with tidbits from the struggling pronghorn herd that shared the graze and the browse.

Four minutes into the screaming, a flash of fur loped from straight downwind. Thirty pounds of hungry surrounded by meat, muscle, and hair. When the yodeler passed behind a juniper, I shouldered the Sako, thumbed forward the tang safety, and prepared to do business. I figured a 52-grain Sierra traveling at a muzzle velocity of more than 3,600 fps would cause the broad-headed dog to lose interest in both beef and antelope.

Mid-March is a poor time to scream for fur. At least it is for me. The coyote had shaken the sugar tree and about every qualified bitch had been impregnated. Dog and bitch, bonded for the season and maybe bonded for life, were involved in the serious business of selecting primary and secondary den sites. Neither will show a lot of interest in the scream. The warming weather, the dogging, and photosynthetic stimulation has caused the fur to singe, curl and shag. No market for that kind of pelt. Even so, I was calling the San Carlos lands during mid-March, exactly the right time to thin the coyote population so that the antelope fawns due to hit the ground within a month would have an increased chance to survive.

Coyote can be a dreadful pronghorn predator. In certain kinds of country, wide open prairie grasslands containing little cover and too many coyote can cause herd survival to be threatened. The Big Prairie was one such habitat. Anderson Mesa, starting slightly south of Flagstaff, Arizona, is another.

Dr. Don Neff, a biologist for the Arizona Game & Fish Department for many years, completed a five-year study documenting coyote/pronghorn interaction in the Anderson Mesa study area; a handsome topography of grassland, ponderosa pine, juniper, and high country lakes. Five hundred square miles of antelope country. Five hundred square miles of Rocky Mountain elk and mule deer country. Five hundred square miles of coyote country.

Anderson Mesa had once housed antelope herds that numbered about eight thousand. Peak numbers, as might be expected, developed during the days when the compound poison numbered 10-80 (deadly on all dogs) was widely used. The banning of that predator control tool caused coyote numbers to become significant. Good times for the coyote caused bad times for the pronghorns. The Mesa pronghorn herd was down to a few hundred when Neff started his study. Evidence suggested the coyote to be the chief culprit.

Spotting scope observation during those crepuscular periods when the coyote was most active confirmed the suspicion. Typically, teams or gangs of coyote would patrol the mesa, searching out doe antelope. One or more of the hunting team would tease the doe into a chase. The remaining coyote would search industriously until the fawn (or fawns) was located. A secret signal would cause the teasers to leave the doe to return and share the meal. The coyote were so efficient at fawn killing nearly no pronghorn fawn survived to recruit into the adult population. Knowing that adult pronghorn does normally deliver twin fawns, biologists see a potential recruitment of 200 percent. Recruitment within the Anderson Mesa herd hovered at a dismal 10 percent. Coyote control measures such as trapping, calling, and aerial gunning, each accomplished during the peak fawning period, caused coyote numbers to diminish. As might be expected, fawn survival increased.

The Neff study ("Effect of Predation by Coyotes on Antelope Fawn Survival on Anderson Mesa," Arizona Game & Fish Special Report #8, November, 1979) established the coyote as a very efficient pronghorn predator. Some biologists believe this wild dog to be an equally efficient predator of young mule deer, young whitetail (and mature deer of both species when snow cover slows the deer to make them vulnerable), and of about every kind and age group of domestic stock. Every coyote called and killed, offers the opportunity of increased life span to about everything that creeps or crawls the land.

Norm Woolsey of the Arizona Game & Fish department paints and collars a coyote trapped during the historic Anderson Mesa Study.

TOP: *An antelope fawn looks worried as he scans the mesa for coyote and other predators. The Anderson Mesa Study suggested that nine of ten fawns born on The Mesa were killed by coyote.*

BOTTOM: *Woolsey watched as a pair of coyote captured and killed this young fawn. Note trauma to head and shoulders. (Photo by Don Neff).*

The coyote is an equal opportunity killer. Coyote depredation on game animals and domestic stock has been well documented. Less well documented, less publicized, is the effect the other major land predators have on prey species. The second largest North American cat (the jaguar takes top honors) is an example.

Felis concolor, also called cougar, mountain lion and gato del monte (cat of the mountain), is mainly a deer killer. Investigate the essentially Western habitat of this big-bodied feline (up to 200 pounds-plus within a part of the range) and you might find exploding deer populations. Sometimes. At other times you might find a few wide-ranging lions patrolling a vast area nearly devoid of deer. Too many lions, particularly within Southwestern areas where deer are water dependent, can cause the deer population to get dead.

Harley Shaw, a lion biologist for the Arizona Game & Fish Department, conducted a radio telemetry study within a central Arizona ranch, Spider-Cross U, and showed that the mountain lion became a very efficient livestock predator when deer numbers diminished. The bottom line? An adult lion

The Apache coyote prospered as they killed and consumed starving cattle.

will make a major kill (deer, elk or cow) about every eight days, nearly one a week. Shaw estimated a lion population of 2,000 adults at that time. You do not have to be a statistician to realize that lion kill a hell of a lot of deer, maybe more. Those who wish to learn more about lion/deer and lion/livestock interaction will find Shaw's "A Mountain Lion Field Guide, Special Report # 9, Arizona Game & Fish Department" to be a good read.

Too deep a predator density can also impact the health and welfare of humans. Many of the states to the west of the big river suffer through periodic flare-ups of the dreaded disease, rabies. Coyote are most often involved. Gray fox and bobcat are also, to a lesser degree. Documented lion and coyote attacks on humans have increased considerably in recent years.

> ***ITEM***: A woman jogger near Cool, California, was chased, killed, partially consumed and covered. An adult mountain lion killed nearby had parts of the woman within its stomach. Locals blame an animal activist-inspired initiative banning mountain lion hunting as the cause.

> ***ITEM***: A two-year-old toddler was taken from his front yard within a California suburb by a coyote and was killed. The mother and neighbors rescued the body before it could be consumed.

ITEM: A teenage girl, waiting for the school bus in a Tucson, Arizona, neighborhood, was attacked and bitten by a rabid coyote. The painful series of anti-rabies injections saved her life.

ITEM: A rabid coyote staggered onto a South Tucson schoolyard and attempted an attack on several children. Custodians killed the animal.

ITEM: A mountain lion attacked an eight-year-old on vacation within the Kohls Ranch area of central Arizona. The father killed the animal using a .22 rifle.

There is more. Too much to cite. Suffice it to say this: In spite of what some animal-lovers say, all critters are not our friends.

And too many predators can cause problems for the predators. A fierce competition for food is the obvious result. The least skilled are undernourished and sometimes starve. Coyote and fox overpopulation can encourage Sarcoptic mange; a disease that causes the hair to fall out, leaving a skin that is scabrous. In extreme cases infection and exposure can cause death. Sarcoptic mange can be transmitted to domestic dogs.

Other epizootic diseases are common to many of the predators. Most within the West carry fleas that can transmit the dreaded bubonic plague to humans. The screaming that diminishes predator populations, the way I see it, minimize problems to humans, to game animals, to domestics, and to the predators themselves.

A high coyote density can encourage epizootics that can cause conditions such as the warty mouth displayed by this former resident of Aguila (eagle) Arizona.

10

chapter 2

Why They Come

The animals I have met during a long lifetime of calling have responded to the screams in about every way possible. I have had eager coyote pups, out on their own for the first time, naive and desperate to get at the rabbit, come at the gallop and nearly crawl into my lap. Other coyote, jaded veterans of February, that are paranoid to the tenth power, come at the sneak-employing the stop and reconnoiter-employing the downwind circle-but still they come.

My occasional calling companion Larry O. Gates and I have had mountain lions come at the sneak and bobcats come at the charge. A cat or two, sad to say, have showed at the back door to climb our shoulders for a short but exciting ride. Animal response, the way I see it, is governed by that animal's nature, prior experience with distress calling, and degree of hunger.

The major reason predators respond to a scream is food-related. Many of the prey animals articulate their terror as they get the close-up look at a set of coyote tonsils, or the equally dreaded beak and talon belonging to an owl, hawk or eagle. Flying predators like hawks, falcons, owls, and eagles, hunt and kill in a similar manner. The prey is located from aloft or from a perch that might be a limb or a lofty cliff top. The critter swoops, stoops or soars to the target, taking hold with razor-sharp talons. Those talons, much of the time, encircle the rabbit's rib cage. Death is by suffocation. The hunter holds tight and the rabbit screams, losing a bit of air. The talons tighten a bit more to further compress the lungs. Scream. Tighten. The process might take a minute or more, substantially longer if the hold is not precise. During all of that time, as air allows, the rabbit or other prey animal screams piteously. Other predators within hearing distance hustle in to have a look, hoping to steal the meal. A hungry coyote, a hungry fox or bobcat has no conscience. Each is likely to kick a red-tailed hawk's butt bad and take away his lunch of succulent cottontail. A hawk that objects too much is likely to join the cottontail within the belly of the beast.

A part of the predator response, I am convinced, has to do with territoriality. About all predators stake out a hunting territory and vigorously defend it from poachers. A boss coyote that has a full belly, as an example, might come running if he believes a neighbor has snuck in to dip a finger in the sugar bowl.

Some come creeping. About all bobcat and some smart coyote come to the call cautiously, hoping to have a meal and not be a meal.

Some critters, mostly of the grocery type, respond to the distress scream because their nature forces a protective response. Deer, antelope, and others of the ungulate persuasion will sometimes come at a charge, fearing a predator has cornered junior and is preparing to munch his tender body. As an example, Larry and I were screaming to a mesquite-choked dry wash during one winter hunt and hooked a hungry coyote. The critter came at the lope, following a serpentine course through the greasewood. When the coyote was decently close, Larry O. pulled the trigger on the Knight Rifle muzzleloader. The critter turned to a rug about twenty-five feet out. Larry continued to scream, hoping to interest a second customer. A few minutes later a fearful crashing of brush announced the arrival of customer number two, an outraged doe mule deer. The doe was only half mad until she saw the coyote carcass. She immediately upgraded to mad-and-a-half. Each and every hair on that outraged doe stood at attention. The ears turned back to attack mode. She suddenly reared to bring the front feet down hard near the coyote's head. Then she backed off to get a run and did it all again. Larry and I controlled our laughter as long as humanly possible and then cut it loose. The doe retreated reluctantly.

The protective nature of the doe deer can cause the distress scream to be a very effective way to hunt mule deer (the common deer around my part of the West). I have had my best luck calling to rutting bucks. Does with the bucks are most likely to respond. The buck tags along to keep track of his harem. The

Child Molester Buck was one such. Read more on this degenerate in Chapter 31, "The Uncalled and the Unexpected."

The little "pig" Southwesterners call the javelina (collared peccary) is a sucker for about any well-blown distress scream. I have had herds (locally called sounders) of the little critters come at the charge, tusks clacking and mouths sending out a fearful grunting. On one memorable occasion, while taping footage for *The Masters' Secrets to Predator Calling*, hoping to prove that staying still was most important when critter calling, I dressed my ample frame in a Santa Claus suit, including red stocking cap with the cute white ball atop, and set out to call critters. A sounder of javelina came at the gallop, slid to a stop twenty feet out looking in amazement at the strangest sight they had seen, and then made a panic run for the border. I laid into the screaming again and they came back, this time to within ten feet of Ole Santa. I am not making this up. Every bit of the action was captured on tape and is included in the video.

The strangest respondent I have had, and the most difficult to understand, is a jackrabbit coming to a jackrabbit distress scream. Common sense suggests a hare hearing the death screams of a brother hare singing his death song would run for home and mother. Not always true. During high hare cycles I have had as many as a half dozen of the long ears hanging around during a single screaming. Why are they there? Don't know. Maybe they're protective. Maybe they come because they know another hare is getting his hairy butt kicked and they want to see it happen.

Critters are a bit like humans in some respects. All do not own the same degree of intelligence. The young coyote of the year is a prime example. Those I have met have been so dumb their butt hurts. One such worked hard to climb

Large predatory birds such as this ferruginous hawk from northern Arizona kill by a slow suffocation that encourages a desperate screaming.

Many prey animals like this Wisconsin whitetail buck might come to the call because of curiosity or as an effort to protect.

atop an old time Arizona caller named Sam Dudley. Sam was hunkered down in a small depression east of Phoenix on one winter hunt when a young-of-the-year came at a charge. Sam and the critter wrestled out of the depression and out of the portable blind Sam carried. Sam flailed away with the barrel of his twelve gauge and managed to inflict a painful wound about mid-barrel. The barrel turned sort of bow shaped. Realizing it was time for the hard sell, Sam turned the ugly end of the scattergun to the coyote and lit the fire. The gun? Sam used it for all of his life, calling it "Singing Sally" (said it sung the critters to sleep) holding Kentucky windage to compensate for the bow.

Older coyote sometimes come in high gear also, particularly early in the calling year. Even though they may have been called the previous season, the passing of time has dulled their recollection of the trickery. As an example, I was calling the slope of an antique juniper push one winter when I sighted two hard-charging bundles of fur coming from far, far away. The critters stayed neck to neck for much of the race, each imagining he or she would be the first to reach the rabbit. Seventy seconds after the sighting, the winner ran up the barrel of the full-choked twelve gauge. The auto loader took the trailer as she stood dumbfounded, wondering why hubby was kicking in the dirt.

Some animals come because they hunger. Some come because it is their nature to do so. Another might come because of curiosity or to protect another animal. No matter what the motivation, some do come, maybe at the run and maybe at the sneak. The excitement provided by that response can be damn fine, a substance that keeps the screamer working through good times and bad.

Even though female herbivores most often respond to a distress scream the ladies can drag along bulls and bucks during rutting season.

chapter 3

Why They Do Not Come

As noted in the previous chapter, animal response can be affected by a bunch of variables. Like response, non-response can be complicated phenomena. Only the critter knows the exact cause, and the critters I have met have refused to talk on that subject. The non-communication may have been because many of the predators were graveyard dead at the time. Even so, knowing the general nature of the critters-and knowing a bit about their lifestyle-I feel qualified to speculate on non-response.

The obvious reason an animal does not show is simple: There is not an animal within scream range. A hunter can pick the best setup, wear the most effective camouflage and blow exquisitely painful screams until he or she gets trombone lip. If no coyote, bobcat, fox, cougar, or lion is within hearing, common sense says none will show. The no-show because of no-hear phenomena is a lot more common in the Midwest and the East than within the West. The reason? Predator density. Much of the West is critter crowded.

Members of the cat family often creep in and creep out without being noticed.

Even when the critter hears the screams, that critter may not have the decency to acknowledge. Non-response may be due to a number of factors or due to a combination of factors. The non-response of a critter that hears the advertisement is most often because the critter is timid (scared scat-less). That fear can come from a lack of dominance within a species (a little guy worries that a big guy might be around to kick his butt), or might come from a lack of territorial access. A coyote from a neighboring territory, for example, might hear the advertisement and might love to come for a bite of hot rabbit. Trouble is, Mean Joe Green owns the joint and turns into an animal when company shows.

Fear can also come because of cross-species dominance. A screamer who imitates the distress cry of a gray fox, as an example, is not likely to call many reds. In areas where grays and reds share a range, the gray is almost always the dominant fox. The same can be said about the gray and the coyote. Grays that do not honor the coyote at every opportunity might as well forget about Social Security and Medicare. Here in the Southwest where the kit fox is the littlest kid on the block, these smallest of the foxes stay deep within burrows during the day and come out at night with extreme trepidation. Nearly every predator, at one time or another, must ask itself the hard question. "Am I going to have dinner or am I going to be dinner?"

Non-response, when you get right down to the bottom line, might be because of something as complicated as the moon phase, or because of the weather. Hell, maybe they just have a headache.

Having said all of that, it should also be stated that the main reason for a lack of interest has nothing to do with any of the above. The most common cause of lack of interest is paranoia caused by a recent and traumatic encounter with hunter screams, moans, groans, and whining.

Gray fox climb to find groceries and to escape danger, accepting a thorn studded saguaro if nothing else is available.

The trauma of those encounters too often ends with a bang, and ends as a 52-grain chunk of copper-coated lead buzzes by at supersonic speed, maybe throwing rocks and dirt dangerously close. Common sense, under such provocation, suggests a desperate run for home and Mother.

My experience causes me to think the coyote is the kind of critter most affected by these close encounters of the .22-250 kind. The foxes, just another dog, rank a close second. Running last, barely in the race, are the cats. Bobcat and the lions I have met have shown a high tolerance for deception, some being so dumb their butt aches. The cat I call the Dumbo of Kinnikinick Canyon illustrates the point.

K. Canyon is a mean gash of a gully that interrupts the somewhat level aspect

Cats that come almost always stick around until they eat the rabbit, or the bullet.

of the wonderfully extensive Anderson Mesa, a vast tract of high country meadowland graced with shallow lakes and fingers of stringbark and alligator juniper. And with somewhat shallow canyons, including Kinnikinick, each decorated with the junipers and with turbinella and Gambels Oak and other low story stuff. Bear country. Lion country. Bobcat and fox country. Hell, even 'coons and cacomistles.

When an out-of-state reader visited, hoping for the opportunity to earball and eyeball the Blair screaming technique, K. Canyon came to mind almost immediately. We planned the drive so that we would be set up and screaming at precisely first light, a dandy time to scream to cats and nearly as good to scream in fox and coyote. Stubby and I settled onto a canyon lip so that we had a decent view of the brush-choked canyon below. I was the screamer and gunner. Stubby was along to listen and to look.

False dawn surrendered to the real thing as I sent out the opening chorus of the tune I call the "Dying Rabbit Blues." Four minutes into the screaming, Stubby shouted a one-word whisper across the fifteen feet that separated us. "CAT." Thinking lion, I looked until my eyeballs ached. Nothing. Stub's angle of vision permitted the sighting. Mine did not. I scooched my butt hard left, and then leaned harder left. Ahhhh. A big-eared bobcat, the pretty kind with the tufted ears and hairy jowls, sat calmly a hundred yards out. I shouldered the Sako and placed the small x of the duplex six below those hairy jowls and prepared to stroke. Even though I was off balance and my position violated every accuracy rule, I knew I could not miss. Through the magic of the magnification the bobcat looked to be as big as a VW Bug. I did stroke and I did miss. The cat continued to set and continued to be calm. I did what too many hunters do under similar situations. I bolted in a loaded round and tried a second off-balance shot. Another miss, although the cat did jerk his head as if to bite at the buzzing bee that sped close. Then the cat renewed his solemn contemplation. Somewhat rattled because of the double miss and because it was witnessed, knowing now the cat would stay until it obtained a taste of the rabbit, I took a second or so to settle my nerves, squared my body to the target, and sent a 3,650 fps chunk of lead squarely into the kitty's necessaries. Walking up, I couldn't help but notice the cat continued to look calm. Tom. Twenty-two pounds. Mature and old enough to know better.

A coyote or fox that answers the call and escapes with his or her life (I am an equal opportunity killer) is naturally disappointed. That critter is also a lot smarter. Even though that one bad experience does not cause him or her to stop being an opportunistic predator, a further advance to a screaming will be done with considerably more caution. Such a critter may come at the sneak, making frequent stops to reconnoiter the country ahead. Those that are upwind will almost surely circle downwind of the screams to let their nose verify what their nature suspects. One sniff of Redman or underarm odor and it is good-bye critter. Supply another lesson or two, and let the pupil escape, and you are almost sure to be dealing with a Ph.D. predator. Most, even though they are on death's door because of starvation, will not investigate even the real thing. The calling and recalling of a coyote is well illustrated by citing the circumstances of the Wildcat Canyon Bitch.

I was on a midwinter hunt within the pushdowns of the Arizona high country the first time I had a look at the bitch. I used the TallyHo tube to call her dog (mate) and used the Sako Forester in .22-250 to make the shot. Continuing to call, as I often do after the shot, I sighted the widow as she wandered about within the juniper push. No chance for a shot. She howled a time or two, talking to the dog, and when he did not answer she skulked away.

This Yavapai County yodeler discovered that weeds were poor protection from a fast traveling .22–250 hollow-point.

I was in the same area a couple of weeks later and used the TallyHo to cause the bitch to come close, backdoor. She saw me before I saw her and made an enthusiastic run for the county line. How did I know it was the same coyote? Didn't, not for sure. Coyote in my part of the country do not wear nametags. The bitch was in the same area and was of the same color variation. I guessed it was her from that.

A week or two later, while on a hunt somewhat close, I visited the bitch one more time. I made the setup atop a pile of pushdowns and did my best to keep my head turning so as to cover every potential approach. Five minutes into the screaming I sighted the bitch making her sneak from two hundred yards out. She hung up at one hundred fifty yards. Her body language told me that was as far as she would advance. I squared, sighted, and stroked.

Calling a coyote once is somewhat frequently accomplished. Calling that same coyote twice within a semi-short time is less common. Calling that same coyote a third time, when the trauma of previous screams is fresh in the memory, is about like bowling a 300 game or golfing a hole in one. Difficult, but possible under precisely perfect circumstances.

I offer a final thought on non-response. A frequent question addressed to the "Question & Answer" column I once did for *Trapper & Predator Caller* magazine (Krause Publications, 700 East State Street, Iola, WI 54990-0001) has to do with critter sophistication. A common phrasing goes like this, "I call my Dad's 600-acre farm and know there are coyote there because I hear them howl. The farm has not been called, so I know the critters can't be that sophisticated. Why don't they respond?" I say this. "Even though your Dad's farm has not been called, it is unlikely the coyote spend all of their life there. Being roamers, it is likely they may have had a bad experience of the screaming kind on a farm many miles away." Generally, here in the West, if I achieve one response during five calls I consider things to be great. Zip codes having a lesser critter concentration will likely deliver even less.

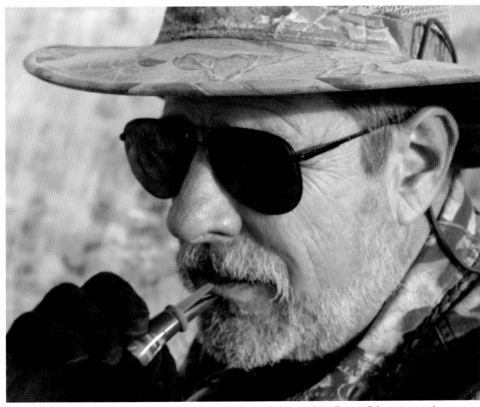

Even experienced callers can run into a 'yote that is wise beyond its years. It is all part of the game we play.

chapter 4

Tubes and Other Screamers

Predator calling has been a popular sport in the West since the early 1950s. A high predator density and vast tracts of public land caused Western hunters to take to the sport as ducks take to the water. Hunters located to the east of the big rivers were less fortunate as far as coyote numbers were considered. Many had ample populations of red and gray fox. Nearly all had more than enough raccoon. Even so, the sport of predator calling lagged. And then a funny thing happened. Big and hungry coyote from Canada started range expansion to the south. Brush wolves appeared within the East and the Midwest in increasing numbers. Yarded whitetail, unable to travel because of snow cover, offered a dandy meal. A big-footed coyote that walked deliberately could travel on top of the snow. The sharp hooves of the whitetail that attempted escape would break the crust to slow the flight. It doesn't take much of an imagination to realize the result.

Easterners, alarmed by the deer depredation, and recognizing the availability of a new kind of hunt, learned a truth long known to Western hunters. Screaming to coyote, and to other predators, can be a most exciting sport.

Many hunters new to the sport of predator calling agonize over call selection. They agonize for no good reason. I have screamed using nearly every call on the market, past and present, and have called critters with nearly all. Tube calls, in certain construction types, are remarkably similar. Battery-powered callers, in certain construction types, send out a comparable sound. I say, with little reservation, that about any mouth call and about any battery-powered caller will send out a screaming good enough to fetch a critter close.

It is also proper to say every screamer, tyro and veteran, will profit from a discussion of tube types and caller types. Later within this chapter I will deliver my opinion on the quality of scream needed to bring a predator close, using any kind of tube and any kind of circuitry.

A wood or plastic tube containing a generic metal reed is the most common of the screamers and is always the easiest to master. The interchangeable reeds stay hidden within the belly of the body. Blowing into the business end of the tube causes the stainless steel reed to vibrate. The scream is produced.

Varying the volume of air sent through the tube can change the sound of the scream. Cupping the hands over the end of the tube can do likewise. Change the cupping and the sound changes. A little, but not much. You want the truth? One mouth sounds a lot like all other mouths when it comes to the sound produced from the metal-reed tube. That device is basically a one-trick pony. It screams.

This lack of versatility can have a bad consequence within hard hunted areas. Critters who have heard the scream from a metal-reed tube a time

Cold weather coyote can seriously impact winter stressed deer and other edibles.

or two can develop a dreadful ennui. Because all mouths sound pretty much alike, critters within those hard hunted areas refuse to play the game.

Metal-reed tubes have other defects. The reeds, being metal, get mighty cold when outside air temperatures chill. Hot spittle (sometimes referred to as "slobbers" in other parts of this book) hit the chilled metal. Frozen slobbers, sad to say, will almost always cause the metal-reed tube to call in sick, and almost always at the most inopportune of times.

About every metal-reed tube on the market uses a generic leaf-type reed, obtained from a common source. Some stainless steel reeds are pre-tuned to send out a good simulation of the jackrabbit distress scream, hoarse and coarse. Growly. A good sound for coyote, mountain lion, and bear. Other metal-reed tubes send out a good simulation of the cottontail distress scream, a more high-toned scream and without a lot of the growl. I prefer the cottontail distress scream for some coyote and for all fox and bobcat. I have screamed using wood tubes and using hard plastic tubes. To my tin ear the resonance of the screaming is about even-Steven. Even so, my records indicate I skin more fur when I scream using the metal reed within the wood tube. Particular favorites are the Weems Wildcall (or a custom made reproduction) or a custom made reproduction of the Trophy Model Wood Circe. Those who suffer from the relatively rare condition called muchomonee might patronize a custom call maker like Jay Nistetter (Rhino Calls), Fred Cronk (Arizona Predator Calls) or any one of a double handful of others. Refer to the custom call makers list located at the end of this book. I have caused some of the no longer available calls to be replicated using desert ironwood or mesquite as a substitute for the original white birch of the Circe and the walnut of the Weems. The sound produced with either is damnfine.

The second kind of common call is a wood or plastic tube fitted with a thin shim of Mylar plastic. The plastic reed is almost always exposed, causing some to refer to this kind of call as an exposed-reed call, or more simply, the open-reed call.

The plastic-reed call is a bit more difficult to master than is the metal-reed call. Strong assets cause that difficulty to be inconsequential in the big picture. I am thinking an ordinarily competent set of tonsils, with proper practice and proper instruction, will be able to master most of the assets of the plastic-reed tube within an evening or two. Assets? The configuration of the open-reed call causes the Mylar plastic reed to be within the mouth, a place where the reed is protected from sub-zero temperature and the consequent freeze-up. The open-reed call is a dandy cold weather call.

Also, changing call position within the mouth will cause the tone of the screaming to vary, offering the asset of versatility. A good tonsil on the open-reed tube will be able to talk fluent jackrabbit, fluent cottontail, damn-fine yips and other pup distress whining, and even the deadly howl.

Even though these three calls carry the same sort of reed each will emit a slightly different tone, such mostly caused by wood density, metal used and by reed tuning.

Finally, no two mouths hold the Mylar reed precisely the same. Consequently, no two mouths send out precisely the same scream. Educated critters are less likely to ignore a call that sounds slightly different. Varying air pressure and cupping one or two hands at the tube end can cause sound variation, just as those manipulations do within the metal-reed tube.

All turkey hunters and some elk hunters will know a bit about the diaphragm mouth call. Few predator callers know anything at all about the diaphragm mouth call. I find that sad. Used properly,

Plastic reeded calls like the TallyHo and the Crit'RCall offer scream versatility and freeze protection.

this inexpensive and versatile call can increase the size and value of the fur collection. A talented mouth can cause the call to send out decent screams, whines, yips, and sometimes howls.

The diaphragm call is made as a thin sheet of latex is stretched over a horseshoe shaped aluminum frame, tautened and secured, and then covered with duct tape of varying colors. Some diaphragm turkey calls hold as many as three layers (a few even more) of the latex. Some contain cuts and notches to cause sound variety. My experience causes me to prefer the single reed and at times the uncut and un-notched double reed for screaming. Diaphragm calls of that character deliver the truest scream and are the easiest to learn.

Even though you may be told you must swallow a diaphragm of each color before finding proficiency, I do not believe such is true. I know of callers who have only swallowed half of the colors. Those that lived turned into decent screamers. Seriously, the diaphragm call is enclosed in the mouth so that the screamer can huff air across the reed(s). Place that sucker too far back on the roof of the mouth, hiccup, and you may have your diaphragm for lunch. The good news? Every diaphragm call I have seen contains zero calories, zero cholesterol, and zero fat.

The final category of mechanical screamers contains a group I call the close-in calls. These low volume models produce a scream or squeak predator ears can hear for a hundred yards or so. Some models have a metal reed placed within the mouth of a rubber bulb. Squeezing to expel air causes sound. Some hunters attach one of the bulbs to the fore part of the gunstock so that they might produce the squeak while holding the gun at the ready.

A second kind of close-in is the one I call the "hummer." Two flat strips of hard plastic hold a metal or rubber band reed within. Placing the call to the mouth, harmonica like, permits the articulation.

Using the natural voice is a final option for the predator hunter. Some who have the needed configuration of throat essentials, those who are willing to practice until they nearly cough themselves into a coma, can obtain a degree of screaming proficiency.

A less difficult articulation is the squeak I have come to call the "Kiss of Death." Lips suck at the hand to produce a high-pitched squeaking. More on this later.

I have not deliberately ignored the class of calls sometimes called electronic calls, but more properly called the battery-powered caller–those that play a cassette tape or play a sound chip. The very next chapter will tell all I know (maybe more) on this versatile screamer.

The diaphragm used to call turkey can work equally well as a coaxer predator call. (Mark Middleton Photo).

chapter 5

Tube Marketing — Cronk

My home state of Arizona holds a plethora of coyote. Literally tons of coyote. Even though I have hard hunted coyote for more than a half a hundred years and skinned more than a few, Arizona coyote continue to prosper. The high and low desert of this middling large southwestern state offers a smorgasbord of beans, fruit and critters, all such being on the coyote menu. The transition woodlands, such composed mainly of a variety of juniper species, pinion pine and Gambel's oak, offer up less than the desert but can be nearly as generous to the dedicated screamer. Even the vast forests of ponderosa pine and the high mountain meadows attract coyote. Considering all of this it is easy to understand why Arizona owns a prominent place within the sport.

Hunters who are long of tooth, as I am, might remember when Jack Cain and Lou Mossinger crafted the beginning of the Circe line of predator calls. Those early Circes' were turned from wood in a variety of configurations. My friend George Oakey of Flagstaff continues to call with a venerable Trophy Model wood Circe, such sounding as good today as it did fifty years ago.

That Arizona predator call making tradition is continued today by modern predator call makers. Jay Nistetter (Rhino Calls) of Glendale is one such craftsman, with each Rhino being custom crafted in a variety of exotic woods. Mark Zepp of Tucson (Zepp's Predator Calls) is another, such being mass produced in an interesting variety of configurations. Fred Cronk (Arizona Predator Calls) is a third. A recent interview with Fred produced a description of modern call making that might be helpful to those who hope to produce predator calls for their own use or as a marketable item. Fred graciously offered the following information about making and marketing a line of predator calls.

"Walt Holt and I began marketing our Arizona Predator Calls a few years back. We chose the name because of the history of predator calling within the state: the Circe line of predator calls, the great rivalry between Arizona and California predator callers and the Arizona State Calling Contests. And, of course, the fact that Gerry Blair lives within and hunts throughout Arizona. We seriously considered other names such as Predator Game Calls, Southwest Predator Calls and others. To us, Arizona Predator Calls seemed synonymous with that treasured tradition.

Around 2000 I bought out Walt Holts' interest in the business as his career in computers caused him to relocate. Walt now lives in Texas and we remain good friends.

As I recall, the original cost of set-up was between three and five thousand dollars. That cost included all of the equipment, as we started with nothing. We could have spent less and could have spent more but decided that this somewhat modest investment would get us moving.

Arizona Predator Calls are turned from doweling. We most often use walnut, cherry or birch. More exotic woods can be used for special orders. I have turned calls using cocobolo, mesquite and African bocati stock.

My method of turning the calls is somewhat out of the norm for wood turning. I use a metal carrier spindle lathe that is set up to turn the call body, drill the step chamber (using two different sized bits) and fine sand the call body. The reed chamber is drilled using a tapered bit which also creates a seating bench for the reed. The call then receives two coats of satin polyurethane inside and out. After drying the JC Products brass reed is inserted. I tune each reed by hand and by ear to insure my customers are receiving the best quality tones from each call. The label is attached and the call is packaged. The equipment I have can produce a completed call (excluding drying time) in about fifteen minutes or so.

The stepped chamber within the Arizona Predator Call gives the call a controlled air flow and reduces vibration. Experience tells me that a straight chambered call resonates and deters from the tonal quality. For the same reason I do not use expandable inserts to seat the reeds. The added metal insert vibrates against the metal reed giving the tone a tinny sound.

There is a multitude of call companies out there, ranging from large mass production manufacturers to the guy next door with a pencil wood lathe in his garage. They will all work.

My greatest satisfaction comes from correspondence. It makes my day when a hunter tells me they have had great success while using one of my Arizona Predator Calls. I make calls because I love calling, knowing that call making is not my main line of income and never will be.

My calling technique starts with the first two series at low volume, each series lasting about five seconds. The third series will be turned up a notch and last for about fifteen seconds. I will continue my call -pause routine for about fifteen minutes. I do not exceed medium volume at any time. Maximum volume, I think, is an error too many callers make. From hilltops, I have witnessed coyote charging to a mere whisper of a call from a mile away.

Calling cats and bear normally require more patience and stands. I usually stay on a cat or bear stand from 30 to 45 minutes, sometimes more. Even so, I stay ready throughout the call, knowing the customer can show at any time. To me, that is what makes predator calling so exciting.

The cats I have called might come to a jackrabbit distress sound but seem to prefer the more highly pitched cottontail or the fawn bleat".

Fred Cronk manages the gun department within the impressive new Cabela's store located in Glendale Arizona (9380 Glendale Avenue). I have found Fred to be very personable and very friendly. I suggest you stop to say hey if your travels take you that-a-way. Tell him Gerry Blair sent you.

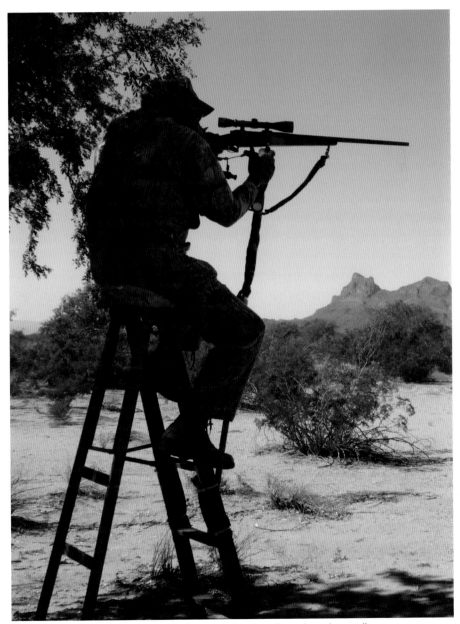

Fred has watched as a coyote travels from far away as he responds to a low volume call.

chapter 6

Plastic Reeded Calls — Boddicker

By Major Boddicker

When I was researching my book: Talking to Coyotes with the Song Dog, which I published in 1996, I spent considerable effort trying to determine the history of modern predator calling.

Records and reports of predator calling before 1950 are few and far between. They consist of scattered references to explorers describing American Indians calling wolves using their voices and blades of grass or sinew between their thumbs. European game keepers did lip squeaking, sucking on their palms, or using blades of grass to call lynx, red foxes and buck deer, recorded as early as the 1400s.

John Opdahl, an excellent varmint hunter from Norway sent me several old references to blading roebuck deer in Europe from the late 1800s. Blading produces a fawn bleat sound very similar to my Crit'RCall Pee-Wee. It is done by placing a leaf or grass blade between the thumbs and blowing on it.

J.R. Alcorn, A now deceased coyote control expert from Fallon, Nevada, published the first article which Alcorn or I could find, describing coyote calling in the

Open-reed style calls work in weather when other calls may not. Major Boddicker with a South Dakota coyote called during a -20 degree day and a 15 MPH wind.

This was Alcorn's first rabbit distress call acquired through a friend, Sidney O. Curtis who bought it from an Indian (probably a Piute) from Wells, Nevada. It is carved from a cottonwood branch with a condom rubber strip stretched across a central hole.

USA, in May 1946. The article appeared in the *Journal of Mammalogy*, a scientific journal that isn't read much by the average Joe Six Pack, and it did not get much recognition.

In the September-October 1950 issue of Outdoor West, Fishing and Hunting in the Sportsman's Paradise, pages 10-11 and 26-27, Alcorn published a similar article.

The 1946-50 period was the time of varmint calling genesis in the USA. Alcorn's first article described both coyote howling and communications and prey distress cries as effective methods of decoying coyotes up to the gun. The methods he describes are the same basic methods we use today. One of the common modern myths has been that coyote howling and communication were finally discovered when the video camera became available in the 1990s. Wrong! Ray Alcorn was starting his coyote calling stands with coyote howls in 1944-46.

Murry Burnham describes his father using lip squeaks to call predators as early as 1904. Ray Alcorn's father was also very effective at using his voice to make rabbit distress cries and coyote howls before 1910, according to Ray.

Ernest Thompson Seton, (original name Ernest Seton Thompson) an excellent descriptive outdoor writer from the 1880s to 1915 era, wrote a book, Rolf in the Woods. It was a fictional adventure about a young man and an Indian companion in northern New York during the Revolutionary War period. He described the Indian, Quonab, calling in and shooting a lynx using his voice, making a distressed rabbit cry.

When I worked in the upper Amazon basin rainforest in Peru in 1997-98. The Mechiguenga and Yaminahua Indians used their voices and lip squeaks for calling javelinas, monkeys and red brocket deer, almost daily. There is no reason to think pre-European era Native Americans did not do the same.

Alcorn credited an Indian from Wells, Nevada, as making the first predator call of which he was aware. The Indian call was a piece of cottonwood limb with the center pith drilled out and a strip of rubber condom stretched over the opening, fastened by a rubber band. By blowing air across the rubber strip holding the cottonwood piece perpendicular to the ground, a nice rabbit squall resulted.

According to A. S. Jackson in the June 1950 *American Rifleman*, a Mexican sheepherder introduced calling to west Texas in the 1930s. The call was assembled with a brass shim reed in a cow horn. Jackson thought that the technique was used rather widely in Texas in the late 1930s, but was a closely held secret.

The modified J-15 duck call was an early type of open-reed style predator call popular with students of F. Robert Henderson during the fifties and sixties.

The calling genie got out of the bottle in the 1950s. Burnham Brothers, Higley, Pied Piper, Circe, Herter's, Olt, Johnny Stewart, and others entered the predator calling market during that decade. All of these calls were closed-reed types except a Burnham close-range call that was a "blade" type call.

I do not know who modified the first Olt J-15 duck call into a predator call, but F. Robert Henderson from Kansas introduced it to me in 1964. Tal Lockwood modified the J-15 duck call and put it on the market as the Tally-Ho in the late 1960s. As far as I know, the Tally-Ho was the first nationally commercially available open-reed predator call.

I used the modified J-15 or D-2 Olt duck calls until 1966 when Dale Wade, a government trapper and student of mine, introduced me to the Boynton's Quanah Famous coyote, cat and fox call. Claude McCready hand-made this little gem at Quanah, Texas. Claude was not interested in making a lot of them, so his call was never widely distributed or recognized. I think he sold most of his calls to government trappers.

When Claude died in 1976 his widow gave me permission to develop the call as I liked. A friend, Otto Shults, and I patented a modified version of the Quanah Famous, and named it the Poudre Piper, from 1976 to 1977. In 1977, we renamed it the Crit'RCall.

Boynton's
Quanah Famous Coyote, Cat and Fox Call

The greatest sport in the hunting field for any one that likes to shoot a gun. Call your game up to any distance that you wish to try your marksmanship. It only takes a little practice to get this call to sound like a rabbit squealing then you have it.

Made by
CLAUDE McCREADY, 1008 W. 3rd Street, Quanah, Texas
79252

The Boynton's Famous coyote caller, popular in Texas during the late forties and fifties, was the fore-runner of the Crit'RCall Standard.

The Pee-Wee model of the Crit'RCall duplicated the notes and pitch of the Quanah Famous Call.

When the Poudre Piper, followed by the Crit'RCall Standard, hit the market the pattern of what a predator call should look and sound like was well established. It had to be a wood or plastic tube with a brass reed thingy buried somewhere deep inside it. You picked it up and blew in one end, which was usually marked so you couldn't miss on which end to use. They all sounded very similar, still do.

Shults and I were told by the Circe folks at the time that varmint hunters were not smart enough to learn to deal with our open-reed call. I refused to believe that.

Open-reed calls, like the Tally-Ho and Crit'RCall have the sound making reed exposed so the caller's lips, tongue, and air flow work directly on it. The hands can work over the barrel in addition to the reed action to modify the sound even more. The result of lip, tongue, throat, air flow and hand action on the call results in an unlimited variety of sounds, from ultra sounds to subsonic frequencies, volume from barely audible squeaks to ear-shattering squalls, all at the caller's instant use, whenever and however he likes it.

Sure, it takes some practice to learn open-reed calls, but once you get the music and technique you never want anything else. Even the most dyed-in-the wool electronics and gadget guys usually have a Crit'RCall on a lanyard around their necks. Why? Because they are totally reliable and of superior quality, if properly used. Also, open reed calls require a lot less exposure and effort to place and use.

From the late 1960s to about 1992, the only open reed calls on the market were the TallyHo and Crit'RCalls. For thirty plus years Gerry Blair, Bob Henderson, Tal Lockwood, Walt Earl, Tom Stevenson and I spoke to the varmint hunting and trapping masses extolling the virtues of open-reed calling to dull stares and disbelievers. A brilliant few became believers and users and won national varmint hunting contests with them.

Space between
reed tip and end
of reed

Reed stands
straight or with a
slight upward
bow

Reed completely
covers air channel

A properly adjusted Crit'RCall reed should stand straight out or have a slight upward bow.

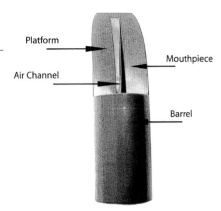

The Crit'RCall Standard body consists of the mouthpiece with reed platform, air channel and body.

Platform

Mouthpiece

Air Channel

Barrel

When my patent protection ran out in 1993, several of the big call makers and scores of smaller call makers started using the open reed design. The variety of predator calls available to varmint hunters is quite amazing compared to what we seasoned old timers had in the 1950s and 1960s.

Open reed calls make hunting, photography and viewing wildlife up close and personal. Of course, I am partial to the Crit'RCall. We make a model for every living critter.

Positioned correctly, the reed is tapered from the barrel end forward to the tip of the platform. The reed should fit tightly, totally covering the air channel. When you look at the call in profile, the reed should bow slightly upward of stick straight out from the reed block. If it does not, either turn the reed or retrain it by carefully rolling it backward and upward with the thumb. Most reed materials have a memory that can be lost because of heat and use; however, it can be retrained or reset. The upward bow scoops air and insures against the reed freezing up against the call platform when blowing it hard.

The reed vibration frequency is the tune you play and the variety is infinite. Every person who blows the call does it slightly differently because of lip, tongue, mouth, throat and breathing variations.

This variety is wonderful. Why? Because it less likely to educate varmints to one sound range. Not only do you sound different from your competition, you sound different yourself at every new stand.

So, the reed vibrates, sends the sound waves down the barrel and through the hand and into the wild blue yonder, hopefully to vibrate the ear drum of the dastardly and wily coyote lying in ambush over the hill. The frequencies of the sound waves are the different flavors of the sound.

Most reeds within open reed calls are made of polyester, a nylon type of plastic. Polyester is tough and is a very flexible and durable material. We at Crit'RCall have tried scores of different reed materials and like polyesters the best. Polyester is virtually trouble free and lasts for decades. Three thicknesses of polyester are useful for varmint calling: .0075", .010" and .015". The .0075"

Major Boddicker with a Rocky Mountain High coyote and a smile.

is great for deer buck grunts, high pitches, easy blow calling, but is too thin for many uses and freezes up in hard blowing situations.

The .010" reed is assembled in the Crit'RCall Standard and is the best all-around reed material. A .015" reed is included with our Standard Model as an accessory. It takes more effort to blow and produces a more gravelly, low pitched sound. Some callers like it better for coyote howls and yelps.

There are many other films which work for reeds within the Crit'RCall models, including clear polycarbonate, opaque fiberglass, phenolic, paper phenolic, linen phenolic. Polyvinyl, (pop and plastic bottle plastics), credit cards and etcetera. That is good because if you should lose a reed a substitute may be close at hand.

Crit'RCalls sells a package of seven different types of reed stock for those who want to craft their own reeds and experiment.

The Crit'RCall operates with the reed up. The reed and call platform is placed into the mouth with the rounded bottom of the platform body resting on the bottom lip and teeth.

The pitch or note level of the sound is regulated by how much of the reed is vibrating. If just the tip of the reed vibrates, a very high frequency (squeaker) sound is produced. If the entire reed vibrates, a very low frequency sound (bawl) results. A huge variety of frequencies can be produced between these two extremes.

The upper lip and teeth, bitten down on the reed, creates the fulcrum, in front of which the reed vibrates when blown. This fulcrum can be moved forward or backward as the call is being blown to the desired frequency by either moving the teeth and lips forward and back, or the call body can be moved forward or back. Tightening the lip and/or teeth bite will increase the sound frequency. Loosening will lower the frequency. Blowing harder on the reed increases the frequency of the sound as well as the volume. Blowing softly lowers the volume and frequency.

The lip and tooth placement and movement on the reed is very important. A tight hold on the reed tip means very high frequency and pitch (mouse squeak). A loose hold using the entire reed means low frequency and pitch (moose grunt).

Moving the tongue, lips and top of the throat also is very useful in producing high quality distress cries and necessary variety. With the lips, do a Bbrrr on the reed. Trill the tongue on the reed. Growl or gargle with the throat like you are bringing up a goober, while blowing the reed. All of this action produces nice sounds of dying critters and that can make the difference in calling success.

Air volume and flow is important. Generally, Crit'RCall works best when held in the mouth with the barrel pointing down at roughly a 45-degree angle. The air flow is straight into the reed and the reed operates with the best air scooping. Tipping the call up or down changes the air flow and sound and adds good variety.

Blowing hard or soft makes great adjustments in the frequency and volume of the call. I purposely vary the blowing effort to produce great sounds. I blow short choppy breaths most of the time but also extended breaths, hold my breath for a count or two, resume louder, softer, as a matter of choice.

Inflection of the air flow is also an important technique in calling. Start with high notes and work to lower notes. Start with short low notes and work to long high notes. You can make bleats, baas, PeeOWW's, barks, howls, yelps, whimpers, whines, squeaks, grunts, wheeps, whaas, buck buck bedock, chatter, gurgles and growls, You can make all of these sounds with the Crit'RCall Standard right out of the package.

Ready? Pick up a Crit'RCall Standard or a similar open reed call, put it reed up in your mouth 3/4th of an inch with your teeth in your upper lip placed on the reed. Point the call barrel at a 45-degree angle downward with the barrel held between the thumb and first finger, with the hand shut.

The lip should press the reed down lightly. Blow into the call from the chest (diaphragm) not the stomach, with the cheeks tight (not blowing out), creating a round, controlled column of air moving directly into the reed. Keep the call barrel between the thumb and the first finger, with the rest of the end open. The reed will vibrate producing a caw sound. Repeat 8-12 times in short choppy breaths. Crows will respond well to this call.

Once that is mastered, repeat, only close the hand over the call barrel and in synchronization with blowing, open the hand gradually at the same speed the blowing is done. This will result in a WWHaa sound. Repeat that 8-12 times. This is the basic rabbit distress cry and works everywhere I have tried it.

If you want a higher pitched rabbit sound, back the call out of the mouth 1/4" and repeat. For a lower pitched rabbit sound, put the call 1" or 1-1/4" back into the mouth and repeat.

Wiggle the lips on the reed as you blow to give the call a quiver.

Gurgle or vibrate your throat to give the call a growl. The variety of sounds you can make is amazing.

To change inflection, to get a fawn or calf bleat, say PeeOOW with your lips on the reed as you blow. A great time to experiment is after you have made a stand on a slow day.

Predator calling is one of the last free acts unregulated in the land of the regulated, home of the brave. There is really no right or wrong way to call varmints. I suggest you try new techniques, analyze what works and what does not. Evaluate and use the tried and true. That evaluation can cooperate with experience and allow you to develop your own secret to success.

The open-reed style call, held in a proper position in the mouth with the lip and teeth positioned, ready to call.

Even skillful screamers like Bill Countess might use a battery powered screamer when circumstances suggest.

chapter 7

Battery Powered Callers

The battery-powered callers available during the early days of predator screaming were mostly miserable little buggers. One model used a bunch of D-sized batteries to power a portable record player. The distress sounds, mostly the manufacturer blowing screams, came on a 45-rpm record. The reverse side, much of the time, held dialogue that explained the basics of this exciting sport. Later generations went to tape but retained the multiple D-battery power source. Taped distress sounds started to appear in the '50s.

You are not likely to be surprised to learn that many serious callers (I was one), visited the electronic store to search for cassette players, amplifiers, speakers, and a power source (six volt lantern battery). The unit I assembled for a couple of hundred dollars did a fine job but was heavy and ugly as a handful of coyote vents. No matter. When the critters were close enough to see "the ugly" it was usually about BANG time. That home-built caller, in spite of defects, caused a good many coyote, cat, and fox to pack for the trip to the big gut pile in the sky.

Those who make and market the battery-powered caller have considerably improved the product since those salad days. Several styles of battery-powered callers are currently available. The tried-and-true cassette player is mainly made and marketed by the Johnny Stewart Wildlife Call Company. The second kind of caller is the innovative chip player, made and marketed by Burnham Brothers, FoxPro and many more. Each of the construction types has all of the assets owned by all battery-powered callers. The caller types present individual strengths. It is best, I think, to offer a general evaluation of battery-powered callers and forego an evaluation of each call type, saying instead that there is currently a plethora of battery-powered players available. Those who are interested in such might examine advertisements in a current issue of *Trapper & Predator Caller*, *Predator Hunting*, or *Predator XTreme*.

Every battery-powered caller has a strong asset. Those who hunt with one have become instantly capable as to the tone and rhythm of the screaming. I emphasize that aspect and that aspect only; but there is a lot more involved. Even those who choose to be relieved of the screaming chore must be hunters and must own that elusive quality called woodsmanship. Even those who use the battery-powered caller must learn the habits and the habitats of the target animal. They must learn setup, camouflage, reading the wind, reading sign, reading animal body language, and more. Finally, when the customer shows, they must be marksman enough to make the shot.

Other assets accrue to the hunter who uses the battery-powered caller. A selection of tapes or a selection of chips lets the hunter choose the sound to be broadcast. Just as a bass fisherman might sort through the tackle box to find a lure that will work within a certain honey hole on a particular day, those who use the battery-powered caller can sort through the tape or chip collection to find a sound that will appeal to a certain kind of animal within a certain kind of country. Critters who have burnt out on the cottontail rabbit distress scream, as an example, might come running to a distressed woodpecker scream. The telling of a true story can emphasize these phenomena.

Robin McIntyre was a tall and lanky rookie policeman whose main claim to fame rested with his ability to ingest food. Robin, as I recall, was a four-helping man. No matter the kind of food and the kind of cooking, he would fill his plate four times and lick it clean each time. I hesitated when Robin asked to go along on a predator screaming. Hell, I didn't know if I could pack enough food for the both of us. I tried, filling the cold case with rolls of summer sausage, cheeses, home baked rolls, Ritz crackers, and such. Even a half dozen cans of the dreaded beanie weenies. Lots of coffee. A chocolate cake. Don't remember what else. Anyway, I felt good about lunch.

I felt less good when the drive to the hunting area was minutes old. Robin, smelling food, started to nibble. The groceries diminished rapidly. When I finally mentioned to him he was eating his and my lunch, he giggled. "Guess I am a lot like a coyote," he confessed. "I am an opportunistic eater." And he was. By the time we set up for the dawn stand, the grocery box held air and not much else.

The first screaming produced a pair of anxious coyotes. Both came at the race and one left at the race. The other fell to the .22-250. Considerably

Frankenhare and a battery powered player can be dandy when it is time to increase the photo files.

All callers, my-own-self included, might use a battery powered screamer to assist some coyote to visit the big gut pile in the sky. (Gordy Krahn Photo).

encouraged, I blew until I nearly got trombone lip during the next half dozen stands. Nothing. Not so much as a crow. The critters within our part of Arizona, I was convinced, had been scream-educated to the point of paranoia.

Even though it was lunchtime we did not stop. Hell, there was nothing to eat except that one early morning coyote, a critter that was beginning to smell more coyote-like with each passing minute. No thanks.

On the next stand (the last of the day, I promised myself) I broke out the battery-powered caller and entered a cottontail rabbit distress tape. Fifteen minutes of that song didn't do it. I slipped the bunny screaming out and entered in a yellowhammer flicker distress, not hoping for much. Ten minutes later I saw fur, a pair of paranoid yodelers making a sneak through the chaparral. Knowing I owed Robin something because of his eating habits, I did not mention to him we had customers coming. I used the .22-250 to "harvest" both. Robin stayed quiet during the ride home. Course, there was nothing to eat. He may have sulked because of that.

The battery-powered caller also shines when it comes to volume. Even though some dam-fine screamers claim volume is overrated, I do not totally agree. Here in the West, where I may be screaming to a coyote in an adjoining zip code, a loud scream does the job. Wind can diminish the carry muscle of tube calls. I like to scream loud with the battery-powered caller during those windy days. Having the ability to cause the screaming to be isolated from the hunter can also be advantageous.

I find the battery-powered callers a good selection when calling to the camera or calling to the camcorder. Isolating the sound causes the critter to be looking over there while I am over here. The customer is less apt to discover the treachery and, consequently, hang around a bit longer, offering extended opportunity for filming or taping. Causing the caller to cooperate with a decoy can enhance the filming or taping opportunity even further. More on this in the chapter on decoys.

I use an identical technique for each of the battery-powered callers. Much of the time, if there is no advantage to be gained by isolation, I keep the calling unit close. I use medium volume at the start of the call and let the screams run continuously for a couple of minutes. If there is no response I assume there is not an interested customer close by. I crank up the volume to full scream. I hold the unit (with speaker attached) high over my head and rotate the unit so that the directional speaker has the opportunity to holler at all points of the compass. Why hold it high? Getting the speaker above the ground cover can free the sound to travel unencumbered.

After I have made the hold-high broadcast, I place the caller on the ground and ready the camera, the camcorder, or the gun for business, permitting the unit to play continuously at full volume for the duration of the setup.

My geezer tape player made by the Johnny Stewart Wildlife Call Company is a compact unit generally consisting of the tape player, an on-off switch, a volume control and a twelve-volt motorcycle battery (rechargeable) within the unit. A plug-in accommodates the attachment of an external speaker. The speaker comes equipped with 25 feet of cord so that the screaming may be isolated from the unit. My cassette caller is the MS-512, a model that has proved to be dependable and durable. These kinds of players reproduce the actual distress sounds of real critters, every one an expert at his or her genre of screaming.

The MS-512 comes with an adapter that permits the battery to be recharged when plugged into a household outlet. An accessory is available that permits recharging through the cigarette lighter of a vehicle, allowing the hunter to recharge while traveling from stand to stand. Such is seldom necessary. You can expect several hours of play from a fully-charged battery. There is more than enough juice to fuel a dawn to dark hunt.

Hunters who work cruelly cold country will find the battery life to be

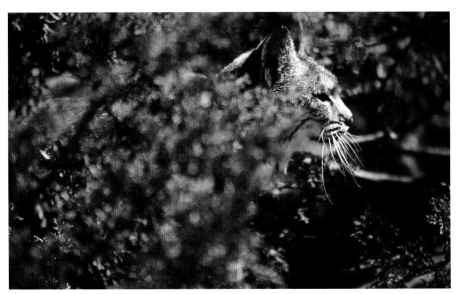

Hang-ups and other bashfuls might beat feet to investigate a low volume and moany close call.

diminished due to the cold. I suggest you carry the battery-powered caller in the warm cab of the vehicle to help the batteries a bit. Also, under such Arctic conditions, a mid-hunt charging might be necessary.

Experience will show innovative ways to utilize the cassette caller. I sometimes record thirty seconds of silence at the start of the tape. Easy to do. Just put the cassette in a standard tape player/recorder, hit record, and time out thirty seconds or so. I then walk out fifty or a hundred feet to the front of the setup, hit the go button, and walk leisurely back to the setup-having ample time to get hid before the music starts.

Another innovation involves the merging of two sounds onto a single tape. Gray fox fight sounds interrupted with cottontail screams or yellow hammer woodpecker screams work well. Such customizing delivers a tape that is unique. The variety of tapes available offers nearly limitless possibilities. That same variety of tapes can cause confusion when it is time to select sounds for the personal collection. Dozens of sounds are offered. At about ten bucks a tape a considerable collection can seriously dent the budget. Some hunters I know have told the kids they can eat a full meal every other day or can have grits every darn day, and use the savings to buy every sound offered. I do not consider that necessary. I suggest that new hunters, or those new to battery-powered callers, start with five basic tapes: the cottontail distress tape, the jackrabbit distress tape, the yellow hammer woodpecker distress tape, the gray fox distress tape and one of the howling locator tapes. Those who live and hunt within 'coon country might add one more tape to that basic list-the baby 'coon distress tape.

Even though the chip player eats a different kind of grocery, much that has been said about the cassette caller can be said about the chip player. The chip player does not play cassettes, not even those you may have collected for the cassette system. Players like the Compucaller pull sound from a programmed electronic chip containing four or more tracks. A switch on the faceplate of the caller permits a quick change of sound. A chip programmed with the jackrabbit distress, the gray fox distress, the cottontail distress, and the bird distress, as an example, can be persuaded to change to any other sound on the chip by moving the indicator.

The screams that come from the chips are electronically produced. The cottontail distress scream is not always a broadcast of a genuine cottontail screaming. It is, rather, an electronic simulation of the real thing. The chips I have heard have a short repeat time. Repeat? The electronic scream sounds for seconds and then repeats that short series of screams. And repeats, repeats, repeats.

I have had the Compucaller I own on several hunts. Even though the short repeats can sound monotonous to the hunter, the animals do not seem to mind, probably because the genuine distressed edibles can get pretty damn boring with their screaming. (I have not heard a single rabbit who screamed as realistically as Rich and Tyler Higgins). That makes sense to me. Those who are about to be eaten have no long time to practice the screaming. The screaming is not a prideful talent passed down from doe to bunny. One short opportunity, much of the time, and that's it. Down the gullet. Considering all of that, their lack of repertoire can be understood.

The asset of scream interchangeability was amply illustrated during a cold winter hunt in the desert lands of Arizona. A rancher who was predictably biased when it came to coyote lost his love's prize poodle to a hungry and hunting pair of yodelers. His bride, having made the trip to the West fairly recently, loved that poodle. Not physically, spiritually. Tanya, as a matter of fact, loved every animal that walked, crept, and crawled the Western wastelands. That included the coyote. Even gophers. Her love of the coyote took a nose-dive when she witnessed the eating and killing of Poopsie (also a recent migrant from The Big Apple). Did you notice I said eat and kill, not kill and eat? Yep, Poopsie was pretty well digested while still alive. You talk about your distress screams. Anyway, such sights and sounds caused Tanya to be sick (physically) and caused her love of God's dog to considerably diminish. Tanya turned ugly. That caused Phil to get out of sorts and he dialed 911, asking for a coyote killer. The game and fish guys dropped my name. And that explains how I happened to be about the dawn desert carrying a new-in-box Compucaller, ready to do business.

The coyote, accustomed to the friendly protection offered by coyote-lover Tanya, were easy. The first came at the gallop. I let him come to sure-kill range and slapped the butt of the Mag 12 (MooseDick, the Mag-10, was in the shop for a tune-up) to my shoulder. The coyote saw the movement and made a frantic yaw to the left, a perfect move to accommodate a right-handed shooter. I placed the barrel bead on the critter's nose and lit the fire. Caught in mid-leap by the load of copper-plated BBs, the coyote did a half-gainer and hit the ground as a rug. I watched the carcass intently for a second or so to insure there would not be one of those miraculous recoveries and went back to work.

The second coyote came a lot less enthusiastically, sliding to a suspicious stop a hundred yards out to deliver the bad eye. Too far out for the full-choked twelve — too far out for a shotgun of any gauge. The yodeler faced straight to the speaker of the Compucaller, displaying the kind of body language that told me this customer would come closer if properly encouraged. I eased one hand to the Compucaller control and flicked the switch to dog distress. Low volume. The coyote keyed in on this new sound, maybe remembering the day she had Poopsie for lunch, and came at the lunge, stopping forty yards out. This time she stood at the broadside, telling me she had come as far as she intended to come. Knowing that 40 yards was about maximum for the three-inch twelve but knowing this was as good as it was likely to get, I took the shot. A few seconds later I was walking out to retrieve the double. Poopsie was avenged. Tanya (she turned out to be a decent sort, even though she later ran off with an alfalfa pellet salesman) would be happy.

I am most familiar with the FoxPro FX5 and will use such as an example. My FX5 carries sound chips that allow a selection from two hundred screamings. The powerful remote control allows the user to change scream and change volume from several football fields away. A press of a button can change from a howl to a scream and one more click can change from a rabbit distress to a bird distress. Jay Nistetter and I used his FX3 during a windy day and fetched in an extra paranoid and extra large (27.8 pounds) bitch that died extra grandly. Other players within the high end can offer similar advantages.

A final comment on the battery-powered caller. Cassette callers like the Johnny Stewart MS-512 can be had for less than a hundred and a half. A new-in-box Compucaller will cost about twice that. FoxPro is somewaht more expensive but has every possible calling advantage without needing to store or carry ordinary batteries, tapes or chips. Either is bargain priced, the way I see it. Such a piddling amount, prorated over a lifetime of hunting, ends up having an inconsequential cost.

As a final comment within this chapter, I feel it proper to mention an observation about the making and marketing of battery-powered callers and other such. Screaming at coyote, fox, cats and all such has caused a proliferation of interest. There are currently websites addressed specifically to the sport of predator screaming. One such (Predator Masters) claims a membership of fourteen thousand or so. Hunt Masters has less but is growing. This increased interest has caused significant change within the industry. The Johnny Stewart Company has been sold to Hunter Specialties. Burnham Brothers has been sold. Lohman acquired the venerable Circe Company, and both Lohman and Circe have been purchased by Outdoor Pursuits. The old Weems Wild Call Company has passed through a couple of companies and is not now active. This increased interest has benefited the sport the way I see it. New kinds of calls are somewhat commonly available, many such offering new insights into call making. Succinctly, the good old days are now.

chapter 8

The Scream

Some who read this might recall I once wrote a question and answer column for the old *Trapper* Magazine (later re-titled *Trapper and Predator Caller*). The question most often asked concerned some aspect of the distress scream. That plethora of questions, often asked but never answered to my satisfaction because of space considerations within that format, cause me to believe it to be worthwhile to devote an entire chapter to that sometimes puzzling part of predator calling.

Knowing that the mind boggling assortment of predator fetching screams available can cause confusion, permit me to say I do not believe that the smartest predator that is, or once was, will categorize a distress scream. Simply put, the predator brain is not constructed to do so. Actually, has no need to do so. Confused? Me too. Permit me to explain. I do not believe a predator will evaluate a rabbit distress scream, maybe thinking, "Hell Farh," (being a southern sort of critter), "that sounds to be a distressed cotton tail rabbit and I ain't toothed a conejo since Hector was a pup. I reckon I might gallop on over and steal a meal." It is more likely the predator will recognize the distress scream as a signal of vulnerability from a creature that might be tasty, a meal needed to provide protein.

Having said such I feel it is important to also say a change of distress scream can cause success. The critters I have met have been somewhat naive but have not been stupid. A coyote, or about any of the meat eaters, has the ability to learn from experience. A predator that has raced to investigate a scream can be mighty disappointed to learn the "rabbit" weighs about two hundred pounds and points a stick that goes BANG. Even so, one bad experience does not often cause a hungry predator to forsake distress screams forever. He does not because he cannot. A carpenter who hammers his finger may say drat and dernamity but will not often retire his saw and hammer. He will instead become more cautious. A predator will often react precisely the same. He will not give up on distressed animals because that is an important part of his groceries. But even a middling smart predator will become more cautious, perhaps to the point that he or she will not respond to the same sounding distress scream. That same predator may respond enthusiastically to a distress scream that sounds to be different. A strong asset of the battery powered player, the way I see it, is the inherent ability to send out a diversity

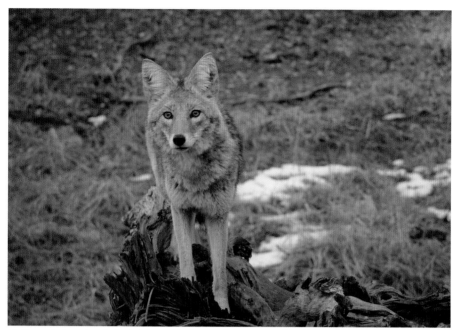

Ph.D. coyote have lost their virginity and hesitate to form meaningful relationships with distressed rabbits.

of screams, some actual and some simulated.

Those who scream using lung power and a reeded call can produce an amazing variety of sound. The Ph.D. predator described above might also respond when an aspect of the scream changes enough to add interest. This change may be accomplished by changing calls, changing reeds or changing the way a call is sounded. As has been noted, those who scream using an open reeded call can change pitch and tone significantly. Moving the lips along the exposed reed can produce the high tenor of a pup distress or the gravelly baritone of a distressed jackrabbit or a gray fox. The mouth has total control over volume and total control over spacing and rhythm. I once used a part of that versatility to cause a coyote to trade his pelt for a taste of the tube.

I was screaming prairie land that lay to the north of the multiple mile high San Francisco Peaks. I had called this juniper dotted country many times over a period of years and had almost always enjoyed action of some sort. On this day a survivor of that action remained discrete within a juniper thicket and howled insult after insult Blair-ward. I was screaming through a metal reeded tube turned from the extremely hard and extremely handsome desert ironwood, such turned and tuned by master call maker Jay Nistetter (Rhino Calls, Blow a Rhino). My screams were the usual cast of characters. Rhythmic screams of medium volume and medium character, the kind of screams the coyote had learned to expect from a distressed rabbit or a distressed hare. The kind of screams that the coyote had learned to hate. After fifteen or twenty minutes of this all talk and no walk I removed the call from my mouth and offered the howler a couple of minutes of unadulterated silence. Time enough to cause Ol Motor-mouth to become curious and perhaps a bit nervous. Maybe even hungry. I returned the screamer to my mouth and sent out a series of low volume moans, each moan lasting about twice as long as the previous scream. Each moan slowly spaced. Five minutes later I sighted a coyote coming my way. Coming not at a gallop, not at a lope but coming at a slow and deliberate creep. When the Doc was a hundred and a half yards out I stroked the three pound trigger of the .22-250 and the Sako bellowed out a hello, and goodbye. Was it the howler? Don't know. I do know the howling stopped when the moaning began. Circumstantial evidence.

I am thinking all of us have experienced instances when the most appropriate thing to say is nothing at all. I have used that technique also to put the hurt to a customer who has become a hemorrhoid (pain in the ass).

I was hunting the high plains of northern Arizona during a December day. I sang my song for the usual fifteen minutes and called using the usual volume and spacing. When El Coyote did not respond I ceased screaming but did not walk away. Fifteen minutes later the paranoid came at the sneak. I did as I usually do when toting the .22-250 and when a coyote wearing a one hundred dollar hair coat stands broadside a hundred yards out giving me the bad eye. How did I know what not to say? Observation, consideration and recollection. I had called the same country early in the season. I was hunkered on a lava blow to gain a bit of altitude and did my thing. When nothing showed I moved about mile away. I sat upon a second lava blow and glassed the countryside as I waited for the prairie to settle down. The Bausch and Lombs revealed a pissant wearing a coyote coat sniffing around the butte I had previously screamed. I observed, considered, remembered and managed to skin the bashful coyote.

Are you ready for the punch line? Stay alert and stay smart. You can bet your fur check the target will do exactly that. The hunter, if he or she is to level the playing field, must do the same.

Now might be the proper time to confess a truth. Gerry Blair would not be likely to win a contest calling event. Why so? Because that Ol Sumbitch of a Beastmaster sounds too much like a distressed rabbit. Contest judges, my own self included, do not often appreciate the monotonous wah-wah-wah articulated by a troubled cotton tail. How do I know exactly how a distressed rabbit sounds? I have listened and learned from more than a few, most such having a foot hooked within the firm jaws of a number two coil at the time. All observed would emit a monotonous wah-wah-wah. That "wah-wah," articulated with passion, with a drop of blood dripping from each "wah" will at times call coyote, fox, bobcat and about every thing with ears. Trouble is, it does not require a high degree of calling skill to do so. Contest judges listen for trills, growls, quavers and all else. Having said such, honesty requires me to say that creative calling will impress judges and also call critters. Is that creative screaming more effective than the basic wah-wah-wah? Don't know. Maybe so. Some critters have been wah-wahed until they are sick of the sound. Innovative calling, being a sound that is less often heard, might cause a paranoid predator to get off his butt and head for the gun.

Rich and Tyler Higgins are a father-son team of screamers who have extended the art of creative calling tremendously. I sincerely suggest you pay close attention to the chapter that follows, such titled Hard Hunting, to gain an insight into current calling conditions and the Higgins solution. Further on, Rich will share his insight into coyote communications.

I never do a screaming with a single call dangling from a lanyard. To do so invites disappointment, can cause missed opportunities, and will almost surely result in an educated coyote. Allow me to provide a for-instance.

I was calling a push-down within northern Arizona when my first disappointment, missed opportunity and education occurred. A California storm front had passed through bringing snow and cold. The radio within my truck claimed the temperature to be eight under. Don't get that cold in Arizona?, you say. "Hah," I respond, "been there, done that and have the frostbite to prove it."

The dawn stand produced a sight seldom seen that late in the season. A gang of hungry coyote responded two minutes after the first scream. Trouble was, they hung up five hundred yards out. I counted five coyote and heard the howls of two more. Jackpot. I placed the end of the metal reeded wood Circe within my mouth and attempted to "wah-wah" the group to sure kill range, figuring I might "harvest" at least one and maybe more. Even though I blew a "wah-wah" into the tube the sound that came out of the tube was ugh-ugh.

downright beastly. The coyote family thought so too, shifting to overdrive and racing for the Coconino-Mohave County line. What happened? Moisture within my breath had hit the extremely cold metal reed and had frozen such shut.

Purists within the readership might wonder why five yodelers would cluster. Winter coyote will do so occasionally. Hunting as a gang offers a hunting advantage, allowing the group to take down prey too large for a single or even a double coyote. In this instance the gang of five probably gathered for a different reason. Later that day I discovered a black angus carcass less than a mile away from the screaming. The crowd, I speculate, were involved in a communal pig-out, actually a beef-out.

If one call is too few, how many calls are too many? I am not sure. I do recall a Globe Arizona hunter who crossed my path during a screaming within the coyote rich San Carlos Apache Indian Reservation. The Globe guy turned out to be a call collector and had his collection hanging from his neck. Even though

it was late in the day I noticed he carried a hell of a lot of calls but did not carry a coyote. Even so, it is better, I think, to carry too many calls rather than carry too few. Sad experience has caused me to carry back up calls, maybe as many as four or five. Such offers a versatility of screams and offers a ready replacement when the main screamer calls in sick.

I began this chapter discussing the kind of scream I most often use to attract predators

Rich joined Gerry for a December 2006 hunt and taught old dogs new tricks

Rich Higgins horny howler speaks fluent coyote.

Fred Cronk's Arizona Predator Calls work well on coyote, fox, bobcat and the amazing etcetera.

Jay Nistetter's desert ironwood calls are awesome.

and some prey, freely admitting my limitations as a creative screamer. At another place within this book, my friends Rich and Tyler Higgins will discuss creative calling and their experience at calling contest events and screaming to critters. Rich and Tyler will reveal the technique they have used to win the hearts of judges, win trophies and win pelts.

Another friend (yep, I have more than one), being a call maker, Jay Nistetter of Rhino Calls, will discuss call collecting.

Finally, Fred Cronk, owner and CEO of Arizona Calls, yet another friend, will reveal another insight. I humbly ask you to pay close attention to what these talented hunters have to offer. There is likely to be a test later.

All coyote, almost all members of the dog family, and a few humans howl when circumstances suggest such.

chapter 9

Howling and Howlers

There are those who are convinced that coyotes howl just for the hell of it. The yips, yodels, and howls heard through most of the West and a part of the East at dawn and dusk, to them, come from the throats of animals so full of themselves they just have to tell the world of it. Even though I do not usually comment on such anthropomorphic drivel unless specifically invited to do so, my experience causes me to think exactly the opposite. No wild critter I have met makes any kind of noise without good reason. They do not gossip and prattle; they cannot afford to do so. Those who earn a living as hunters, and at times reluctantly accept a change of roles to become the hunted, cannot be much of a blabbermouth. To do so can cause prey animals to be alerted. To do so causes those higher on the food chain to have an improved target. Articulation, to a critter, is a basic of communication. Even though few humans understand every nuance of the coyote language, it is probable each sound carries a specific message to another coyote.

Dawn and dusk howling is the coyote vocalizations most often heard. Those sing-alongs are mostly territorial in nature. Coyote have found a survival advantage to homesteading a particular territory and then defending that territory from poachers and other encroachers. A territorial coyote, often a territorial pair, learn about every aspect of their piece of ground. That knowledge can cause a critical advantage when it comes time to search out groceries, or to escape when the hunter comes to call. The howling announces continued residency to the coyote in adjoining territory. Such non-aggressive territorial claims reduce confrontation between neighbors.

How do I know all of this? I read and I observe. Wildlife professionals, and those who aspire to be such, sometimes fit captured critters with a radio telemetry device that allows a discrete spying when the animal is released to the wild. One such Peeking Tom conducted a territorial study involving certain coyote within a favored coyote habitat. Nope, not Anderson Mesa but the pinion juniper woodlands surrounding the mesa uplift. One such coyote tagged as Number 97, a handsome male trapped near the Wildcat Canyon mud tank, was released to the wild when he was a vigorous two-year-old. That dog, becoming wise in the way of survival, lived to the ripe old age of seven-years-plus. Number 97 suffered through a really bad day during the winter of his seventh year. It happened this way.

I was in the push-downs slightly to the east of Wildcat Tank to scream at winter coyote. Prime pelts from this high country habitat brought big dollars from the fur trade, an inducement that added incentive to my hunting activity. I was there with a Flagstaff city police supervisor to demonstrate my hunting and screaming technique. We set up to the front of a pile of pushdown string-bark junipers and started the screaming. Minutes later Number 97 charged into view, handsome in the prime of his coyote-hood. I lip-squeaked to stop the gallop, carefully sighted upon that place behind the shoulder and midway between back and chest bottom, and stroked. Number 97 died well.

Noticing the ear tag, I made an inquiry and learned a bit about 97's reputation. A wildlife biology major from Northern Arizona University had trapped and ear tagged Number 97 while he was a two-year-old (the coyote, not the biology major). Released, the coyote established dominance, took a mate, and did coyote things for the next five years, entirely within about a three square mile area surrounding Wildcat Tank.

That same study established a fact of coyote territoriality. A coyote identified as Coyote A was territorial. Coyote B occupied an adjoining territory. Both were fitted with transmitter collars. Coyote A and Coyote B honored rigid territorial boundaries for all of Coyote A's life. Finally, the radio collar attached to the neck of Coyote A sent a sad message. Coyote A had stopped moving about and was presumed to be dead. Coyote B, sending out his territorial howlings and receiving no answer from Ol' A, trotted over into A's territory to have a walk about.

Dawn and dusk howls, and howls at other times, can communicate circumstances other than territoriality. Such can announce degree of dominance, gender and even sexual receptivity. Through much of their range, particularly when coyote populations are crowded, only the most dominant of coyote pairs are permitted to breed. Coyote, like other wild dogs, mate pretty much for life, or at least until one of the pair dies or loses dominance. A dominant female who has lost a mate, or who has one who is too old to shake the sugar tree, may announce her needs to surrounding ears. It does not take long for Handsome Hairies to come at the gallop.

An easily identifiable coyote vocalization is the distress yip, sometimes called the pup distress. These high pitched hurtings signal trouble and ask for help. I have heard distress yipping when a dominant coyote disciplines a submissive. Politically correct body posture (the avoidance of eye contact and a slinking posture, at times laying on the back with belly and throat exposed) combined with the yipping can communicate complete submission. I have also heard the distress yips when a coyote suffers a poor hit from rifle or shotgun.

The coyote vocalizations mentioned above, the territorial howl (called the challenge howl or the dominance howl by some), the female invitation (love invite) and the distress yip (pup distress) are those most helpful to the coyote hunter. I have used all three to cause a coyote to come close.

Coyote Number Ninety Seven lived long, prospered and all such until along came Blair. (Duane Rubink Photo).

A northern Arizona study suggested a female coyote losing a mate might howl to advertise her availability. (Duane Rubink Photo).

The territorial howl can be used to attract dominant male coyote during the dogging season that begins here in the Southwest about the last of February and is likely to begin later as latitude changes. Dominant dogs have come running to the challenge during that season. I have had less luck howling in coyote outside the breeding season. I use the dominance howl then mainly as a locator call, relying on the following technique.

Even though it is illegal to shoot coyote during the dark here in Arizona (also illegal in many other Western states and within some Eastern and Midwestern states), I find it to be helpful to drive through good coyote habitat during the dark, stopping to howl about every mile, using my natural voice, a howler, or playing a howl tape through a battery-powered caller. Experience has suggested a wait of five to ten minutes after each howling as some response is delayed. Howl-backs are noted as to mileage (or milepost) and direction. Some howl sites produce a multiple response. That information is also noted. When daylight comes I retrace the route, setting up to call to the howl-backs. A number of advantages accrue. Having heard the recent howl I am somewhat certain there is a coyote within hearing to be called. Having pinpointed location, I am able to set up using that knowledge to good advantage. I choose a hide that causes wind direction to be beneficial and that offers vision and shooting lanes located along probable approach.

The female invitation howl, like the dominance howl, is most effective during the dogging season. Used then, the howl is a dandy way to bring in males at a gallop.

The pup distress is also most effective during the time the pups are at the den and within the company of Mom & Pop, maybe April through September. The adults respond, I think, because they fear a creature is munching on Junior or Sis. They come to protect. The pup distress can be used effectively throughout the year, although response will be less vigorous than during the pupping period. The pup distress, correctly used, can be a call for all seasons.

Imagination will extend the usefulness of the pup distress. A report of an actual hunting experience illustrates.

I was screaming to a pinion juniper hillside during an early season hunt (about the first week of October, as I recall) hoping to fetch in a dumb pup or two. Dispersal happens about then, and the nearly adult-size pups of the year have the typical teenage appetite. Most lack sophistication. Even though the pelts obtained from early October coyote are not one hundred percent prime (the leather being still somewhat gray), the under fur and the guard hair are well developed, cooperating to produce a saleable pelt.

I was three or four minutes into the stand when I sighted a flash of fur coming at the gallop, actually two flashes of fur racing to the scream. Trouble. The lead coyote was at least a hundred yards ahead of the trailer, causing it to be difficult to take both. I did as I usually do under similar circumstances. I waited until the leader passed behind a stringbark juniper and used that opportunity to shoulder the Sako, centering the small x of the duplex six at about expected reappearance. When the coyote showed in the sight, I lip-squeaked (The Kiss of Death) to cause the critter to stop. A second later the sight was centered on the critter's necessaries — back of the shoulder and about midway between back and brisket. Death came a trigger-twitch later.

Moving fast I shifted to pick up the trailer, now running desperately for home and Mother. No shot. Almost by instinct I used my natural voice to send out a decent pup-distress-screaming. The runner slowed, stopped, and started the circle, hoping to taste the wind. When the coyote stopped two hundred yards out to deliver the bad eye, I braced my elbows across my drawn-up knees, sighted, and took the shot. The pup distress screaming caused my fur production to double on that stand.

I will make no effort to describe the sounds involved in the various coyote language, knowing that such description is not all that helpful. I suggest, instead, that those who are serious about howling invest in one of the howl instruction tapes. See the listing at the end of this book for recommended sources.

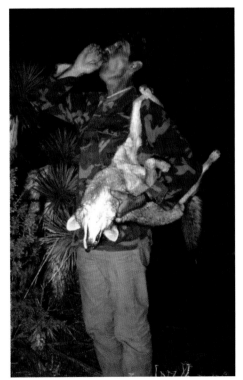

The right kind of vocal cords can cause a human howl to sound coyote-like.

chapter 10

Coyote Communications-Higgins

1. A Scientific Perspective

Over the course of fifteen thousand years, Canis latrans, in all twenty plus variations, has evolved a complex and varied social structure, which requires a complex and varied communication system. Dr. Phillip Lehner, a professor and research scientist at Colorado State University, stated that "The coyote's ability to adapt to a changing environment is ultimately a consequence of it's complex behavior, especially it's manifold communication system."

Coyote communication is indeed a manifold system and is comprised of visual, olfactory, tactile and auditory signals with the latter being of primary interest to predator callers.

Dr. Franz Camenzind, during his five year study of unexploited coyote populations on the National Elk Refuge in Jackson, Wyoming, identified nine coyote vocalizations. Dr. Lehner identified eleven vocalizations as did legendary ADC trapper Bill Austin.

Dr. Lehner classified the coyote's vocalizations into three categories, Agonistic, Greeting and Contact.

Agonistic is defined as aggressive or defensive behavior between individuals of the same species.

Anyone who has observed aggregations of coyotes around carrion knows and understands the meaning of agonistic.

He further classified them as Long Range and Short Range communications and Universal and Individual vocalizations. Evidently coyote puppies are born with an innate understanding of certain vocalizations. Whether they are born c.latrans umpquensis in northwest Washington, c.latrans var. in New Hampshire, c.latrans frustror in east Texas, or c.latrans ochropus in coastal California, all of their puppies, regardless of subspecies or geographic locale, are apparently born with an instinctual understanding of Universal vocalizations. Individual vocalizations are those that are taught by the parents to the pups or by one coyote to another. In addition, I am convinced that Universal vocalizations have Individual modifications; that coyotes will lend their personal "accent" to certain howls.

Dr. Lehner defined coyote vocalizations as "a graded continuum, both within and between vocal types, and vary in intensity through changes in amplitude, frequency, and vocalization type." Dr. Lehner listed his eleven vocalizations in order along a physical continuum as follows:

A. Agonistic
  1. Wool
  2. Growl
  3. Huff
  4. Bark
  5. Threat Bark-Howl
  6. Yelp
  7. Whine (h-f)

B. Greeting
  1. Whine (l-f)
  2. Greeting Song
    (wow-oo-wow)
  3. Group Yip-Howl

C. Contact
  1. Lone Howl
  2. Group Howl
  3. Group Yip-Howl

Drs. Jaeger, Mitchell, Makagon, and Barrett published a paper titled "Information Content of Coyote Barks and Howls" in which they conducted discriminant analysis of spectrograms of recorded coyote howls and barks. They concluded that because of the variations in the length, shape, and volume of the supralaryngeal vocal tract, coyote vocalizations are individually specific, meaning that coyotes can identify the howls of coyotes that are known to them. Their study and others have determined that highly specific information regarding identity, size, age, sex, and emotional state are encoded in coyote howls.

Kathleen Fulmer's Master's thesis is titled "Characterizing the Functions of Coyote Vocalizations Through the Use of Playback"

Her objective was to investigate coyote responses to broadcast vocalizations. Ms. Fulmer and her associates broadcast recordings of lone howls, group howls and group yip-howls to 113 radio-collared coyotes in ten territories on the ALE in Washington State.

Fulmer reported that coyotes responded vocally more to group yip-howls than other vocalizations and responded with physical approach more to lone howls. Coyotes responded more often to playback broadcast within their territory than to playback broadcast along or outside of their boundaries. Resident coyotes often repositioned themselves more toward their core area before responding either vocally or with an approach. Most environmental factors (presence or absence of moonlight, barometric pressure, humidity, and precipitation) were not significantly correlated with coyote's movements in response to playback. Movement varied significantly with wind.

2. A Caller's Perspective

Most of the eleven vocalizations can be successfully used to either entice a physical approach from coyotes of all social groups or to evoke a vocal response from resident members. It is important to know that transients and nomads, which make up as much as 70% of the population at certain times of the year, are generally non-vocal, that announcing their location is usually not to their benefit. Subsequently, when we hear howls we can be fairly certain that they are being issued by resident coyotes and we callers can use that knowledge to our benefit.

Because coyote vocalizations vary widely in meaning and intention, it would follow that their application to calling would also vary widely. Some vocalizations are of limited utility in that they appeal only to coyotes of a specific status within a specific social group, while others have a much broader appeal to most if not all coyotes. Coyotes will respond to vocalizations for one or more of at least seven different motivations with social issues and territorial concerns being foremost.

The following is a brief description of each vocalization and the manner in which it can be used on stand.

AGONISTIC AND ALARM
1. Woof

The woof is a short range, low intensity threat and/or alarm and is the sound that the parents use to send the pups into the den or cover.

I use it to stop or position coyotes that are very close to me without scaring the Bejeezus out of them as a loud bark will often do.

2. Growl

A short range, low to high intensity threat. I use this in the same manner as the woof and often in combination with it.

3. Huff

A very short range, high intensity threat that is produced by the forceful and rapid expulsion of air through both the mouth and the nose simultaneously with the resultant effect of blowing snot and spit in the face of the current object of their discontent. It is produced in a rapid series that results in a chuffing sound.

I don't attempt to use this sound because of the context in which the coyote uses it. If any readers do attempt to use it, I recommend that their rabies vaccinations be current.

4. Bark

This is a short to long range, low to high intensity threat and/or warning. This is one of the most controversial of all the vocalizations among callers. One well known calling video producer states that when he hears this sound he gets in his truck and drives at least five miles before making another stand. Many callers agree that hearing a bark in response to calls means that the caller has been "busted," detected and identified. In reality, coyotes bark for a number of reasons, including to increase their sense of security when confronted by a sound, sight or smell that intimidates them, whether it is identified or not. Lap dogs bark frantically at unidentified noises and people whistle while walking along a dark street for much the same reason. A barking coyote can often be approached from a different direction and called in or, in open country, an approach can be made by utilizing a "gorilla" walk or an "ugly cow" walk. These are performed by squatting or bending over under a net to obscure the human form and then "duck walking", closing the distance by zigzagging into range. By approaching at a 45-degree angle, rather than directly toward the coyote, we can often approach surprisingly close in full view of the coyote.

Scott Huber, an ADC trapper for the state of South Dakota says that he does not use barks with his howls because he feels that many coyotes will perceive those barks as intimidating and will not approach. I rarely use barks on a stand to elicit an approach for the same reason and I will address the reason for this when discussing the next vocalization. I do use barks to stop and position a coyote where I want it.

5. Threat Bark-Howl

This is probably the least understood and most mis-used of all vocalizations. It is often called the "Challenge Howl" which I believe is a misnomer and contributes to the confusion associated with this vocalization. Many callers consider a "challenge" to be an invitation to do battle, similar to the elk challenge bugle. Elk issue these "challenges", coyotes do not. As stated earlier, vocalizations are a graded continuum and escalate in intensity as the encounter intensifies. If we consider the barks to be warnings to stay away and not approach closer and we know that those barks can escalate into threat bark-howls, then we can consider the threat bark-howl to be exactly that, a threat and demand that the intruder leave now or else, rather than a challenge, then it helps to put the sound and it's application into a proper perspective. This vocalization can be spectacularly effective if you set up a stand near a den during denning season and reports of those responses at that time are probably the reason that so many callers insist on using it. I often hear "I knew coyotes were in the area and I blew a challenge howl, but nothing showed up". Quite simply if you set up a stand in overlapping home range or along boundaries or even within defended territory and loudly demand that every coyote within hearing "leave now or else", they quite probably will. Transients, nomads certainly will and at certain times of the year they comprise as much as 70% of the total population. If you are primarily interested in calling in the greatest number of coyotes then this vocalization will be counter productive, if your goal is the selective removal of the alphas and you know that you are within the groups core area then this can be an especially productive call.

6.Yelp

This is a high intensity submission or startle response.

From a calling perspective, adult yelps can be alarming to coyotes with a low security level and would probably be most effective within the same scenarios as the threat bark-howl. Puppy yelps or puppy distress, however, are one of the most effective sounds in the callers repertoire. They will effectively call in coyotes of all ages and social groups as well as fox, bobcats and probably many other predators.

7. Whine (high frequency)

This is a short range, high intensity submission.

I do not use whines as a primary call. I do use them as coaxers, enticements and curiosity draws in conjunction with other sounds.

GREETING
1.Whine (low frequency)

This is a short range low intensity greet from subordinate to dominate animals.

I use this whine in the same manner as the high frequency whine.

2. Greeting Song

This vocalization perfectly demonstrates the complexity of coyote vocalizations and behavior. Dr. Lehner and Bill Austin both named this the "wow-ooo-wow" because it is a mixed sound that apparently results from an oscillation between motivations. The result is a vocalization that grades back and forth between a low frequency whine, which is a low intensity submission, and a growl, which is a low intensity threat.

Duplicating these sounds with hand calls and howlers will be an extraordinary feat and beyond my meager talents, however a recording of the greeting song broadcast within a pack's claimed territory would surely be investigated by the residents.

3. Group Yip-Howl

This is a multi-faceted, graded, fluctuating greeting. This is one of the most important vocalizations to the coyote's social structure. As the other greetings escalate in excitement, the dominate coyote will generally initiate the howls and is gradually joined by the other group members as the intensity escalates. The howls become modulated and yips become more frequent and other sounds are included which have been described as "gargles" "screams" and "laughs". I have witnessed a greeting ceremony that escalated to such a high level of excitement that at least two of the subordinate coyotes began yelping as if they were being injured. The social intercourse that this ceremony develops plays an integral role in strengthening social bonds and reaffirming status within the pack.

CONTACT
1. Lone Howl

This is the jewel in the callers repertoire because it is an entire lexicon within itself.

Biological research is subject to peer review, which probably results in conservative conclusions by many researchers. I have seen papers that describe the function of the lone howl as "announces location." We lay persons, however, are not held to strict standards and we are free to speculate as much as we wish. One electronic call manufacturer has 33 coyote vocalizations in their catalog. Eighteen are lone howls with names such as "female solicitation howl", "male domain howl," "adult female western territorial howl," "dominate male rally howl" and "Lost Mate." These names are descriptive and may or may not correctly identify the purpose and intent of the issuing coyote. The inflections, modulations, frequencies, and different durations of the howl change the meaning. A short, low frequency howl that ends on an ascending note has an entirely different meaning than a short, low frequency howl that ends on a constant or declining note. One may be a "Lost Puppy Howl" the other may be what Gerry Blair calls a "Bite my Butt, You're a Dork" howl. Until discriminant analysis of vocalizations can adequately identify the purpose and information broadcast in the howls, Gerry's interpretation has as much merit as the call vendor's does. Dr. Lehner proposed that "the large intra-individual variations of howls might obscure inter-individual differences between coyotes." This is significant in that it suggests that the research biologists do not know if those large variations and differences are within the howls or between the coyotes.

Because howls are individually specific I don't believe that we can fool any coyote into believing that we are their lost mate, lost puppy or any member of their pack. Since coyote howls contain specific encoded cues, I am at a loss as how to encode the information that I am a two year old, 23 lb. female that is lonely into my howls.

Since we can not know with certainty what information we are conveying to the coyotes with our howls, we simply try to convince all coyotes within hearing that we are an unidentified coyote sounding off. Most howls, regardless of how they are packaged and promoted, will accomplish that.

A non-aggressive howl and it's presentation are of utmost importance when appealing to the greatest number of coyotes to investigate the source of the howls that the caller issues. The caller does not want to intimidate or even diminish the sense of security of the betas, omegas, or transients/nomads and discourage their approach. The caller does not want to blast out a hairy-chested bark threat-howl from within overlapping home range and send every coyote within hearing packing; the alphas for their defended territory and the transients for deep cover. I use a howl that is so non-threatening that it even brings in twelve week old puppies to investigate the source. Follow it up with prey distress or a curiosity trigger. Simple.

No, this is not a sing along. Practice makes for perfect howls.

2. GROUP HOWL

The group howls are lone howls performed by two or more coyotes following reunion or in response to distant howling.

I don't bother with the group howl on stand because the lone howl is more effective in eliciting an approach response and the group yip-howl is more effective in eliciting a vocal response.

3. GROUP YIP-HOWL

This is, I believe, the most interesting of all vocalizations. It is useful for spatial distribution, passive territorial defense, increased pack cohesiveness, establishes and affirms rank within the pack, and even influences reproductive rate. In addition to all of the social functions that it serves, the coyotes just love doing it. Major Boddicker aptly calls it the "Joy of Life Call."

Because it announces the occupancy of a territory by resident coyotes it can be considered to be a territorial claim or declaration. As such it informs all transients and adjacent pack members of the residents presence which encourages those coyotes to move along, which in turn facilitates spatial distribution. I know of three studies that have suggested that "excessive howling" reduces litter size and encourages dispersal.

This is the vocalization that researchers use to locate resident coyotes because it elicits a like response more than any other vocalization.

My son Tyler and I can reproduce these howls with our hand calls and howlers and occasionally do so to locate the current position of known packs. However to simply locate coyotes in unfamiliar territory we will broadcast at high volume a recording of a group yip-howl from a speaker held outside the truck window while driving slowly toward the coyote's suspected location. The resident coyotes seemingly hear an approaching pack of coyotes that are claiming that territory and this technique literally rips a vocal response from the residents. Very much like a loud emergency vehicle siren rapidly approaching their position will often do.

As more hunters and more callers exert more and more pressure on coyotes their comfort zones become smaller and more remote and their security levels diminish. These coyotes become reluctant to respond either vocally or by approach. Social issues and territorial concerns still must be addressed and a skillful caller can often utilize the proper vocalizations with the proper presentation to motivate a resident and even an occasional nomad to investigate the source.

In conclusion it would probably be prudent to quote two gentlemen who are not shy about sharing their opinions either.

"Of course, this is just my opinion. I may be wrong." — Dennis Miller.

"Only the Yippers know for sure and they aren't telling."

— Scott Huber

Some coyotes are reluctant to come. This one should have been more so.

chapter 11

Blowing the Wind — Nistetter

The dawn howling and screaming began during a dismal daylight. The drab short grass prairie was a same shade gray, decorated by equally gray and equally drab sagebrush. I hunkered within the cold and friendless arms of a stringbark juniper and shifted the Sako to a more comfortable hold and listened as Jay Nistetter worked his magic, screaming a Rhino of his own making. The howling, sad to say, was from a somewhat steady twenty five MPH south wind that gusted to maybe twice that. All such creating enough noise to diminish the bloody screams. You want the truth? Even though Jay's screams were as good as could be, I did not expect a hell of a lot from the stand. A coyote who could hear the screams above the moaning wind, I figured, would have to be close, so close we could smell the hungry on his breath. And even then, having heard the screams, must be desperate enough to risk terminal frostbite of the credentials as he traveled to meet the bullet during this precisely arctic high country Arizona morning. I shivered a bit deeper into my camo's and tried to convince myself I was having fun.

Fifteen or so minutes later my expectations were fulfilled. Nothing showed. Jay, being a gentlemanly kind of killer, un-hid and horsed me upright. We gratefully abandoned the stand and walked to the warmth of Jay's four by four Dodge, such not an antique but getting there. Minutes later we bumped along the dirt ranch road headed for stand number two.

I had called this country when I was youngish, maybe sixty or so. The ranch had been owned by the Babbitt bunch then and the ranch foreman was a friend of mine. The ranch had been sold since then and the new owner was the Hopi Indian Tribe. We were upon the Hopi land hoping to call a coyote or two, hoping to off at least one, and hoping the worldly remains of the recently deceased would offer an opportunity for proud hunter photos and all such. Why bother? I was gathering material to do a radical revision and update on my Predator Calling with Gerry Blair. Jay was there to help.

I used a technique called thinking to select a location for stand number two. As is the case with many (maybe all) cattle ranchers, sick and semi-sick cattle are enclosed within a corral somewhat near the ranch house, having them handy for doctoring and such. Sadly, not all of those mother cows, calves, steers, heifers and even bulls survived. Those that bit the big one would be

Nistetter with coyote that came a running.

dragged to a dead dump and left there for those critters who enjoy a meal of well aged beef. The coyote I have met during a long lifetime of predator control were almost always an eager participant,

We set up upwind from the place where the dead dump used to be and hopefully still was. I snugged into the stingy comfort of a rocky crest holding the .22-250 at the ready, a place that offered a decent view of the sage decorated short grass prairie. And then I watched as Jay walked the FoxPro battery powered caller fifty yards out into the sage. Why would a pair of experienced screamers use a digital? Hell, the extra volume delivered by the FoxPro, we figured, would somewhat compensate for the wind. And it did.

Jay returned and set up ten or fifteen feet to my right, hunkered over the viewfinder of a camcorder, punched the selector button, punched the go button and relaxed to enjoy the music.

The jackrabbit distress screams were the worst I have heard during more than a half a century of predator hunting. Bad in a good way. Blood covered every note. Sad enough to bring tears to any mother's eyes. Hell, there were tears in my eyes but it might have been because of the wind. I could not check out Jay's eyes as he wore his trademark sunglasses.

Eight minutes into the screaming my peripheral vision revealed a flash of fur to the right. Jay's side. The patch of fur was occasionally visible as the critter negotiated among the sage. I followed with the 4.5X Bushnell, and as the fur entered a somewhat open area, sucked a lip squeak. The customer froze, leaving the body within the sage but the head and neck visible. I centered the small X of the duplex on the neck and caressed the three pound trigger on the Sako.

Making the retrieve I paced off 78 John Wayne steps. A piece of cake for the muscular .22-250. The 52-grain Sierra hollowpoint entered the neck and shattered the cervical vertebrae. There was no exit. Jay Nistetter's digital scales registered 28.7 pounds, large for an Arizona female coyote.

We took our photos loaded our junk and headed for Flagstaff. During the one hour drive we talked.

There is a lot to like about Jay Nistetter. A lot to admire. Jay is a hunter who has thirty years of experience hunting predators. He is a custom call maker and turns out the very handsome and very screamful Rhino Calls (Blow a Rhino). Jay is also an award winning video producer. Jay wrote the book on predator call collecting. He and Al Lux cooperated to construct *Predator Calls: The First Fifty Years*, such being a thick hard cover filled to overflowing with color photos and filled with information that is bound to be of interest to call collectors, wannabe call collectors and about all who have an interest in our exciting sport. Those who hanker to contact Jay can do so by keying in rhinocalls.com.

As a favor to me, Jay authored the following on predator call collecting.

The inquiring nature shared by predator hunters and other armchair dreamers can trigger many a question and induce a wonderment. Questions about the quarry and the tools of the trade abound, yet without one single tool, the task would be daunting. That single tool is the Predator Call. The predator call is an instrument used to lure the fearless fox, the cautious coyote, the bashful bear or the cunning cougar.

Predator calls, affectionately called "Screamers," are the heart and soul within a special breed of hunter that transcends far beyond the challenge experienced by most sportsmen. Within the proper mouth those "screamers" make much more than noise. Each blood curdling scream shouts an account of the timeless contest between predator and prey, a contest that delivers life to one and death to the other.

Any predator hunter who has scents knows a delicious scream when he hears one and also knows that in order to call a song-dog, he must be able to sing a song. Some of the pioneer screamers of the '40s and '50s learned several of those songs and sang many a critter to the big gut-pile in the sky. The somewhat crude instruments (crude by today's standards) have evolved into collectible treasures.

Predator calls are gaining popularity within the world of collectibles. Some old calls might be found at garage sales. Others might be discovered within sporting goods stores, perhaps hiding amidst the dust of a neglected shelf. Sometimes, as is the case with many treasures, prizes can be acquired at bargain basement prices.

Age, condition and availability are important factors to consider when determining the value of wildlife calls. Age alone does not make any call a prized collectible. Conversely, a modern call may become extremely valuable when the history is well defined. Hidden within this last statement is probably the most important factor affecting the collectible value of virtually all wildlife calls. If no one knows about a certain call, then in all likelihood, that call will be ignored. Information can cause that call to become appealing to a collector. Trivial statistics are the backbone by which a collectible survives. Whew! What did I just say? To put it in a nutshell, when word gets out that someone has something, another person will want it.

The earliest commercial predator calls were designed and advertised as "deadly on fox". During the early days of calling predatory animals fox were the common critters within many areas. At some point in time, El Coyote took center stage and the sly fox took a back seat.

Since the commercial advent of wildlife calls specifically designed and marketed to attract predatory animals, many shapes, sizes, colors and materials have come and gone.

Call companies were constantly under the gun to improve their products, expand production, move to better locations, change materials and add new items to their product line in order to meet the demands of the newly crowned "predator hunter" and increasing competition among call makers.

During the late forties and early fifties (of the last century) the earliest available commercial calls were made of wood and some cow horn fitted with handmade reeds. Scattered among the woods and horns were calls made of Tennite and Bakelite. Calls made of these plastic-like materials were heat hardened within molds. As the rapidly growing sport of calling predatory animals grew, so did the number of call makers. The seventies saw the decreasing use of wooden calls and an increase in the number of manufacturers producing calls made from plastics, which yielded greater profits.

Collecting early calls can be both rewarding and frustrating. Many of the early call manufacturers have long since gone and unfortunately so have their history. Labels, boxes, instructional sheets and decals sometimes denote subtle changes and that clue can suggest rough time lines. Examples of this are easily overlooked and may be discovered by a mere address change, the addition of the zip code (1963), color and size variations of their logos, special edition coloring, specially contracted merchandise, brochure changes showing a 45 rpm record instead of the older 78s, old clearing house catalogs, hunting magazines and more.

The mystery surrounding early predator calls has caused a curiosity. That mystique, as you can see, paves the way for a collector's dream come true for three obvious reasons. First on the list would be that collecting predator calls is virtually an untapped market making it fairly simple for a beginning collector to acquire a collection of desirable calls at a bargain basement cost. Second, many of the originators and early students of this sport are still with us today and are sometimes willing to share historic tidbits. Third, and probably most important, is the fact that the number of predator calls made is many times less than that of duck calls, for example. As the number of collectors increase, it is only a short period of time before the value of predator calls skyrocket. I can envision some calls commanding four digit prices very soon.

Many of the old predator calls can be easily overlooked, but with a keen eye for detail, you may score huge, giving you a piece of the history of this exciting sport, bragging rights and a seat closer to the pickle barrel."

chapter 12

Fur Guns/Rifles

I was after monster mule deer on the North Kaibab when the song sang from a ridge a quarter of a mile away. Nope, it wasn't the fat lady. It was almost surely a coyote. I interrupted my walk long enough to dig into the coat pocket to retrieve the nearly new Burnham Brothers Long Range Fox Call. Seconds later that sad song I call the "Dying Rabbit Blues" raped the northern Arizona high country. Not that good, as this was my first serious attempt at screaming. Even so, a couple of minutes later an out-of-breath coyote showed at the run. Amazed, I watched the advance. When the yodeler was fifty yards out he stopped to make a reconnoiter. I shouldered the ought-six deer gun and sent a custom-loaded 165 grainer through the critter's necessaries. As might be expected, the coyote was killed much more dead than need be. The corpse, sad to say, retained little dignity. That experience taught several valuable lessons. Yes, the rabbit distress scream does cause coyote to come close. Yes, about any centerfire rifle will kill a coyote graveyard dead. Yes, mule deer and elk guns like the .30-06 and all others of like genre do a messy job when it comes time to do wet work on coyote-sized critters. Kinder and gentler calibers abound.

That experience atop the "Mountain That Lays on Its Side" caused me to set out to learn all I could about the exciting sport of predator screaming. And it did even more: I set out almost immediately on the search to find the perfect fur gun.

My years of experience since the "harvesting" of that first called coyote have convinced me of the cold hard facts. There are a lot of good fur calibers available to those who squeeze the rabbit. No one caliber, at least none I have used, can be considered to be a perfect fur gun for all facets of predator screaming. No such caliber, the way I see it, exists. A caliber that does a dandy job on long distance coyote weighing thirty pounds, maybe the .22-250, does less well when the target becomes an eight-pound fox that begs for the rabbit from twenty steps beyond the gun bore? The best a screamer can do is to choose the gun (or guns) that most often meets expectations, forgetting the perfect gun and settling for next best, the nearly perfect fur gun. A nearly perfect fur gun, no matter the caliber, must be accurate. If you can't hit 'em you can't kill 'em.

The right kind of cartridge can reach out to touch a long distance customer, maybe do so twice. Perry Shirley of Flagstaff, AZ.

Out of the box accuracy can be decent among about all of the calibers marketed as varmint guns. I write mainly of those that have an appetite for the .224 diameter bullet. The newly resurrected Hornet, the .222, the .222 magnum, the .223, the .22-250 and the .220 Swift, shooting factory made ammunition, owns enough accuracy to deliver a killing blow to a coyote, a bobcat or a fox at moderate range. Trouble is, the critters I have screamed into gun range do not always cooperate and come to moderate range. An almost perfect fur gun, the way I see it, should have enough talent to consistently take critters at moderate range and have the extended talent needed to take occasional critters at immoderate range.

Considering the above, I believe it important to comment a bit more on extended-range targets. Nine out of ten of the coyotes I call will come so close I can smell the mutton on their breath. Bobcat and fox are more so. The coyote, bobcat, and fox you call will approach similarly. That tenth critter is the one you should prepare for. While on a hunt with a well-known Nebraska publisher we discovered Number 10 to be a paranoid coyote that galloped broadside at an honest 300 yards. I amazed the publisher (and myself, although I made no comment at the time) when I cleaned the earwax (and all else) from the critter's ear using a 52-grain chunk of copper-coated lead. On another hunt a Babbitt Ranch cowboy and I were calling the Redlands when a big male coyote swaggered to a ridge top five hundred yards distant. Again, Number 10. Aiming at the moon I triggered a desperation round that found the coyotes' engine room. Luck? Mostly. I feel it important to say the luckiest people I know are those who are best prepared. Knowledge of the gun, knowledge of the cartridge performance, and ability to judge range permitted me to place the bullet within the ballpark. Luck did the rest.

When it gets to the bottom line, screamers who hope to salvage fur from called critters do not aim at the critter, they aim at a specific part of the critter, usually the part of the rib cage immediately behind the shoulder on broadside critters and within the center of the chest on facing customers. A correctly loaded round that causes either hit is likely to penetrate the critter's necessaries and explode without exiting, providing an instant and humane death. An imprecise hit, even with one of the nearly perfect calibers, can cause fur to fly into adjoining zip codes.

Hunting with cartridges handloaded to match the appetite of a particular fur gun, and handloaded to respond to the challenges of fur hunting, is critical to ultimate fur hunting accuracy and pelt-saving performance, in my opinion. The factory loaded round is handicapped by popularity. The many who buy those mass-produced cartridges hunt through the broad spectrum of hunting opportunity. The factory-produced cartridge must address each of those opportunities to deliver characteristics that permit a decent performance within all.

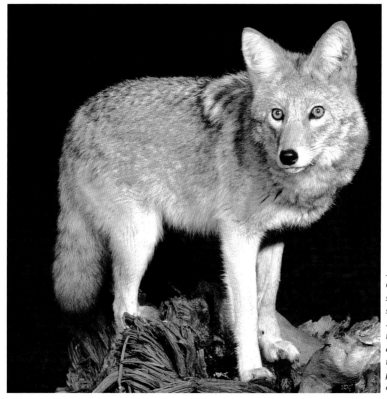

Coyote killers such as those shooting the .224 diameter bullet can cause a kill that leaves the pelt in pristine condition.

I have heard it said that reloading is a way to save money. I do not believe such to be so. Considering initial investment, considering the cost of components, I do not believe there is a substantial savings to be found unless the reloader shoots a hell of a lot (and maybe more). The main strength to the reloaded round comes from the provided ability to tailor a round to the appetite of a specific gun and to the job ahead. And, I consider reloading to be a pleasant part of fur hunting activity. A hunter who commits to reloading is likely to shoot more. That increased shooting will almost surely cause him or her to become a better shot, an asset that can cause an increase in the fur collection.

Certain mechanical manipulations can cause an almost perfect fur gun to move a bit closer to perfect. The attachment of a quality telescope sight is an example. I freely admit a bias to the lower power magnifications. A nearly perfect choice is a variable that ranges from about 1.5 to 4.5. Isn't the gunner who throws a 52-grain chunk of copper-coated lead at a three-hundred-yard coyote handicapped by such low magnification? Not really. Here is a sad truth, learned the hard way. The critter you want to kill is not that big brute in the glass. The target, always, is that little bitty booger you see with the naked-eye. The lower magnification sights, in my opinion, cause me to aim more precisely. That same lack of magnification is almost always an asset when a critter comes bootstrap close.

The right kind of rifle, the right kind of cartridge and the right kind of pelt preparation deliver a pelt that looks good to the fur buyer and looks good on the wall. (Bill Musgrove Photo of Gerry Blair).

Careful attention to the trigger can also improve accuracy. I freely admit to being a trigger man, hating all of the eight-pound factory triggers, most likely put there by the maker to escape a degree of liability. A good trigger to me is one that crisply releases at a bit less than three pounds of pull. All of my collection of fur getters (Sorry Sarah Brady would call it an arsenal) have crisp and lightweight triggers, factory triggers adjusted by a competent gunsmith or replacement triggers installed by the same.

Gordy Krahn, editor of North American Hunting Magazine, *offed this handsome baileyi 'bob while hunting with the author upon the San Carlos Apache Indian Reservation (central Arizona)*

Knowing an evaluation of fur calibers must be made within this chapter, I reluctantly turn my attention to that. Why reluctantly? Choice of caliber is mainly subjective, the way I see it, a bit like deciding upon a blonde or a redhead. (Personally, I love both.) Those who have established caliber priority within the mind are often inflexible as they defend. Some, sad to say, have not learned to disagree without being disagreeable. Even so, my own very subjective evaluations follow.

Knowing that some will want to know, I start at the small end to write upon a round that falls far below the minimum velocity and energy needed in a fur gun. I write of the ubiquitous .22 rimfire.

The .22 Rimfire

The .22 rimfire is a dandy gun for tin cans, for tree squirrels, and for cottontail rabbits. Even shooting the .22 long rifle in hollow point, the round does not offer the range and knockdown needed to cleanly kill even small coyote, small bobcat, and fox of any size consistently. Twenty-two rimfire lovers might wonder if my opinions would change if the rifle shot the reduced lead and increased powder round sometimes called "The Stinger," sometimes called "The Yellowjacket," and sometimes called something else. My opinion stays constant. Even though such manipulation results in slightly increased velocity (and almost always in a drop in accuracy), the increase is not enough to cause the round to hunt with the big dogs. Sorry.

The .22 WRFM

I hold an improved opinion of the improved .22 rimfire muscled up to become the .22 WRFM (Winchester Rim Fire Magnum). Under some circumstances, within certain range limits, I consider the .22 WRFM to be adequate for close-range fox, close range 'coon and close range cacomistle (ringtail cat). Sort of. When the hit is precise. Equivocal? Sure.

Even though the gun might be shooting the 40-grain hollowpoint to a muzzle velocity of 2,000 fps, providing an impressive 364 foot pounds of energy, few critters are shot at the muzzle. That same 40-grain hollowpoint has substantially changed character at 100 yards. Velocity has been reduced to 1,407 fps. Energy has been reduced by about half, to 176 foot pounds. A precise hit on a fox or 'coon will usually result in a somewhat sudden death. An imprecise hit will not.

There was a time (a very short time) when I thought the .22 WRFM might be a dandy gun for close coyote. I was working a pushdown during an early morning scream. Never heard of a pushdown? Such is an area of pinion juniper woodlands ravaged by a pair of D-8 Caterpillars connected by a hundred feet of anchor chain. The dead and dying trees were bulldozed into mounds. Those mounds, after fifty years of aging, have turned into favored habitat for cottontails, rock squirrels, bushy-tailed wood rats, and a mind boggling assortment of mice and voles, all critter edibles.

I had snuggled my big body into the generous arm of a long dead juniper to make the scream. A flash of fur caused me to focus fifty yards out. I locked onto the coyote at about the time he stopped to beg for the rabbit. I took the facing shot offered, centering the crosshairs of the H&R Model 700 to the precise center of the chest. The yodel dog went down as

The .22 WRFM can cause clean kills on some fox but lacks the muscle needed to consistently kill coyote.

if pole-axed. The entry hole was .224 caliber. There was no exit. No muss and no fuss. I was convinced I had come upon the ideal close-range coyote killer.

My enthusiasm was radically diminished by day's end. That day of screaming hooked three more coyote, all coming somewhat close. The first was a 65-yard opportunity at a running coyote. The auto load asset of the Model 700 permitted more than one shot. It is possible I missed, although I do not believe I did. The coyote was sure I did. He made the desperate run for home and Mother, and made it. Maybe.

The other two opportunities were at about the same range. Both were at standing coyote. Each was solidly hit in the chest. Both staggered. Both made the escape. I have not used the .22 WRFM on coyote since.

The Insects

The years preceding the Big War (WWII) caused a proliferation of insects to descend upon the shooting fraternity-the .22 Hornet (1932), the .218 Bee (1938), the .219 Donaldson Wasp (1941), and the slightly earlier .219 Zipper (1937). All of the above were somewhat similar except the Hornet (early models were chambered for the .223 bullet) shot the .224 bullet. All shot decently at close range. All were moderately successful for a few years. The popularity, in my opinion, came from concept, from marketing, and because no sensible alternative was offered. All languished when improved calibers became available. You want to know why? You want the truth? None, with the possible exception of the Hornet, maintained accuracy when range was extended. When the highly accurate .222 debuted in 1950, critter killers were damn glad to go to it. Bench rest shooters too. More on the deuce a bit farther on.

As a point of interest, Ruger restructured their Model 77/22WRM rifle during late 1993 and early 1994 to resurrect the .22 Hornet chambering. Sales have been phenomenal. Production has not kept pace with demand. If the Hornet is the best of a bad bunch, as noted above, why the popularity? I can answer only for myself. I bought my Hornet because I didn't have one. I bought the gun because I wondered how it would perform on called gray fox and the occasional raccoon. I bought it, mainly, because of nostalgia.

Screamer Martin Hendrix of Flagstaff bought his Hornet (Savage-Anshutz) for about the same reasons. A talented reloader, Martin has punched sub-minute of angle Hornet groupings (about 1/4") from the bench using Nosler Ballistic Tip bullets.

The .17 Caliber

The .17 can be a dandy gun for short-range fur and can be a fair caliber for mid-range fur. Remington legitimized this smallest of the centerfires during 1971. The .17 is a fast little booger and that speed is its main asset. A hot-loaded 20-grain or 25-grain bullet can be caused to leave the muzzle at an impressive 4,000 fps. Such will provide spectacular blowups on small critters.

The slowed triple deuce does dandy on fox and raccoon but sacrifices long range punch power.

Such speed, as might be expected, causes the load to be flat shooting. That same speed can cause excessive pelt damage on furbearers if the hit is not precise. Reducing powder will cause a slow down and might improve accuracy. Doing so, however, causes trajectory to be less flat. Even so, those who shoot a lot of thin-bodied fox, and do so at moderate range (maybe a hundred yards or so) will find fur damage to be minimized.

The bad news? The petite pill will not buck much of a headwind and is likewise affected by staunch crosswinds. The .17 does not own the ability to take long-range fur, not as well as do most of the .224s. The small capacity of the case causes loadings to be critical. A half grain overload can increase velocity significantly and might result in an alarming pressure increase. The bottom line? The .17 is fun to shoot and does a decent job on critters out to about a couple of hundred yards.

The .222 Remington

I believe the deuce to be the most accurate of the mid-range calibers. The caliber has been a favorite of bench rest shooters since its introduction in 1950.

Hunters were likewise impressed. Much of the time a factory gun fresh from the dealer's shelf would deliver minute of angle accuracy. Unlike predecessors, the deuce accuracy did not appreciably diminish as range extended.

I see the .222 as an almost perfect fur caliber for all of the East, all of the Midwest and parts of the West. Loaded close to maximum, the .222 round does a dandy job on coyote out to about 200 yards. Downloaded, the round becomes dandy for close range fox. Sadly, as I was creeping into geezer-hood, not paying attention, the major manufacturers conspired to cause the ceuce to turn belly up. Those who hanker for a deuce must currently deal with custom gun makers or custom barrel makers. Those deuce lovers who are not insistent on virginity have the option of adopting an experienced Remington Model 700, an experienced Model 77 Ruger or some such. Check local sporting goods stores, maybe a mega-store such as Cabela's. As a final option, examine the listings within a publication such as *Gun Digest*, published by Krause Publications, 700 East State Street, Iola, WI 54990, www.trapperpredatorcaller.com.

The .223 Remington

The .223 Remington is ballistically close to the .222 Remington Magnum, the case being a bit shorter and holding a hair less powder. I see the .223 to be about as good as the deuce and maybe a bit better in some aspects.

As many know, the .223 was developed for the military during the late fifties. Remington presented the caliber to the civilian market at about the same time. Although the round is labeled a .223, the gun shoots a .224 bullet. Commercial guns deliver good accuracy; many of the military autoloaders do not. A strong asset of the .223 is the availability of once-fired military brass. Commercial reloaders often offer reloaded .223 military at a bargain price. The case capacity of the military brass, fortunately, is about the same as the case capacity of brass intended for civil use. My .223s (including the H&K Model 630 autoloader) group both 50- and 52-grain match hollowpoints well.

The .222 Remington Magnum

The .222 Remington Magnum has a twenty-percent greater case capacity than does the .222 and has about a five percent greater case capacity than does the .223. The caliber was in competition to become a military cartridge but did not succeed. A short time later (1958) the caliber appeared as a civilian offering.

The performance of the Mag-deuce is about midway between the .222 and the .22-250. The .222 Magnum delivers accuracy that is nearly equal to the legendary accuracy of the .222 and has the added advantage of increased range, out to about 275 yards.

The .222 Magnum has not enjoyed the same degree of popularity as either the .222 or the .223, and probably never will. Even though the magnum is ballistically superior to the standard deuce, the eight-year head start enjoyed by the latter causes .222 Mag sales to lag. The .223, being ballistically similar, owns the advantage of military recognition. That, and the availability of once-fired brass, causes the .223 to be most popular.

The .22-250 Remington

The .22-250 began life about 50 years ago as a wildcat. The caliber is essentially a necked down .250 Savage with a slight increase in shoulder angle. The .224-grain bullet leaves the barrel at speeds superior to the old .250-3000 Savage and delivers increased accuracy. The chambering has become the most popular varmint caliber ever developed. Considering all of that, it is surprising to note that no major gun manufacturer offered a factory chambering for this rifle until 1965, even though the .22-250 had outdistanced the popular .220 Swift years before.

I see the .22-250 as the almost perfect caliber for Western screamers. The caliber owns impressive assets. Legitimate 300-yard plus range. Outstanding accuracy, near that provided by the .222 and the .22 Magnum. Enough muscle to take the biggest coyote and the biggest cougar.

Larger Calibers

As noted at the start of this chapter, a caliber of any size can do a decent job of killing a called predator. I have used the .30-06 mentioned and have also used the .25-06 (still do, at times). Screamer friends use the .243 and the .257. Such, in my opinion, can cause it to rain fox fur for a week. If such a caliber is all that is available, and if you wish to salvage the fur, download as you reload so as to avoid bullet expansion. Expect an exit hole on every shot. With luck that exit will be one that can be repaired using patience, needle and thread.

WILDCATS

There are shooters among us who find fun while tweaking rifle and handgun calibers to cause them to be all they can be. Such tweaking, in the past, has led to the creation of calibers considered to be the tamest of cats currently. The love of my own life, the .22-250, evolved as a shooter tweaked the venerable .250-3000. There is a hell of a lot (maybe more) of calibers that can be suitable for fur taking, all such not mentioned within this abbreviated listing. Does that mean I consider such to be Ka-Ka? Nope, not at all. It means I have not tested such on paper and on fur and therefore refuse to write an evaluation. Those who have an interest in radical wildcats are referred to the many information sources on the Internet and to the many reloading manuals that offer all you ever wanted to know. Maybe more.

chapter 13

Fur Guns/Shotguns

It was a desert day to be remembered. A November night rain had traveled from Baja to water the desert. Giant saguaro, as they almost always do, took a greedy drink through their stingy root system, causing the ribbed exterior to swell with delicious enthusiasm. The long-limbed ocotillo (being a bit crazy by nature) thought the rain to be the signal of spring. Bare limbs turned new-leaf green. A few of the hard-core crazies produced flowers of a brilliant red, so pretty I could only stand to look with one eye. Ahhh, the desert after a rain.

That night rain freshened the ground and the air, causing both to look as pristine as on Creation Day. I scrunched a bit deeper into the friendly limbs of the creosote bush and sang my favorite song, "The Dying Rabbit Blues."

I heard the customers coming before sight was possible. The wet ground and the cleansed air cooperated to cause the thumping of the gallop to be drumbeat loud. A pair of storm-hungry coyote, I figured. I raised the massive maw of the ten-gauge autoloader I call "The MooseDick" and readied myself physically and mentally. Seconds later the desperate duo became an intimidating presence not more than thirty yards out. The first pattern of tightly-choked, copper-plated BBs took the leader (the easy one) full face. I was swinging to the trailer a semi-second after the boom, following as the critter made the desperate turn to begin the run for home. The second shot connected before that turn was fully complete. Those few seconds of action caused a pair of prime silver-bellies to hit the ground graveyard-dead and provided hunt excitement. The shotgun, I am convinced, deserves much of the credit for the clean kills. Knowing my limitations, knowing I am not the greatest offhand rifle shot in the world, I am betting I would not have collected two coyote on that screaming if I had carried the rifle. Hell, I might as well be totally honest. It is possible I might have missed both.

The shotgun is my gun of choice when I scream shotgun-friendly country. What kind of country is that? Tight country. Creosote-choked desert flats. Chaparral. Winter woods stripped of leaves and ground cover providing some

---

OPPOSITE PAGE: All big bore shotguns and some rifles do the dirty deed without scattering coyote hair and coyote-burger into adjoining zip codes.

Gerry Blair has used the muscular ten gauge magnum and the three-inch twelve to "harvest" more than a few coyote.

vision opportunity, all at close range. Any kind of country where the customer has to come sure-kill close to get a look at the rabbit. How close is sure-kill close, you ask? Depends, I answer. Sure-kill range varies as the body size of the target varies, as the gauge of the gun varies, as the constriction of the bore varies, and as the nature of the gunner varies. Permit me to share opinions on each of those considerations.

Gauge is an easy explanation. The screamer who hunts coyote-size critters (30 pounds or so in the West and 40 pounds or more in the East) will do best when equipped with one of the gauges I call the big bangers. I refer to the 3.5" ten-gauge, the 3.5" twelve-gauge, and the 3" twelve-gauge. Each of those bangers has the muscle needed to reach out and touch a coyote at reasonable ranges. The bigger the bore, the way I see it, the better the banger.

The gun I call Moose-Dick can be a sensible choice for hunters who scream a lot. My gun is one of the older Ithaca Mag-10s, a big junkyard-dog kind of a gun having the assets needed to rug out a mature dog coyote at surprising range-out to about fifty-five yards, at times a bit more. When stuffed to capacity, one of the ten gauge hulls holds two full ounces of BBs, maybe more. Even though the gas-operated autoloading action drains off a bit of recoil, the kick can be substantial. I do not mean to say the Mag-10 will kill at one end and cripple at the other. I do say that those who have the correct body size will find the recoil to be tolerable, particularly when you consider that screaming shot opportunities might be limited to a half a handful a day. What is the correct body size for the ten gauge? I consider my own to be dandy. A six-foot frame of substantial weight. A hunting incident illustrates the good body/bad body equation.

I was on the hunt for a pair of raccoon who amused themselves by robbing the corncrib on a Texas ranch. Wildlife biologist Bill Del Monte and I traveled to the area to do a bit of night screaming. Minutes into the hunt four eyeballs showed in the beam of the Nightlight. Nope, it wasn't the rare four-eyed 'coon. It was, instead, a pair of two-eyed raccoon coming at the lope, shoulder to shoulder. Bill handled the light and illuminated the corn lovers when they paused for a reconnoiter thirty yards out. Knowing that the first shot would be easy and the second shot less easy, I gambled. I placed the barrel bead between the two heads. A trigger twitch later and both 'coon were rugged. "Holy Moly!" Bill exclaimed, "That was impressive!" And then he asked a fateful question. "Does that gun kick you?" I admitted it did not and offered Bill the opportunity to see for himself. He took dead aim at a stump and lit the fire. The recoil bruised his shoulder, backed him up and hurt his feelings. "I thought you said the gun didn't kick," he grumbled. "I said," I answered, "it didn't kick me." Even though the gun kicked each of us equally, Bill's 150-pound body was affected more than my own 250-pound body.

An auto-loading shotgun can be an asset when responding to multiples of raccoon, fox and coyote within brushy country.

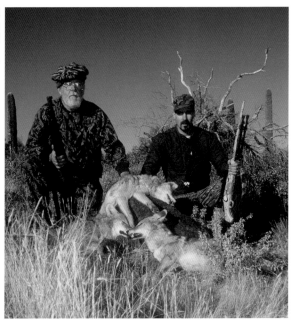

Moosedick killed two of these central Arizona coyote while Gordy Krahn offed the third using his scope sighted .243. (Gordy Krahn Photo).

The assets provided by the ten-gauge autoloader are obvious: range and knockdown power. Each of those allows a clean kill at extended range. The autoloading feature permits a couple of fast follow-up shots if need be. Not often required when dealing with a single customer but almost always needed when the coyote, the fox, the bobcat, and the raccoon come like grapes, in bunches.

Ten-gauge defects can be equally obvious. Recoil has been mentioned. The cost of the gun and the cost of the shotshells can cause a hernia to all but the most muscular budgets. The ten-gauge autoloader, as most know, is currently made and marketed by the Remington Arms Company, using the old Ithaca Mag-10 configuration. Purchase price will trash out a thousand dollar bill, maybe leaving enough leftover for a few boxes of fodder. The buying of that fodder, sad to say, can cause a cold wind to blow through the bank account. I figure each bang out of that big booger blows a dollar bill. Reloading, for those who are so inclined, can cut the cost in half. That's the good news. The bad news? Unless you shoot a hell of a lot (maybe more) the cost of equipment can cause savings to disappear.

Hunters who work the flyways for high traveling honkers and other waterfowl, particularly those who hope to steel the goose, will find the ten gauge to be dandy. Other all-season hunters will be less pleased. The ten gauge is not a grouse gun. It is not a quail gun, nor is it a rabbit gun. Hunters who own the small gun safe, those who must make do with one general-purpose smoothbore, are advised to think twelve.

The recently revived 3.5" twelve-gauge, best typified by the Ulti-Mag pump gun made by Mossberg, can be a sensible substitute. The 3.5" hull, as long as a ten-gauge hull but not as fat, delivers decent punch out to about fifty yards. All that was said about the ten-gauge can be said about the 3.5" twelve, reduced by about 15 percent. I see one important defect in the 3.5" twelve. Factory fodder offerings are limited. The 3.5" twelve, like the 3.5" ten, was engineered to be a steel shotgun for waterfowl. Shot shell manufacturers do not offer much for the critter caller.

Thinking positive, the cost of a gun such as the Ulti-Mag can be less than half the cost of a gun such as the Remington SP-10. And unlike the ten, the 3.5" twelve will accept the less long shotshells — the 3" twelve and the 2 3/4" twelve. Even though guns designed to handle the long twelve hulls are big and somewhat clubby, such can be crammed with reduced load shotshells and pointed at about any kind of game susceptible to a smoothbore.

The tried-and-true twelve fitted with a chamber long enough to accept the 3" shell can be a dandy choice for screamers who intend to make one gun answer all smoothbore needs. Experience causes me to favor the autoloader, typified by the venerable Remington Model 11-87 SP. The SP stands for Special Purpose, a designation applied to guns made specifically as ambush guns, all having a non-glare metal finish (sometimes achieved through chemically altering the metal and sometimes achieved through camo painting) and all have a low luster finish to wood or plastic parts.

The three-inch twelve, in autoloader or in pump gun, does a decent job on called critters and on flyway waterfowl. Stuffing the magazine with 2 3/4" loads of the proper shot size can cause the gun to turn attention to a mind-boggling variety of feathered and furred critters.

Ammo cost can decrease when big banger hulls are reloaded.

Experimentation has caused Blair to believe a loading of copper plated BB's to be bad medicine for coyote, fox and raccoon.

Even though I mention only the autoloader and the pump, I am aware of other shotgun configurations, the single shot and the stack barrel and side-by-side doubles. Those who own that kind of gun will likely find the gun to be decent, subject to the limitations noted during the discussion of other shotgun types.

And even though I have discussed only the ten-gauge and the twelve-gauge, I am aware lesser gauges exist. I consider the sixteen-gauge, the twenty-gauge, the twenty-eight-gauge, and the .410 caliber to be unsuited for heavy-duty predators. I am not saying such cannot be used. I say, instead, that those lightweights cause the job of critter killing to be more difficult than need be.

Some mention must be made of barrel constriction, commonly called degree of choke. Tightly-choked guns cause the shot disbursement to be delayed, delivering a dense pattern at a surprising distance. Super-tight chokings have been made available to those who hide in the bushes to make a noise like a turkey's girlfriend. That kind of hunter calls the gobbler to somewhat close range (25 to 35 yards) and aims for the turkey's head — a target of about hardball size. Too large a pattern spread can cause a miss. Those tightly-choked turkey guns can do a fine job on called critters, delivering a dense pattern to the animal necessaries.

A tightly-choked gun delivering a dense pattern offers an advantage. That advantage may turn to a disadvantage. A careless shouldering or a careless aim can cause the dense pattern to be off target. Some screamers compensate. They add an extra barrel bead and sometimes fit the gun with open or glass sights. More on that within the chapter dealing with sights.

chapter 14

Fur Guns/Primitives

The fur takers mentioned to this point have been the kind of killers that cause the killing to be less difficult. Fast and flat shooting centerfires like the .222, the .223 and the .22-250, shotguns of the ten and twelve gauge subspecies. Knowing there are those who find pleasure in doing the difficult, this chapter will discuss screaming critters close to the front stuffer, the handgun, and the stick and string. I say at the start I do not intend to say a lot on the subject of screaming to the primitives, knowing that those who have answered this extra challenge will be a somewhat small percentage of the readership.

Those who enjoy the smell of black powder will find the muzzleloader to be a decent fur getter. There is the obvious handicap caused by the one-shot capability. The reloading, even using speed loaders, offers sufficient time for the slowest of foot to make the escape before the powder is poured and patched, before the lead is ramrodded home and before the capping or priming. A second disadvantage comes from the relative inaccuracy provided by even the best of the black-smoke belchers. None I have handled offer the pin-point accuracy provided by the deuce or by any other of the .224 genre.

This high country yodeler was called sure-kill close within the short grass prairie of northern Arizona.

The question of caliber is one that can be confusing to those not familiar with the ballistics of the muzzleloader. The slow speed of the projectile does not offer the advantage (or disadvantage) of expansion. A .36 caliber ball, a .36 caliber maxiball, a .36 caliber chunk of rock will deliver a .36 caliber entry and a .36 caliber exit. All of the above in .54 caliber will deliver an entry and an exit of .54 caliber. What is the difference? Not a hell of a lot, speaking furwise. I shoot a .54 caliber for all of my big game hunting and use that same .54 caliber on called critters. The entry and exit fur tears are easily repaired. The big chunk of lead delivers the big whack, causing the recipient to be graveyard dead in an instant.

Those who handgun hunt will find paranoid predators to be a hard get. Shooting from the set can be difficult. The target, much of the time, is on the move, compounding the degree of difficulty. Here is the technique I use to handgun fur, a technique that works, some of the time.

I find it best to buddy hunt when I head out with a holstered handgun. I find it to be too tough working alone — not enough hands to do all that needs to be done. A solo hunter can do about as well if he or she trades the tube for the battery-powered caller. I find a comfortable set that places me against a tree or to the front of a bush, anything to cause my big body to blend, and set so that my body is squared to the anticipated approach. I draw up the knees and use those drawn-up knees to support the arms. Using the two-hand hold I stay ready for customers. If the critter comes running, as most do, I lip squeak, growl, or cuss to cause the critter to slide to a stop. Then I take the shot.

Taking a coyote, cat, or fox using the bow and arrow is a most difficult endeavor. A certain amount of motion is needed to make the draw and take the aim. Releasing the hold causes the arrow to fly and that causes a movement that can alarm the customer. A quick-footed coyote, sad to say, can dodge an arrow and have time left to scratch a flea. What to do? Take a tip from the archers who take stick and string to the spring turkey woods, the turkey being about equal to the coyote in degree of paranoia-use every advantage available.

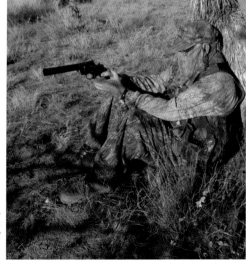

Delicious screams and proper technique can cause handgun hunters to take javelina and about all animals with ears.

Even though the distress scream can cause coyote to come close archers who are not fully camouflaged will have trouble connecting.

As noted in the discussion on handguns, it is important to have the screaming isolated from the shooter. This can be done by having a buddy call or can be done using the battery-powered caller. It is also important to give the customer something to look at when he or she comes to do business. A coyote coming to the screams expects to SEE something. If they do not, they will not stay around for long. Consider the use of a decoy, preferably one that moves, to satisfy expectations. That decoy can deliver a second advantage: Looking at the decoy makes it less likely the critter will look at you.

The use of a brush or commercial blind, each provided with shooting ports, can be critical to success. The blind hides necessary (even unnecessary) movement from the critter. Finally, and this is important, cross the fingers. If it is in your nature to do so, pray. Taking a coyote, a fox, or a cat using bow and arrow can be REALLY difficult.

chapter 15

Calling Equipment

I checked for snakes. Seeing no big ones I used the toe of my boot to kick away sticks and stubs and wallowed my big butt into the depression. I was beneath the cap rock of a desert rim and was halfway through a walking trapline. It was beanie-weenie time.

Minutes later I was munching happily, eating slowly to make it last. At about that time a coyote howled from across the canyon. Don't be asking me why a coyote would howl at noon-thirty on a hot desert day. Hell, maybe it smelled the beanie-weenies. Anyway, I grabbed for the Circe and blew soda crackers, beanie-weenies, and screams right on top of the howl. I nearly swallowed the tube when a gaunt desert dog popped up on the far rim of the slot canyon, maybe a hundred yards off. My only gun being a trap gun, a four-inch S&W

A Sako Forester and a 52-grain reloaded .22-250 caused this northern Arizona coyote to die with dignity. (Mark Middleton Photo).

Back-up calls are handy when the main screamer calls in sick.

Model 63 in .22 rimfire, I did not draw and did not shoot. I stared at the yodel dog as he stared at me. The stare-down ended when the 'yote figured a half can of beanie-weenies was not worth the walk over. Watching him walk, I discovered a critter-calling truth. It is not wise to mess with a critter unless you own the equipment to deliver the extreme sanction.

The equipment carried on early fur hunts was Spartan, barely enough to get the job done. I carried a call, carried a gun and carried a knife. That was it. No camo, no facemask, no nothing. Even so I called critters. Lots of critters. (Honesty causes me to explain there were a hell of a lot of critters to be called then and not as much competition.) And then a funny thing happened. Not funny, odd. The more I called, the better I got at it, and the more equipment I carried. Not because I really needed it, mainly because experience taught hard lessons. Calling accouterments, much of the time, causes the calling and killing of predators to be less difficult. Some such helped to put more fur on the stretcher. Others offered convenience. Some, truthfully, were neat to have. The following listing of calling accouterments helps me during my screaming. I am betting they will do the same for you.

I never hunt without carrying more than a single screamer. I carried only one until hot slobbers hit the super cold leaf of the Circe reed to cause a freeze up at a time when I had a herd of coyote coming. I hunt now equipped with a metal-reed tube or two, a similar number of plastic-reed calls, and maybe a diaphragm; and my mouth, to make the Kiss of Death, the growl, the moan, and all else as needed. I never leave home without it.

Most of the time I use only one call at each stand, alternating only when the one within the mouth calls in sick. I might alternate calls during the day to offer the critters (and my own ears) a bit of variety. Carrying that collection of calls offers a further asset. Having all of those backups available brings contentment.

I also carry a collection of guns in the truck, although never less than three. Why three? I carry my main squeeze, MooseDick, knowing that substantial circumstance of wood and steel might whine like a whipped cur if left at home. And I carry a long distance getter, usually the .22-250 Sako Forester to have

Carrying a back-up rifle or back-up shotgun (maybe one of each) can be dandy when sights become misaligned during a far away hunt. (Gordy Krahn Photo).

the right gun for open country. I take a second centerfire, that to be decided prior to the hunt as I stand to gaze and be amazed at the contents of the gun safe. That choice, much of the time, is a dandy H&K Model 630 in .223, such being the pretty one from H&K-an accurate little sumbitch, good for putting a lot of lead into the fur, and doing it quickly.

Why a backup centerfire and not a backup shotgun? I have not had a shotgun call in sick during mid-hunt. Centerfires, particularly those fitted with glass sights, can be less stalwart. I offer an example.

I was far from home, far from the truck, when I attempted a half gainer from off the ice-slicked rock. Olympic judges (even the Russians) would have awarded a high score for technique. Even though naturally clumsy, I did not hit the ground head first, but came close. The Ruger went into orbit, did a couple of dandy flips, and landed so that most of the reentry impact went to the Weaver K-6, causing it to come loose from the mounts and rattle among the cold rocks in a most depressing way. Me? Hell, I was bruised and pissed off, but no broken bones. The telescope sight was another matter. I examined, cried my tears, and started the trudge back to the truck. But, no backup gun there.

I did the same thing nearly, during one of the payback hunts mentioned earlier; it was another cold-weather ordeal. I was wearing wool army gloves to cause my hands to freeze less solid and made the mistake of grabbing the Sako by the barrel. Wool on cold steel did not offer much of a grip and that lovely .22-250 slid to hit butt first on the hard surface. The scope popped, the buttplate broke and a hairline crack extended from butt to rear sling stud. I was sad and glad. I was sad because of the damage to one of my good friends; I was glad because I had a backup available.

Unlike some who write, I do not consider myself to be the world's greatest offhand rifle shot, not even in print. I stay constantly envious of those sure shots who consistently whack far off critters (all such being a half-mile away on the windy day-all at the gallop) the first time every time.

I am not that kind of shooter and have not hunted with one who was. Dirty Harry has said a man must know his limitations, and I do. I take every advantage when it comes time to start the wet work. I set up so that I can brace arms across drawn-up knees. I borrow trees, posts, anything handy, to add stability. On one stand, having been offered a somewhat awkward angle, I leaned across Grandma Dog's broad butt. Took me 30 minutes to catch up to her after the shot. Not the coyote, Grandma Dog.

I have also used many of the bi-pod accuracy aids. Such, I am convinced, have permitted the taking of extra fur. Look for a listing of bi-pods and shooter sticks in the back section on equipment.

Those fortunate screamers who have viewed the Beastmaster tape know I dressed as Santa one December day to scream in a sounder of javelina, did it twice, got it all on tape. (The rumor Larry O. hummed "Jingle Bells" during the screaming is false, even though he might have if he was not busy with the camcorder.) I screamed while wearing that ridiculous costume to prove a point. The hunter who sits still as a mountain (California excepted) will remain discrete even though not wearing camo. Can a screamer enjoy success while wearing street clothes? Sure. I have done it. George Oakey does not own one piece of camo, probably never will. Why wear camo then?

You wear camo to become even more discreet. A lack of camo clothes might not bother some critters. Experience tells me it absolutely does bother others. Some, the ones I call the Ph.D.s, will start the desperate run for home and Mother at the least excuse. Camo clothing, including facemask and gloves, makes sense. Shotguns and rifles of the non-reflective configuration need no

A self made bipod can enhance accuracy and do so at low cost. Bill Countress of Colorado

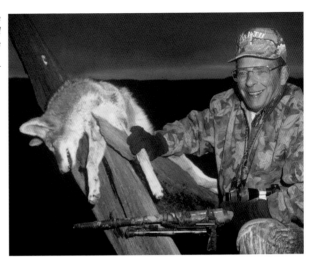

supplemental camouflage. Guns with a more flashy finish do. Such can be subdued using paint, using camo tape (I like the cloth kind best.) and using a camo sock. Maybe other ways I have not heard of.

Some customers come from downwind. Others come from upwind but circle downwind to take a taste of the air, hoping to taste rabbit. Those will almost surely spook if the air tastes a lot like Gerry Blair (Oreo Cookies) or Larry Gates (Raspberry-filled Fig Newtons). Using a scent masker like pure old unadulterated skunk musk, or using an imitation like Tex Isbells CoverScent (available from Johnny Stewart Game Calls) can cause the coyote nose to stay trustful.

The critter country I hunt is of two types, the desert being one. My desert is the kind of place where everything green has stickers or spines, sometimes both. A hunter who bare-butts it is likely to end up (snicker) with a rear that looks as though it has been porcupined.

I hunt high country also, a place that can be snow-covered during prime fur time. Placing a somewhat warm rear within that snow can cause a meltdown, not of the rear but of the snow. The wet rear almost always freezes; not all that uncomfortable during the freeze but damn painful during the thaw. Carrying a cloth-covered section of foam or a section of scrap carpet, something that can be placed between the butt and a hostile surface, can cause a degree of comfort.

I hate to skin on the ground, saying so within the chapter on skinning. I carry a dog choke chain on every hunt so that I might skin in the field and do so in a way that suits my nature. Those who require increased sophistication should consider the carrying of a skinning gambrel. I also carry a tail stripper and a tail splitter, each available at low cost through advertisements in *Trapper & Predator Caller* magazine.

While on the subject of skinning I feel it proper to mention a technique I call safe skinning. There was a time when I did my skinning barehanded, the way real he-men and he-women did it. I do not remain that macho. I carry surgical gloves (S-M-L at pharmacies) and pull those skin-tight rubbers on when I skin (I call it safe skinning). The gloves protect the hands from blood, intestinal material, and (ugh) the ever-present poop. Thus protected, the skinner stays semi-safe from epizootics. Cleanup, when the skinning ends, can be as easy as removing the rubber gloves.

The deadeye Richards mentioned earlier seldom need backup ammo, every shooting resulting in a one-shot kill (usually in the ear). Those of us who are less gifted need to carry enough ammo to make at least one reload. Carrying those reloads within the pocket can be natural. Such can be inconvenient. The sitting hunter might find it to be awkward to make the retrieve. Worse, such might do as I did on one stand. It happened this way.

I missed the running coyote four times within about as many seconds, each shot coming close enough to encourage an increase of speed. I got lucky on the fifth shot (Law of Averages) and made the connection (not in the ear). I was all happy, telling myself what a good sumbitch I was, when I sighted a second coyote headed my way. (Reckon he wanted to know what-in-the-heck I had killed.) I made a dive for the front pocket of a somewhat tight pair of Levis jeans, a place containing extra .22-250 rounds. The first grab brought out the key chain, three quarters, two nickels, a muddy piece of quartz collected on the way in, and several fired cases. I tossed all and went back. Two trips later I had my reload, but, too late.

What's the point? The point is, the screamer who is serious about the kill needs to carry backup ammo in a convenient location, maybe one of the clever shell holders offered by Michaels of Oregon. (See equipment listing in the back of the book.)

Want more? I carry a sharpening diamond to return the edge to the skinner after each peeling. I carry a few gallon-sized ZipLocs® to receive the pelt, placing it within the ice chest if weather is warm. I carry Wet Wipes (within baby supplies at pharmacies) so as to have an instrument to remove disgusting matter from the hands. I carry an accurate field scale (Cabela's) to reduce the size of those fifty-pound bobcat and eighty-pound coyote. Your own experience will likely cause you to discover other aids. If so, drop a line (in care of Krause Publications) so that I may know. I am the kind of hunter who continually strives to improve.

Accurate scales can cause a twenty pound fox to be reduced to half that.

chapter 16

Decoys and Other Flimflam

The coyote came at the charge. Fifty feet out from Frankenhare the anxious critter slid to a stop. A right front foot was in the air, causing me to be amused. "That damn fool 'yote thinks he is a pointer," my brain said to itself, and then that brain chuckled. At about then the coyote began a deliberate sneak, and that sneak continued until the critter was somewhat close. Suddenly, when the sneaker was ten feet out it launched to land exactly on the unconcerned decoy, that decoy being a very modest effort at taxidermy-a soft plastic form covered with the ratty hide from a black-tailed jackrabbit.

Even though the decoy did not look all that good, it apparently tasted worse. The coyote began a trot that would take the prize to a place of privacy. That trot was stopped after a step or two and the coyote spit out Ole Frank, then slunk off into the greasewood of the Papago. Hell yes, it happened. I was there. So was Chuck Spearman. We saw it all.

A second coyote-decoy interaction took place some miles away, later in the day. Chuck and I made a stand in somewhat crowded greasewoods; a place decorated with isolated clumps of prickly pear cactus — the kind that makes the pretty yellow flowers and then the succulent red fruit. Anyway, Frankenhare was fifty feet to the front, looking mildly amused (as he always did). Chuck and I were within the scrawny arms of a creosote bush, our Canon auto-focus cameras at the ready.

The coyote came at a gallop, making what I call a run-by-a maneuver that lets the critter maintain full speed as he makes the reconnoiter. The coyote saw the decoy and his eyeballs sort of popped. The 'yote locked in on the decoy but continued the run by, a situation that can lead to excitement when in cactus country. And it did. The coyote ran full speed into a prickly pear. Chuck and I laughed out loud as the critter made the retreat. Decoys are like that, we agreed. They keep the hunt interesting because the screamers never know what in hell will happen next.

Having said all of that, it is also proper to consider a couple of other aspects to critter-calling decoys-mainly, are they all that good? Will they help to put more fur on the stretcher? I say maybe and no, and then qualify. My experience with decoys causes me to think such can be dandy for those who scream to the camera or scream to the camcorder. A critter that comes to the call, the way I see it, is responding to an audio. That critter expects to see the picture when he gets close. When they do not, the light bulb lights and they get the hell gone. Such is not a great problem for gunners. A predator that comes close enough to see the rabbit is usually close enough to kill. You are not likely to kill that critter one bit deader if he loiters to gaze at the decoy. Such action, at times, can permit a more precise shot placement.

Even so, the main strength owned by a critter-calling decoy goes to the cameraman. Some critters that come to the call, when they see the decoy, do goofy things. A good many stick around a lot longer than they might otherwise, providing the opportunity to burn up a lot of tape or a lot of film.

I have experimented with decoys of varying personality. Frankenhare has been mentioned. Frank started his decoy-hood as a hunkered hare, a critter that sat to think pure thoughts while a coyote made the sneak with murder on his mind. The original Frankenhare was not all that good. You want the truth? Many of the customers ran in and ran out and never saw Frank. Oh well, back to the laboratory.

Frankenhare II was somewhat improved. The hare hide was stretched over a running rabbit form, lending the suggestion of movement but no movement.

Beauty and the Beast. Wisconsin resident Pat Akey holds Frankenhare, an entity that encourages critters to come close, and die.

Frankenhare III did better. Larry and I modified the running rabbit form to permit movement. We placed a steel rod through the middle of the body, extending the rods so that an inch or so protruded beyond the body. Those rod extensions were positioned within stirrups that came up out of the base. The least tug on the nose would cause Frankenhare III to nod his head agreeably. I screwed an eyehook into the nose, tied on monofilament line drawn from a Zebco reel, took the reel back to the setup, and tugged when a customer came. That little bit of movement allowed about every customer a good look. Most reacted. We became encouraged.

The concept of the moving decoy was extended. The next effort involved a battery-powered, hair-covered bit of nonsense marketed under the name "My Lovely Puppy." ("She walks and turns her head, she barks and wags her tail." I am not making this up). The little critter came with a leash (actually, a cord containing the controls) and a cute pink ribbon. $12.95 (on sale). Figuring the price was right, figuring what the hell, we bought a couple.

My Lovely Puppy was not an immediate success. The short leash caused her to sit close to the gun during the screaming. A critter looking to see her walk, bark and wag her tail was bound to see the two big guys hunkered close by.

We messed around with Lovely Puppy, hoping to make her better. We tied into the cord and inserted twenty-five feet of telephone wire, small diameter stuff. Reviews were mixed. One bobcat and a few fox appreciated our puppy. Most coyote customers did not. We moved on with the search to find "the perfect decoy."

An inexpensive jackrabbit form can be united with a hare skin to produce a rabbit-like enticer.

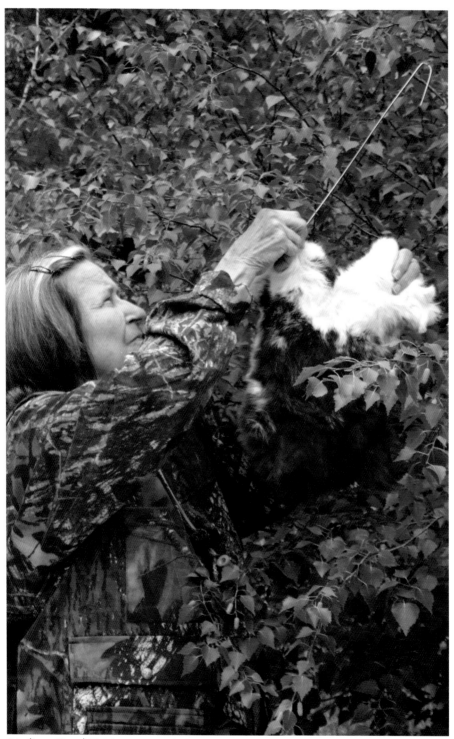

B.jo (Sweet Thang) Blair hangs a tanned rabbit skin to a brushy branch to serve as an El Cheapo decoy.

Our next effort was high tech — at least it cost considerably more. I bought a radio-controlled (about a hundred dollars or so) toy 4x4, whip antenna and all. In the field I covered most of the plastic with a tanned gray fox hide. I was ready.

The coyote came from out of the greasewood, maybe a hundred feet or so out into the overgrazed meadow, sending the bad eye over the two or three hundred yards that separated us. Figuring it was time to give him a look at the secret weapon, I pushed a button to make the motorized fox move a bit, not a lot but enough to show life. I pushed the wrong button. The 4x4 took off at the race, fox fur flapping, antenna to the rear like some damn stinger, headed right at the coyote. The coyote turned and started a desperate depart with the 4x4 fox in hot pursuit. I have not seen a coyote (or a 4x4 fox) run so fast.

Somewhere in there we also tried out Frankenyote, another home taxidermy effort. It does not embarrass me to say we made a mistake or two. Mistake One: Being hooked on the trophy aspect, we chose the hide from the biggest coyote we had and placed that hide on the biggest taxidermy form. Mistake Two: We combined our meager talents to deliver a dominance demeanor. We realized our miscalculation the first time afield.

We set up within open greasewood at a place we had called coyote before. Frankenyote snarled from maybe fifty yards out. The coyote, either a pup or a little bitch, came at the run but slid to a stop when it saw Frank. Turning tail, the little coyote made a desperate retreat. I am almost sure I heard a pitiful yipping, but Larry says no. Turns out the sound I heard was Larry giggling. Anyway, trying to sort things out, we agreed that a big and dominant male coyote decoy is not great. Think about it. How would you react if you came upon John Wayne with a toothache?

Other experiments were modest. One involved using a frozen road-killed jackrabbit as a decoy; a technique that wasn't that bad early in the day but turned nasty by afternoon. We also used the tanned hide of a gray fox, laid upon a rock or draped across a limb. One configuration worked somewhat. We used monofilament line to tie the skin to the slender branch of a greasewood, leaving several inches of line between limb and fox. The least bit of wind would cause the fox to move. Several called critters, mostly coyote, showed appreciation, making an attempt to trash the fox.

Where do we stand now on the use of decoys? Sort of at the idle. Somewhere in my head there is one more decoy idea. I see Frankenhare mounted on a platform, sharing space with the remote control mechanism from a model airplane. I see that contraption out front with the Beastmasters hid in the brush, Larry manning the Camcorder and me holding the controls. A coyote appears, I push buttons to cause the rabbit to gyrate. The coyote goes crazy, charges, and runs off with all, with me and Larry in hot pursuit. Ahhh, dreams.

chapter 17

Calling Camouflage

I sat in the sun and away from the sanctuary of greasewood and mesquite to do the screaming. Faithful companion Larry O. Gates stood behind, encumbered by the substantial weight of the Panasonic AG-460, an enhanced camcorder with an appetite for the Super VHS 1/2" tape. When the TallyHo screamer was near to my beard-covered lips I turned to ask a final question. "Larry O," I says, "I want the truth. Do I look stupid sitting here in the open, in the sun, wearing a bright red Santa Claus suit (even though it was not Christmas) while making a noise like a coyote's supper?" "Yes, Gerry, you do," Larry answered truthfully. Satisfied, I turned my broad back to the camera and started the screaming.

An extra long face mask can disguise a bare hand holding a call. (Bill Rice Photo).

Minutes later a small sounder of the pig-like critter called javelina came at the gallop and the growl. The half a handful of peccaries came ten yards close, reconnoitered and reconsidered, then trotted off while coughing out indignant whuffs. Not willing to leave well enough alone, I laid into the 'Ho one more time, sending out a delicious series of short and choppy screams. The pigs, nearly out of sight, paused, listened, looked and threw it into reverse. Seconds later the lead boar (I assumed him to be the Boss Hog.) had his sensitive snout at my boot soles. Not willing to have him become too close a friend, I waved a hand and whuffed out a warning. That pig, and all others, made a second noisy retreat.

That encounter provided two benefits. Benefit number one was the knowledge that peccaries and other wild animals will come close to a screamer who wears a bright red Santa suit and sets in the sun, as long as that hunter sits as still as a rock and stays as quiet as a cactus. Benefit two? Superb footage for the video on predator calling we were taping.

I do not advocate the wearing of the Santa suit or any other conspicuous clothing during a screaming for predators. I did so in this instance to make a point, and I made that point. Having done so, it is proper to also say that the hunter who goes on the hunt for fur will be most successful if he, she, or it does so while clothed to be as inconspicuous as possible. That discrete appearance,

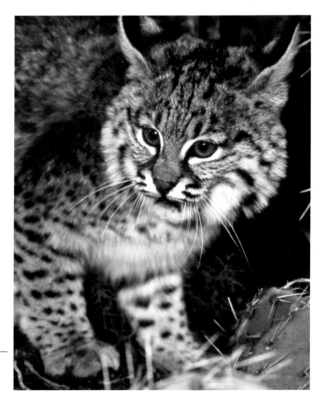

A fill-in flash causes this Arizona bobcat to lose about all of it's natural camouflage.

A well camouflaged hunter carrying a camouflaged gun offers little to alarm the most paranoid customer. Gordy Krahn Photo).

it seems to me, will be best accomplished if the hunter wears one of the carefully crafted camo patterns available to the sport; Jim Crumley's Treebark, Toxey Hass's Mossy Oak, Bill Jordan's Realtree, and others. Each of those has been fashioned using varying contrasts of neutral and non-reflective cloths. A hunter who wears such, the hunter who sits as still as a rock and as quiet as a cactus, will be invisible to the eyes of the most paranoid of the predators.

Even so, there is more to competent camo than the wearing of pants and shirt. Complete camo calls for camo gloves, a camo head net, camo hat, and a properly camouflaged gun.

Even the best of the tan-colored camo can be in poor taste under certain conditions. Various-colored camo does a fine job when the hunter hunkers within the shadow of a leafed-out hardwood to toot the tube. Change the setup to a snow-covered plain and that hunter will be as obvious as a college sophomore on his first date. The thing is, the thinking hunter matches his camo to the country he or she mostly hunts.

There is more to complete camo than sight camo. Nearly every predator depends on their sense of smell and sense of hearing to keep their butt safe from bigger predators. It does little good to disguise against sight and fail to disguise against sound and smell. Stay tuned while I talk (actually, write) a bit about my philosophy of complete camouflage.

According to some wildlife biologists, the coyote and many other animals do not see color, at least not in the same sense as the human eye sees color. The peccaries that came to the screaming Santa probably did not see a red Santa. It is likely they saw a black Santa. Coyote, bobcat, fox, and some other predators would have seen Santa about the same. The smart hunter, it seems to me, should not worry a lot about the color or lack of color within his or her camo. That same smart hunter should also know that animals do see contrast. An extreme example would be a midnight black cat standing atop a snow bank. That critter is obviously visible to human eyes and to animal eyes. Put

Blair's bare hands and bare face did not alarm this customer but might cause some paranoids to head for home and Mother. (Gordy Krahn Photo).

a pale pussycat on that same snow bank and camouflage has been accomplished.

A medium red fox standing in a mostly grey background, conversely, is likely to be nearly invisible to the predators that see only blacks, whites, and shades of gray. Knowing that, it makes sense to match the camo or the clothing to the CONTRAST of the hunt setting and not spend a lot of time fretting about matching to the COLOR of the hunt setting.

Honesty causes me to say that certain kinds of "street clothes" will work about as well for the predator screamer as will the most expensive of the camo patterns in some instances. A close friend and occasional hunt partner (George Oakey) does not and has not (not even one time) worn patterned camo to the screaming. Even so, George is a very successful screamer who has called and killed a ton of fur.

My own screaming costume, during the days when I was recently retired from the Arizona Highway Patrol and hunting fur to complement a meager retirement income, consisted of forest green trousers that exactly matched the shaded junipers where I did much of my screaming, or khaki tan trousers that precisely matched the brown of the autumn prairie. Much of the time I would wear a shirt to match. Calling snowfields caused me to break out a set of painter pants and shirt. During those times when I screamed the midnight I would opt for dead black, becoming the Mutant Ninja Screamer. This is all common sense stuff.

Gloves of some kind are needed to disguise the flesh tone of the hands. Those same gloves can be an asset when the temperature turns frigid. Those same gloves can create a pair of problems. Problem one has to do with the "feel" of the trigger finger. During my early days as a screamer I bought a handsome set of gloves that did a dandy job of keeping hands and fingers toasty warm and did an equally admirable job of hiding the flash of the flesh. Trouble was, the gloves completely destroyed my feel for the three-pound trigger of the Ruger .22-250. During one memorable hunt I managed to miss eight coyote in a row. To make matters worse I had a buddy along who witnessed the humiliation and felt obligated to tell all who would listen about how Blair missed a charging coyote that was 20 feet out. Those tales caused me to consider giving up screaming for good. And then, I realized my lack of marksmanship started on the day I first wore the gloves. I tossed them into the truck box, called, and shot barehanded, and skinned eight of the next ten critters called. Nope, my talkative friend was not along to witness THAT part of my marksmanship. Dammit.

The second handicap that comes from the wearing of gloves has to do with the volume and tone of the scream. Gloves that cover the palm of the hand used to make a sound chamber for the tube will cause the volume of the scream to diminish and will cause a change of tone. What to do? I sometimes call with the soundbox hand (the same hand fitted with the trigger finger) bare. If I feel a glove on that hand is critical, I will use a glove that has the palm part cut out. A longitudinal slit in the trigger finger cover allows that most important digit to stay snug and warm until circumstances call it to action. It is a simple matter to slip that booger out to help with the wet work. A second option, available to those who call in somewhat warm weather, is the wearing of net or mesh gloves-lightweight so that the trigger finger is not stifled, with enough flesh available to decently "box" the screams.

Camouflaging the face is not essential when calling country where the critter does not come so close you can smell the rabbit on its breath. Many of those long-range opportunities let the shooter do the dirty deed before the

Face paint, as used here by Susan Wells, can be effective but is almost always messy.

customer has a chance to spook because of a non-camoed face. Place that same hunter in tight country, a setting where close contact is the norm, and the non-camouflaged face can cause paranoia that will cost in lost fur. I compensate on the side of caution by wearing one of two types of face covering on every stand. Those two types are the head net and camo makeup.

Head nets are available in a mind-boggling variety. I have used the pullover kind with no eyeholes and no mouth hole, the same with holes, the Bandido Mask, masks fitted to eyeglass frames, and masks attached to camo caps. All will work. Some work better than others. I do not favor the pullover kind, with holes or without. The kind without holes, while doing a good job of hiding the flash of my eyeglasses, causes the moisture within the breath to fog those glasses during cold weather screams. Bad. And those with no mouth opening do not offer access to the tube. Double bad. Those pullovers having appropriate holes are a bit better but will also cause fogging. And turning the head almost always causes the eyeholes to squirm around to pay an unauthorized visit to the ear. The best kind of mask, at least the best for me, is one of the Bandito types, a mesh that covers the face from the eyeballs down. Pulling the camo cap low on the forehead causes most of the forehead to hide, leaving only the eyeballs uncovered. I like the kind of mask that has cloth hanging to the upper chest, leaving a lot of room so that I might move my calling hand (usually bare) up under. Doing so causes the overhang to effectively hide the flash of the flesh as the fingers flutter to provide quaver.

Camouflage makeup is a second option. Blacks, browns, and greens are applied so that flesh tones are disguised and the focus of the face is mottled. The camo creams I have used have done a decent job of hiding the face. The lack of a more substantial face cover causes the glasses to stay fog free. There is no obscured vision as in the case of full-face covers. Disadvantages? Only one I know. The stuff is messy, rubs onto clothes, and might run when sweat-provoked. Finally, those who run around with such makeup can cause observers to be brutally frank.

I was driving a backcountry road during one hunt when I encountered two cowboys chousing a small herd of Herefords. I stopped the truck to relinquish right of way, as is my custom. One of the 'pokes moved his grulla in for a close look. We talked for a minute or more before he made his comment. "Feller," he said, "you are the queerest looking sumbitch I have ever seen." Knowing he was right, I did not take offense.

Wearing a camouflage that neutralizes a critter's nose can be a bother but can, under certain conditions, cause an increase in the fur collection. Some critters, the real paranoids, those who have previously discovered the deception of the predator screamer, will manage to approach from dead downwind, or will approach from upwind and circle downwind to take a taste of the air. Those kinds of critters, almost always, will head for home at the faint smell of Old Spice aftershave, Listerine mouthwash, or even the dreaded B.O. Even those

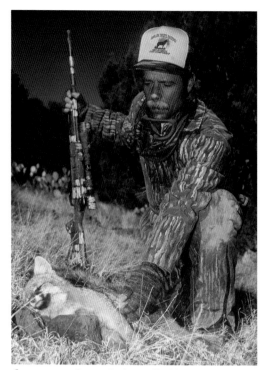

Gun camo can disguise the sheen of highly polished wood and steel. (Gordy Krahn Photo of Gery Hull, Saldotna, Alaska).

among us who feel compelled to bathe weekly (whether they need it or not) can emit an odor that causes the paranoia to hang onto a coyote like ugly hangs to an ape.

Gun camouflage was mentioned in the chapter on shotguns. That mention mainly said there are factory-camouflaged shotguns available from Remington, Winchester, Ithaca, Mossberg, and others. All also offer shotguns and rifles (sometimes called SP for Special Purpose and sometimes called by another name) in a non-reflective finish, both stock and metal. Those who have guns, rifles or smoothbores, owning a high polish on wood and metal have options. Camo tape is inexpensive and easy to apply (not quite so easy to take off). I prefer the cloth tape over the paper tape. Such is more durable and will last longer than a part of a season. Some manufacturers offer pullover camo elastic (Gun Chaps is one) that does a decent job of hiding the shine. A more permanent camo job involves the use of spray paint on wood and metal, best done, I think, when the gun involved is a beater that can only be improved by such. Finally, a competent gunsmith can take the prettiest of guns and uglify that sucker so that it is coyote friendly.

Some mention must be made of sound camouflage. Predators hunt using all of their senses. Every one I have met has owned a highly developed sense of hearing, some being able to hear the footsteps made by a white-footed deer mouse wearing Reeboks. That sense of sound can cause the critter to react to the distress screams while more than a mile away. That same sense of sound can cause the critter to ignore the best of those screams. What kinds of sounds are most apt to spook a paranoid critter? I do not play the radio, the tape, or the CD while in calling country, particularly during times when vehicle windows are partly open. The truck bed stays free of those roll-arounds that might cause clanking.

I also make it a point to maintain absolute silence when walking to a stand. If you call with a companion, convince him or her of the value of silence before the hunt. Ask that the companion not slam the door of the truck. Say, seriously, that in the event he or she inadvertently laughs, coughs, burps, sneezes, or otherwise exercises the vocal cords you will immediately grab a stout juniper limb and begin to beat upon his or her body until he or she whines like a whipped hound. If that does not do the trick, get ugly.

The rule of silence should also be observed during the walk back to the truck. I took a neighbor to the junipers one fall day to scream at coyote. I called a pair of chargers and got lucky, putting both down with the .22-250. On the walk out my companion begin to relive the action. His voice spooked a big bobcat that had come back door. I had a tough shot at the bob' running at 200 yards. Even though I almost always miss during such opportunity, the law of averages compensated in this instance and I connected. That lucky shot, the way I see it, saved my companion's life.

Smart hunters, like Raymond Branch, Winslow, AZ and the author, remain silent during the walk-in and walk-out, knowing a relative of the deceased might be close by.

chapter 18

Woodsmanship

I have alluded to the craft of WOODSMANSHIP within other chapters. Even so, I feel such to be critically important if a screamer is to be all he, she, or it can be. Certainly important enough to address specifically.

Permit me to say at the start I disapprove of the word woodsmanship as it is applied here. Much of Arizona, as even a snowbird knows, is without woods. Treeless essentially, unless one labels the giant saguaro cactus as a tree as some do. Much of the state consists of vast tracts of high and low desert, such being decorated with a mind boggling variety of the thorny succulent called cacti by scientists and called #&$@!! by about every one else. A part of the desert does have trees of a sort. The giant saguaro has been mentioned. Other more typical trees grow upon drainage borders. Those borders are as dry as a popcorn poot for most of the year but can flow bank to bank due to summer monsoons and spring snow melt from neighboring mountains. That deluge of welcomed water can cause mesquite, catclaw, green and blue palo verde, palo christi, ironwood and other such to hold to life tenaciously.

The cactus can appear as a plethora of forms. Prickly pear can be somewhat common. So can Teddy Bear Cholla, the cactus that has been accused of jumping to dig the claws into a passerby. I have not seen this cactus jump and doubt that it does. Even so, the staghorn cholla, the way I see it, is much better behaved and therefore more likeable than the Teddy bear.

Bobcat prefer cottontail rabbit but will substitute as circumstance permits.

Those who love beauty, as I do, will surely find pleasure as they view the spring display of flowering cacti. The prickly pear offers egg sized yellow or chartreuse blossoms that will eventually transform into a handsome and succulent purple pear. The ground hugging hedgehog usually presents a like sized lavender blossom. Fire engine red plumes decorate the slender tips of the ocotillo. The desert, particularly during a wet spring, can be handsome and a half.

Some readers are likely saying who the hell cares? Or perhaps Ho Hum, when do we get to the good stuff? I care is the answer, and so should you if you hope to reach your full potential as a hunter and most particularly as a predator hunter.

Finally, (please pay attention), the good stuff follows.

Every creature that walks the land, swims the water or slithers on its belly like a dern reptile must adapt to its environment if it hopes to live long and prosper. As an example, even though some see the coyote as a despicable and carnivorous opportunistic killer of rabbits, hares, rats, mice, voles and all such (which he is) the coyote is more than that. The coyote also savors the young (and sometimes the old) of herbivores such as deer, elk, antelope, sheep and the delicious etcetera. The truth, however, is more complex. The coyote and other members of the wild and domestic dog family are not truly and totally carnivorous. The coyote I have met have been omnivores, a creature capable of extracting nourishment from a wide range of plants. Also, I speak (actually write) of the fruit and the pulp of the aforementioned cactus here within the southwest. I realize all who read this do not live and hunt within the southwest. I use the southwestern example because I do live and hunt mostly within the southwest. Those who do not can extrapolate the message to apply equally to habitat that might contain a paucity of cacti but does contain a plethora of hardwoods that produce nuts, wild and domestic trees that produce fruits, and bushes that offer berries. Even fields that offer corn, melons and the tasty etcetera.

Back to El Coyote. What does the barking dog eat when meat is not on the menu, you ask? About anything that fits in it's mouth, I answer. Southwestern yodel dogs eat a gracious plenty of the sweet purple pears found on the prickly pear cactus during late summer and early fall. Nourishing? Hell yes! And having an added advantage of included liquid, a definite plus here in the southwest, a place where water is in short supply.

At a slightly higher elevation many coyote make it through the winter by munching the turpentine taste of the bitter berries of the string bark juniper, eating the berries from low growing limbs early in the fall and gathering the berries from the ground after drop down. The point is, knowing where the critters gather to find their groceries allows the hunter to spend his or her time within that very productive kind of country.

The Arizona black bear is like the Arizona coyote in at least a few

Weather patterns and moon phases can influence hunt success.

characteristics. Both the bear and the coyote are omnivores. Knowing that bear within a certain part of the state moved into prickly pear thickets during the fall of the year, enabled me to be in the right place at the right time to scream in a decent sow (175 pounds) and make the shot. I included sketchy details about this San Carlos Apache bear hunt because this version will contain added information that will be helpful to those who hanker to hunt bare (bear, that is).

Mike Mell might be the best bear hunter within Arizona. I would say so even if Mike had not been one of my late wife's favored cousins. Even if I had not aimed a camera at Mike's marriage to "whats her name," and Mike had not offered a hunt upon the bear rich San Carlos Apache Indian Reservation as recompense. All of the above explaining, sort of, how Mike and me and a black powder toting sidekick happened to be making a dry camp along the bank of Ash Creek (also dry) at midnight thirty on a middling hot mid-October night.

In spite of the long day previously we were up before sun up on a hilltop with Mike looking into the lens of a 20X spotter while I scanned with a pair of 7x35 Bausch & Lombs, the kind advertised as being capable of illustrating an apple on a limb at a mile or more away. Maybe. I myself have not actually seen that mile or more apple. Certainly powerful enough, however, to identify a bear at a distance of near 3 miles. Seeing such, I whispered (do not ask me why I whispered when the bear was three miles away but I did) to alert Mike. Maybe I whispered because the guys on the hunting videos always whisper and it seemed the thing to do. Mike homed in on the bears part of the prickly patch and verified.

One might wonder about the early up. Two good reasons. Mid October is warmish on the San Carlos. A critter wearing a bear suit is not apt to hang around long after sun up. Choosing instead to laze away the hottest part of the day within the friendly shade of a brush-choked canyon. Reason number two has to do with temperature also. The high desert heat causes shimmering heat waves to distort the view offered by the glasses. We figured we had an hour, maybe an hour and a half, of somewhat clear vision.

We sighted the bear at about sun up thirty and watched that pissant sized speck as he or she wandered within the prickly pear patch. A short time later the pissant gave it up and mosied into the maw of a brush choked canyon.

We returned to camp, gobbled down a lumberjack breakfast, strapped on a day pack loaded with water and other necessaries, and started a meandering march that would eat up a good part of the day. The good news? We made it to the scene of the crime at about three p.m..

I scrunched my big butt into the desert debris doing my best to avoid the worst of the stickers, stobs and mean natured rocks. I performed a careful inspection, intending to discover any extra large scorpions or tarantulas, any adult rattlesnakes and Gila monsters of any size. An hour later I felt I just had to scream.

Several screams later a black blob discharged from the canyon mouth and headed our way at a medium fast mosey. The blob paused one time during the amble, backed up to a bug sized (VW Bug) boulder and proceeded to scratch the bear behind vigorously. When Miz Bear was a hundred or so yards away I centered the small x of the duplex scope upon the bear's ribcage and lit the fire. Mike did the dirty work, we divided the load and arrived at camp about midnight thirty.

Carrion dumps can cause coyotes to cluster to do a communal stink-out.

Hunt the deer to find the lion is good advice but the big cat will kill and consume other prey as circumstance allows.

The technique I use to hunt cats is somewhat similar to the technique I use to hunt bear. Not the prickly pear part but the part where I seek out habitat that caters to the cats need for protein.

I watch the ground a lot when I hunt, hoping to discover a fresh track in sand, dust, mud or snow. I watch for the distinctive scat offed by mountain lion and bobcat. I spend much of my time within country that offers the kind of grub preferred by cats, deer for mountain lion and cottontail rabbits for bobcat. And I look for the kind of country that abets the sneak and dash kind of hunting favored by lion and the flush and dash style of the bobcat.

Some predators are totally tied to a certain kind of country. As an example, the pee-wee fox called a kit must live within a tightly structured habitat. The kit fox I have met have mostly lived within burrows. A part of the time those burrows are borrowed from a digging machine called a badger or maybe even dug by a coyote. Some of the time a kit must do his own digging even though the kits pathetic toe nails are poorly suited to such. Those facts cause the kit to cluster within habitat covered by a loosely packed alluvium. Easy digging.

That same semi-soft alluvium is friendly to kangaroo rats and other favored kit fox foods.

Why is the kit fox dependent upon burrows? A couple of reasons. The kit, being the little booger on the block, must have a sanctuary that protects the kit from hawks during the day time, owls during the night time and coyote and bobcat at any old time. The burrow also offers a less hot hideout from the torrid rays of a daytime desert sun.

Are you ready for the bottom line? I suggest you learn all possible about the flora and fauna within the area you hunt. The knowledge gained will permit a process called thinking and such will surely cause you to be a more efficient hunter.

Be a friend to the cowboy and other land users and they will be a friend to you.

chapter 19

Masking Scents

Olga spent her summer days throwing bales on her daddy's farm. A good part of the nights were spent with me. Rawboned and muscular, willing, having considerable stamina, Olgie came from sturdy stock who figured a man or woman who took a razor to the armpits was some sort of sissy. There was always the smell of honest sweat to Olga, an odor I did not find offensive then and do not find offensive now (as long as it is somewhat fresh). The thing is, Olga could never sneak up on me. I could smell her coming. Years later, when I became addicted to screaming to predators, that early life experience with Olga taught me a valuable lesson.

Every human, even those who shave the underarms somewhat regularly, have an odor. If our nose was long like a coyote nose, containing all of those super sensitive odor eaters, I am betting we could recognize Aunt Martha or Cousin Jody from a couple of hundred upwind yards. Don't believe it? I can't count the number of times I have had a paranoid coyote come to that distance and have him (or her) turn tail to make the desperate run for home. Other coyote might come to an indecent distance, being upwind, and quarter to make the circle that will allow a downwind reconnoiter. Looking for the opportunity to taste the wind. Good-bye customer. Good-bye to a substantial part of the fur check.

When I tired of those smart alecks who used their nose to save their butts, I got serious about a deodorant of the coyote kind. The stuff old-time trappers almost always called skunk piss; in actuality the amber fluid that fills the marble (taw) sized glands that decorate each side of a skunk's pooper. Using that odiferous abomination as a masker can cause some of those nose-hungry coyote, fox, and bobcat to stick around long enough to get dead.

Honesty causes me to report a divergent opinion. I know callers, some of them damn good callers, who disagree, saying the predator nose is so sophisticated it can cut through a five-gallon bucket full of skunk phew to discover the human hiding within. Maybe so. My experience has convinced me that using a masker causes me to skin extra fur every season. Coyote number 97 is a good example.

Old 97 was a husky dog that hung out in the standing and pushdown stringbarks on one of the Babbitt spreads east of my Flagstaff home; a chunk

Skunk musk can be an effective human scent masker.

of real estate heavy hit by hunters. Screamers are so numerous during the early part of the season you almost have to take a number and wait your turn. Coyotes who do not get dead get smart. Calling there during January is about as satisfying as eating raw carrots.

Knowing better, not knowing where else to go, I went to hunt, armed with the trusty .22-250 and a film cassette filled with cotton and skunk stink. I made the first call at daylight, setting up on the edge of a stand of stringbark juniper and staring out into an area of somewhat open pushdowns. I hung the skunk on a low juniper branch (downwind of course) and slobbered out the first stanza of the "Dying Rabbit Blues."

Five minutes later I eyeballed a flash of fur from dead downwind. Here comes this big coyote at the gallop, having murder on his mind. I welcomed the brute by poking a 52-grain chunk of copper-plated lead through his necessaries. Walking out to make the retrieve I discovered an aluminum tag within one wooly ear, #97 stamped thereon. Inquiry showed Old 97 had been trapped (about 200 yards from where he died) as a two-year old by a graduate student attending Northern Arizona University, five years before. That old dog was seven years old and had survived those seven years within a heavy hunted chunk of territory. Even so, 97 came from dead down-wind and came at the trot. Senile? Maybe. I prefer to think superior calling and the judicious use of a masking scent caused his demise.

A certain kind of masking scent does a decent job of disguising the obvious pheromones of human stink. The only effective masker I have tried has been pure and unadulterated skunk musk or a chemical facsimile of the same. How does one go about obtaining THE REAL THING? It's somewhat easy if you have access to a skunk and can convince your Karma to do a bit of skunk milking. Here is the way I go about it. RULE #1: Never milk a live skunk. Be sure that sucker is one hundred percent graveyard dead before making a move to the marble-size glands located on each side of the anal vent (sometimes called by more colorful names). Wear surgical gloves (available at most pharmacies) to keep the hands somewhat stink free. Place a glass or plastic container to the vent opening and press gently on each side of the gland to cause the amber fluid to squirt into the bottle. Stop when the amber fluid flow stops and is replaced by a milky concentrate. Cap the bottle using a plastic or rubber closer. RULE #2: Do not pick your nose (or any nose) before removing the gloves.

If you are not into skunk milking, consider the purchase of a chemical substitute such as CoverScent marketed by the Johnny Stewart Company. This excellent product comes as a two-part liquid, each innocuous alone but turning nose-ugly when mixed.

In either event, use an empty 35 mm film cassette container (available at film processors if not otherwise) and fill that plastic container with cotton or cotton balls, maybe cloth, well just about anything porous. Add a few drops of the skunk musk or of the imitator and cap, quickly. Opening the container and placing it downwind during a screaming can cause fewer of the paranoids to escape.

Less reliable alternatives are more available. I have used liquid garlic and have used pine oil, each available at many super markets. Or rub a raw onion on your shoes. None of the above will work as well as the skunk, but each is better than nothing.

Common sense suggests other cautions. Those neat-nicks who insist on bathing once a week (whether they need it or not) should avoid the use of smell-goods like cologne or aftershave if they intend to hunt the next day. Gas up the night before to be sure you do not, (while half asleep) slosh gas on your boots (or on anything else). Lay off the cigarettes on the drive out and during the hunt. Don't hog down a half a pot of limas the night before the hunt. Stay clean. Once clean, there is stuff available to make your body smell like about anything you can fantasize. Maybe a sow bear in heat. I am not making this up. CAUTION: Not recommended during the bear rut.

Take the time to remove all reflective adornments before heading to the stand. I leave rings and bolo ties at home, knowing that each can cause a light flash that might alarm the most paranoid of the customers. Same deal on reflective watchbands, belt buckles and eyeglass frames. The fur hunting I have done has convinced me of the truth of the old adage. It is better to be safe than sorry.

WARNING: Never attempt to milk a skunk that is not one-hundred percent graveyard dead.

chapter 20

Calling the Weather

The wet clouds hugged the sere slopes of the Date Creek Mountains to create an aspect of unusual beauty. Water rich cumulonimbus, the kind cowboys call waterdogs, flowed to fill the shallow canyons. There was the smell of rain. Larry and I left the 4x4 in the sand bottom of an inconspicuous dry wash and loaded the daypacks. A barely bright cloud to the east announced daylight was imminent. Minutes later we were hiking the boulder jumble that marked the boundary between desert and mountain. As we hiked, knowing we had a ways to go, I turned my thoughts to the screaming ahead, and thought of the effect the changing weather would have on predator response.

I had screamed to weather fronts before. And on about every one of those hunts predator response had been good. There is something about the aspect of an arriving or departing storm that causes the critter appetite alarm to sound. Maybe it is the smell of rain or the barometric pressure?

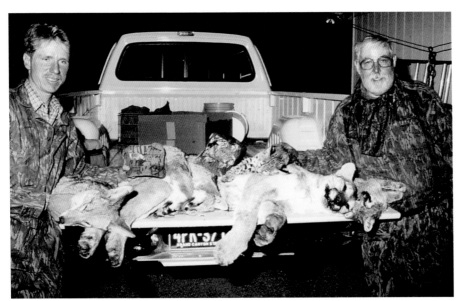

The right kind of weather within the right kind of country can offer up a truck load of multi-species customers. Larry Gates of Wickenburg, AZ on the left.

Bobcat can use the back door to come uncomfortably close.

Critters feed before a front, I think, because they sense unsettled weather and sense that prey animals are likely to be less active, causing their own hunts to be less productive. Maybe the predators are smart enough to know a storm is on the way, but lack the sophisticated receptors that can define a major storm or a minor storm. Not knowing when they might eat again, maybe they go on a feeding frenzy to be safe. Hell, maybe they just don't want to get wet.

A half-hour later Larry and I set up among the granite boulders, some as big as a two-bedroom house (with den), facing down desert to discover the coyote we knew would come — sending out the first chorus of the "Dying Rabbit Blues." There is something about wetted air that causes the tone of the distress scream to be uncommonly fine. The screams are fulsome and each note is exquisitely rendered. I was working the TallyHo, working well, when the bobcat showed. Backdoor.

I did not see the cat coming-nor did Larry. One instant the bug-size (VW) boulder was bare, the next the cat was atop, creating a handsome cooperation that approximated the finest of taxidermy. A prickling of the neck hair caused me to look back. I lip-squeaked to Larry. The camcorder light lit and the 10x lens swiveled smoothly to take in the tufted-eared boulder. When I was certain Larry was on target I went to work with the call, doing my best to cause the cat to come closer. Catlike, the bob' stayed still, hoping to discover if he was going to get supper or be supper. I scooched to square to the target and made the shot. That number one stand provided hunting excitement and delivered a prime tomcat. And as a bonus, several minutes of dandy footage for the *Masters' Secrets to Predator Calling.* We were three miles from the truck by noon-thirty and had made a half-dozen stands. That effort had added a pair of handsome gray fox to the bag. The two had come to a single screaming, each bounding across the boulder jumble in a most picturesque manner. I took one at thirty-five yards and took the other as he attempted escape at about one hundred yards. Larry worked the camcorder and captured the first kill on tape.

Two miles more, one hour before dead dark, we paused again. The afternoon screaming had added a pair of coyote to the collection. A bad camcorder angle made it impossible to tape either. Total take for the hike was one bobcat, two grays, and two coyote — pretty good all right. We could have called it quits right then and probably should have. We were one hour away from dark and two hours away from the truck. One half of the return would be made on a stormy night that showed no moon. We were in cactus country and knew it would be slow (and perhaps painful) going. We would have done precisely that if Larry had not found a fresh lion track on the soft sand of a dry wash.

Walking all of the way to the truck in the dark instead of only half way, we figured, was not that bad. We set up in the boulders to scream one more time. Larry did the screaming as I relaxed to enjoy the music, appreciating the quaver put into the TallyHo screams. Ten minutes later I perceived a slight change in tonal intensity. I looked diligently but saw nothing. I settled back for more screams.

Thirty minutes later Larry was still screaming. That screaming was interrupted when Larry's .22-250 reported. Larry was on his feet almost instantly. "Did you see him?" he shouted. I nodded a no. "Lion," he said as he headed for the ridge top at the lope. I followed. We did not see the lion when we gained the ridge top but did see a boulder jumble that could hide a lion. Investigation showed a crevice containing a smudge of blood, about shoulder high to a cougar. Larry, being brave, lit a gopher match and crawled into the crevice. Seconds later the lion made a desperate run. Larry crawled backwards and gave chase, eventually baying the beast within a second boulder jumble.

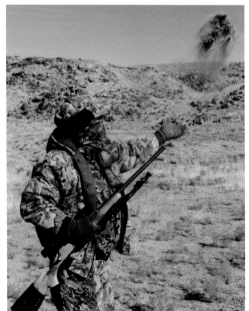

The second shot from the .22-250 was well placed. The tom weighed 135 pounds, an impressive weight for a desert lion.

Walking out we talked on the dandy day of screaming and talked of the effects weather can have on the quality of the hunt. Our good luck on this day, we agreed, was mostly due to the imminent storm.

Calling on the day a storm leaves can be nearly as good as

Some customers taste the wind to avoid unpleasant surprises. Smart hunters call with the wind in their face when such is possible.

calling the incoming front. Predators and prey, much of the time, lay up to miss most of the bad weather. Those predators that do hunt during the storm often have to hunt for damn little reward. Clearing weather finds the predator population with empty bellies. Being anxious to eat, they can come to the screaming with enthusiasm.

Certain kinds of weather can adversely affect calling success. The worst, the way I see it, is wind. I do not refer to the mild five or ten mph breeze that can actually encourage critters to hunt but stays moderate to avoid bad side effects. I am talking big-time wind — the kind that makes the ground shake (or at least the limbs of trees) and the ocean roll. Such adversely affects a screaming in more than one way. The noise that is a common concomitant to such wind can cause the range of the screaming to diminish. Critters upwind, those most likely to come, cannot hear the advertisement. Critters downwind can hear a bit better but have the advantage of the wind in their nose. They are not apt to come close.

Winds that shake the limbs cause a further negative. Predators and prey alike look for movement. Prey animals do so because movement is a warning that can signal the approach of danger. Predators look for movement for the same reason but also watch for movement to signal the presence of prey. When every bush, every limb, every weed, and every leaf moves, both predator and prey become really nervous. Predators that are stressed are not likely to gamble on a distress scream. Those that do, almost always, come at the paranoid. You want the truth? Windy day calling makes me nervous too. I do not call the wind if it is practical to postpone. Having said that, honesty causes me to say I sometimes call the wind, maybe during a hunt that starts out during perfect calling weather but degrades. Maybe when I have a hunt scheduled that cannot be canceled. Experience has caused me to use techniques that can cause the screaming to be somewhat effective. I compensate for the reduced range of the call several ways. Way one: Knowing I will not cover as much country with each screaming, I shorten the distance between stands. Instead of making a screaming every mile or so, as I would on a windless day, I make the calls every half mile-maybe each quarter of a mile. Way two: I put away the tubes to break out the battery-powered caller, feeling the amplification delivers more volume. Way three: I do my best to select sanctuaries: hills and ridges on the lee side of the wind; hollows and basins that are somewhat protected. Way four: I sometimes position the battery-powered caller downwind a couple of hundred yards from the setup, then set up somewhat high so that vision is improved. The customer will sometimes come close to the caller and not smell the gunner. Shot opportunities under such conditions can be long range.

I do not often call during a rain because it is not pleasant to do so. I sometimes do, when a mild and intermittent rain is a concomitant to a front. Doing so can be dandy, as described at the start of this chapter. I do call during a snow, particularly when that snowing is somewhat moderate and does not come with wind. Driving remote roads during a snow, or following a snow, can be dandy – sometimes damnfine. A moderate snow does not usually discourage predators. They seem encouraged to move about and hunt. Road hunting to find tracks (always fresh) permits the hunter to scream within an area that is certain to hold a target. The response can be immediate and enthusiastic.

Cold weather, really cold weather, can cause critters to go on a feeding frenzy. Nutrition requirements go up. It takes a good many calories to keep from freezing to death. The simple act of walking or running can be more difficult, causing the expenditure of increased calories. As good as it can be, extremely cold weather can have an effect on the calls. Metal-reed calls collect spittle from the breath and will almost always freeze. A plastic-reed call, Crit'RCall, TallyHo, Lohman C-250, the Johnny Stewart PC-6, that sort, do better. The plastic reed stays snug within the mouth during the screaming, preventing freeze-up.

The battery-powered caller can be a sensible choice when the weather turns frigid. Hunters need to know that cold weather can cause battery power to diminish. Always hunt with a fully charged battery. Carry the unit in the cab of the vehicle between stands to cause a warm-up. Plug in the 12-volt charger to replace lost battery power as you travel.

Screaming a track within a fresh snow can be dandy.

chapter 21

Calling Big Game

Almost all predator callers know a screamer used within the right kind of mouth and the right kind of country might cause coyote, red, gray and kit fox, bobcat, bear and even the cat the Mexicans call Gato del Monte (cat of the mountain) to come close to the gun, the camera, the camcorder or maybe just the eyeball. Actually, about all predators that walk the ground or fly the sky sometimes come sure kill close. A second side of predator calling, however, is less well known. Many non-predators, species commonly called prey animals by we humans and called supper by about every true carnivore and some not so true carnivores, might come a running when the screamer is used within the right kind of circumstance. How does Gerry Blair know all of this? Heck, he knows because he has been there, done that and has the Tee-shirt to prove it.

A decent pronghorn buck demonstrated his rutting strut as I screamed accompaniment.

It would be boring, the way I see it, to present a laundry list of the edible creatures I have screamed from the woods (and the desert) to the freezer. And it would be unfair, I think, to simply say I have called a hell of a lot and maybe more. A careful consideration suggests I present abbreviated hunting experiences and endeavor to explain when I deemed it needful to scream and why I considered such to be so.

The Child Molester Buck and his too young harem answered the scream.

Members of the deer family can be particularly vulnerable to a screaming. Those who are somewhat familiar with the southwest, most particularly Arizona, know that great state houses mostly mule deer, some such reaching record book stature. Less common is the diminutive whitetail deer called the Coues (please say cows). I have not actually had a Coues deer come running to the scream. I sometimes use the screamer, however, to flush a Coues from a brushy daybed. The hunt with hard hunter Robert Flamme illustrates.

The hunt with Robert (don't call me Bob) Flamme took place within the high desert canyon country that borders the south side of Apache Maid Mountain. We were up and at it shortly after sunrise using binoculars and spotting scopes to investigate the ridges and canyons. I became lucky when the eyepiece presented a better than average three point buck (western count) feeding on a canyon side a mile or more away. That three point buck, to the east of the big rivers, would classify as a true eight pointer. We packed up our things and made a march.

The buck, unfortunately, was no longer visible when we arrived at the scene of the sighting. Rather than kick a rock and say shucks and darn I mouthed a Trophy Model Wood Circe and screamed enthusiastically. The Coues was bedded within the shade provided by a mini-cliff and bounced away as if all the hellions of Hades were in pursuit, which they were. Robert made the shot and the buck died grandly. A later taping suggested the Coues measured an impressive 110 B&C points, high enough to make the Boone and Crockett book if we had bothered to submit.

The screamer can be a deer hunter's best friend when the target is Rocky

Mountain Mule Deer or even desert mulies, particularly when the hunter totes a black powder smoke belcher or some other kind of primitive. My screamer proved to be precisely that when I lugged a .54 caliber Knight rifle into the foothills that border the north edge of the Harquahala (land of many waters) Mountains.

That December hunt took place during a part of the desert mule deer rut, a good time to be out, about and screaming. I had still hunted until well after sun-up and had found zero excitement, excepting the time I nearly stepped upon a lethargic Western Diamondback rattlesnake big enough to swallow a VW Bug who had left his (or her) den to sun a bit. Our encounter proved to be a draw. The snake did not bite me and I did not shoot the snake with my rifle but did shoot it with my Canon.

At about mid-morning thirty I scrunched into the shade of a mountain mahogany and did a screaming. A similar sized mountain mahogany down slope exploded, such causing a dern decent four point (ten point eastern) and a couple of comely does to head my way. I stroked the three pound trigger of the Knight and the Child Molester Buck (the two does appeared to be under age) hit the ground. The teenage does stood around and looked glum.

Skeptics might say not so. The truth is, I have screamed in mule deer many times in Arizona, having had one such approach taped within a VHS marketed by Krause Publications. Other responses have been documented by photographs. One buck came so close my 300 mm telephoto lens would not focus and I was required to sneak away from the buck to get the picture. I am not making this up.

Rutting bulls often follow cows as they answer the scream.

I readily recall a time when I flew to, motored within and walked upon the vast state of Alaska pursuing a part of the Illeamna Barren Grounds Caribou herd. I glassed an impressive bull as he traveled at a right angle about a half mile away. I did a screaming and caused the bull to head my way at a ground eating walk. When he was one hundred yards close I touched the trigger of the .25-06 and sent a 110 grainer through the necessaries.

Can you stand one more about Alaska? When the caribou hunt ended, my partner and I motored about, taking in the sights. One part of our travels revealed a roadside wildlife park south of Anchorage. A portion of the exhibit housed a semi handsome Sitka buck. Trouble was, the buck was bedded within a shaded area that offered limited camera appeal. What did I do? Yep, you guessed it. I screamed out a few moany groans. The buck stood, moved my way at a stiff legged walk and paused to glare from about 15 yards. The 300 mm auto focus Canon glared back and delivered a very pleasing image of this seldom seen (in Arizona at least) member of the deer family.

Knowing you are likely sick and tired of deer tales I shift now to a time when I used a screamer to tie my tag to the horn of the bison some folks call a buffalo. I was on the east side of Kaibab Mountain at a place where the State of Arizona maintains a hundred head (and also one hundred tails) of the shaggy beasts. Knowing full well the free roaming herd would reproduce beyond the habitat, Arizona allows hunters to apply for a herd thinning hunt. Easy meat? Hardly. I hunted from first light to last light for the longest time and did not discover a buffalo or even a fresh buffalo track. Not even a fresh turd. Finally, the day before the hunt ended, I discovered a fresh bull track. I followed that somewhat fresh track for more than three hours as

Gerry Blair tracked the bull and screamed to stop him for the shot.

the bull wandered to investigate enticing smells. Sensing he was being stalked the bull eventually resisted wanderlust and bee-lined for the sanctuary of the Grand Canyon National Park. I climbed the bank of a dry stock tank and sighted the bull's rump headed for safety.

Shooting at the broad expanse of a bull's butt is not my idea of a clean kill. I whipped out the trusty screamer and did my thing. The bull paused and turned broadside to deliver the bad eye. I shot for the lungs and the bull continued to stand. I shot for the lungs again and the bull continued to stand. I shot again and the bull did not have the decency to even flinch. As I was cranking in yet another round the bull sank to the ground. Each of the bullets penetrated the lungs within an area that could be covered by my palm. Tough? Hell yes.

Even though the bull was old, even though the bull owned a super tough constitution, the flesh was sweet and

The javelina unhid, puffed, huffed, clacked his tusks a time or two and charged.

chewable if the chewer had a full set of teeth and strong jaws. As I recall it took me and the rest of the Blair's about three years to work our way through that 1500 pounds of protein. Why so long? We chewed each bite for a long, long time.

No chapter dealing with screaming for groceries would be complete without a bunch of words dealing with the pig-like critter called the collared peccary by some, called the javelina by others and called the $%&@* by a few grumpy ranchers. If javelina had money. I am convinced I could earn a fortune selling them the Grand Canyon, Meteor Crater, the Petrified Forest and all other such found within this very scenic state. When it comes to screaming the javelina is so dumb his (and her) butt hurts.

I was on a javelina hunt within the Date Creek Mountains of central Arizona when my companion drove the jeep along a ridge. Sharp eyes caused us to glimpse a hairy behind disappear into the mystery of a brush choked canyon. We parked and walked the lip hoping to encounter the pig at a range suitable for the .54 caliber front stuffer. No such luck. I placed a custom made ironwood tube (actually, blew a Rhino) to my lips and sent out screams that would surely bring tears as big as horse biscuits to any mothers eye. The javelina caused every hair on his hairy body to stand erect and charged from a couple of hundred yards away, clacking his tusks in a most fearsome way. The Knight Rifle belched smoke, fire and a hefty hunk of maxi-ball and the threat display ended.

Another time I was shooting footage for the video to be titled *The Masters' Secrets to Predator Calling* when I enjoyed another encounter of the javelina kind. Hoping to make the point that sitting still would cause animals to come close even if the screamer was wearing something totally ridiculous, I went afield wearing a red and white Santa suit. Even though I was screaming to coyote the sounder of javelina responded. An entire herd of javelina responded. Javelina were bouncing within the greasewood at about every angle. Two aggressive adults came within ten feet of my Redwings. And did so several times. Others did about all they could do to play ugly. I felt myself to be lucky to escape unharmed and escape with some dern fine footage.

I wish I could find the words to explain how I know when to scream and how I know the kind of scream that will be favored by the customer. I suppose I do so based mainly on an intuition tempered by a long lifetime of hunting and about that much time spent screaming to all sorts of ears. That intuition is further fine tuned because of the knowledge obtained observing animals in the field, reading scholarly texts about animal habits and habitats and relating all of that to the situation at hand. All such causes me to intuit correctly some of the time and miss by a mile at other times. The good guesses usually out number the bad guesses and the success ratio is good enough to keep me screaming.

I regret I am unable to offer more precise guidelines that might help other hunters determine when to scream and when not to scream. The truth is, almost all animals will run when they hear the scream. Maybe run to the scream and maybe run away from the scream. My advice is basic. Scream when you feel like it. Maybe scream as a last resort when all else fails. You may be pleasantly surprised.

chapter 22

Calling to the Camera

Screaming an invitation to pose for the camera, the camcorder or any such can be enjoyable. At the very least imaging wildlife provides a way to recall the excitement of past hunts and a way to share that excitement with friends and relatives.

As is the case with about all enterprises, obtaining enjoyable or saleable images is facilitated when the screamer uses appropriate equipment and appropriate technique. Exactly what is and is not appropriate? The answer is dependent upon intended use. An image suitable for home viewing and the family scrapbook requires a minimal amount of sophisticated equipment and a bare minimum of talent. Your goal is to please yourself. An image intended for the market will require more sophisticated equipment and a more polished technique. If you feel as I do you may wish to cause the images to be as good as can be. An image intended for the scrapbook today may turn into a marketable image at a later date.

Gerry Blair is a geezer who has hidden behind a 35mm SLR camera loaded with Kodachrome or Velvia for much of his life. That same Gerry Blair operated his own darkroom for most of that much. Even so, I recommend the concept of digital cameras. The new crop, the way I see it, will satisfy about every need. Digitals offer convenience, are economical (because they do not use film), deliver a quality image, and have the added asset of versatility.

As an example, I own a handsome image of a gray fox, such showing a background of a clouded blue sky. Sharp eyed readers might recall seeing a similar image within the chapter on gray fox. The original image was taken during the darkest part of a moonless midnight. I used computer technology to slightly alter the stump and to cut and paste a new background, such borrowed from one of my cloud photos. Why bother? I wanted to show that grays might hunt both day and night and might answer the call at any time.

Not every digital camera model is created equal. The high quality models offer an increased pixel rating. Most of my images were shot using a five mega-pixel camera. I have recently purchased a nine mega pixel model.

Many of the newer model digitals offer the zoom range demanded for some wildlife photography. I have found a telephoto range of 10X (such translating to about 300 mm within film cameras) to be adequate.

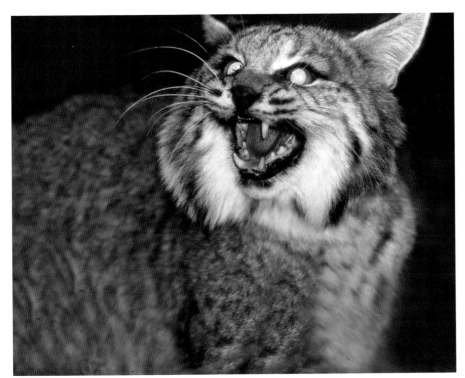
Trapped animals can be encouraged to smile and offer a fine photo opportunity.

Pricey? Sure! Expect to pay between five hundred to a thousand dollars, less than you would pay for a high-end 35mm SLR film camera and auxiliary lenses.

Honesty causes me to include a codicil. The image captured by a many mega pixel digital can be mighty good but not quite as good as the image captured by a quality film camera. Close but no cigar.

As digital technology progresses, many knowledgeable people predict the digital will equal and exceed film camera performance and do so within the foreseeable future.

Calling to the camera instead of the gun offers a number of advantages. Much of my life I have killed the customer at the earliest opportunity. Doing so does not teach a hell of a lot about critter nature, excepting the response to the distress scream and the ability to die grandly. Not killing the customer, as is the case when calling to the camera, allows a glimpse into critter character.

I have had puzzled coyote come to the call, sneak to pounce upon a decoy, urinate and defecate on my battery powered caller, and even leap over my prostrate form and allow a glimpse of their most private parts.

I have had bobcat come backdoor and leap to brush a companions shoulder, stand at a companions heel as he operated a camcorder, sneak to make a pounce on one of my Redwings and snarl enthusiastically at the rear of my right shoulder, such causing me to slightly soil my camos.

Calling to the camera also allows access to sanctuaries, places where gun hunting is not allowed. The creatures within, much of the time, are naive and cooperative. I have written elsewhere about parts of a day and a half hunt upon the Papago Indian Reservation. Chuck and I called a counted forty two coyote within that day and a half of calling and obtained photos that continue to be treasured.

I have also called within urban areas, within gated communities, within state and national parks, within some national monuments and upon at least one military reservation. Almost all will allow entry when you carry a Canon instead of a cannon.

Even though I prefer to call using a reeded tube when gun hunting I switch to a battery powered model when calling to the camera. Why so? It is difficult to handle a call and a camera at the same time. The battery powered caller frees up my hands, allows the customer to focus on the caller and not upon my mouth and encourages the customer to stay around for the longest time, allowing the opportunity for multiple exposures.

Some of the newer remotely operated battery powered callers are damfine. My FoxPro FX5, as an example, has an impressive two hundred screams. Placing the unit out away from the gun can cause the customer to focus on the sound and not upon the blob behind the camera. An oversize keyboard permits a changing of the sound, maybe from jackrabbit screams to a distressed pup sound and do so discretely. Volume can be similarly controlled.

I have found the quality of my images improve when the camera or camcorder is tripod supported, or at the least, mounted upon a mono-pod. Camera shake can be a problem when cameras with telephoto lenses are handheld.

Animals that respond to a distress scream are sometimes naive but are not often stupid. A customer rightly expects to see something distressed after running a half mile or more to investigate. Much of the time a disappointed customer will take a look and leave. Some may even howl out insults. I have found it helpful to offer something interesting to look at. Perhaps something as complex as a rabbit look- alike that does the jitterbug and maybe something as simple as a tanned rabbit hide attached to a piece of monofilament fishing line.

Do not hesitate to be innovative. One of my most successful attempts at animal photography involved a feeding station outside an office window at my Flagstaff home. That window looked out upon a part of the Coconino National Forest and that forest was home to an amazing variety of wildlife, much of such being nocturnal. My son Michael and I moved an assortment of stumps to within six or eight feet of the window, removed the window pane, replaced the pane with thin plywood, cut a lens sized hole in the plywood and placed a tripod mounted digital camera at the hole. The good news? The customers could not see the man behind the camera. Now for the bad news. We could not see the customers. My son Michael attached a small television monitor to the camera viewfinder and we were able to watch live action as raccoon, gray fox, coyote, ringtail cat and skunk came to taste our offering of dry dog food, a honey and cornflake mixture and about anything else we wanted to donate. An electronic shutter release kept our hands away from the camera.

Lighting was somewhat of a problem. Mike and I experimented with flash photography but were not satisfied with the results. We settled on a flood light arrangement that eventually numbered four. We placed a single light at the start and added additional lights as our customers became adjusted to the light source.

The first night of image taking was not successful. At the beginning of night number two I set up a battery powered tape player and used a series of medium volume rabbit distress screams to advertise the new buffet in town. Eyeballs began to appear from among the ponderosa pine and the Gambel's oak. We were able to identify raccoon and a single ringtail cat. The third night we enjoyed action at the bait station and were able to obtain several high quality images. Action would begin at dead dark thirty and continue on until two or three a.m.. Much of the time there was a critter or two waiting when we went out to feed.

Eventually we had collected a plethora of images showing animals eating dry dog food but hoped for something a bit more interesting. Michael would place his finger on the shutter release and I would moan through a reed-ed tube or maybe kiss out a close up call. Either often caused the customer to look at the camera and appear interested, hungry, suspicious or pissed off. One customer, a particular perky coyote, delivered the raspberry. Michael, owning the fastest finger in the west, would grab the image, much of the time more than one.

That same set up worked very well when the day shift came on duty. A bunch of birds showed for sunflower seeds and or water including the showy acorn woodpecker and the seldom seen bandtail pigeon. Abert's squirrels, rock squirrels and chipmunks also cooperated. The images obtained were actually high quality animal portraits.

Knowing that some predator callers who read this book also trap I feel it proper to mention that a trapped animal can offer a fine photographic opportunity. Those who wish to market the image should endeavor to leave the trap out of the image. I have had good luck photographing trapped animals when I have had a partner along to divert the animals attention from the guy behind the camera. Having the decoy human approach somewhat close to the critter can cause snarls, growls and howls, all such looking good within still pictures and even better on the camcorder.

At times I would add an element to the script to improve photographic potential. I recall a time when I collected a road killed cottontail rabbit as I drove to check the traps. The first set held a handsome baileyi bobcat. I tossed the rabbit carcass close to the 'bob and obtained several saleable images. I did about the same thing at another time and taped the bobcat as he ate the offering. The sound of the purring cat and the sound of crunched bones cooperated with the visual to produce extra fine footage. A portion of that footage was used within my video *Masters' Secrets to Predator Calling*.

Do not hesitate to be innovative. I clearly recall a coyote collecting trip to one of the cattle ranches adjacent to the Petrified Forest National Park within northeastern Arizona. As I walked away from a non-productive set up, I discovered a very handsome western collared lizard sunning on a section of petrified log. I dug the camera from the day pack and took several exposures. Later, a second boomer scurried beneath another section of petrified wood. I used my hat to snare the lizard, built a corral out of wood and plastic wrap, and released the lizard within. The images were damfine. At sessions end I released the lizard and wished him (or her) well.

As outdoors oriented people, we are offered a rare opportunity to enjoy wildlife. Preserving those images, to me, makes sense.

I have used those images, and others, to illustrate books, articles and slide shows. I have used some of those images on stationary and some on business cards. Hell, even Xmas cards. I have used the camcorder footage to produce predator calling videos. As callers and trappers we are offered a unique opportunity to photograph wildlife. As you might notice, as you examine images within this book, the product can be worth the time, effort and expense involved.

A corral made of sticks and plastic wrap caused this Western Collared Lizard to play nice.

chapter 23

Night Calls

I shrugged my double-XL shoulders a bit deeper into the thorny arms of the Wait a Minute Bush and screamed. Nope, not because I was in pain (I was), but because I was there to scream. I was night hunting for predators and that is what night hunters do. Without a warning the great horned owl swooped to caress my cap with a furled primary. I had hardly recovered when a rustling to the rear asked for attention. Was it a snake? A snake with rattles? It was early in the fall and still warm, too high a temperature to encourage hibernation. I forgot the owl and concentrated on the crawler.

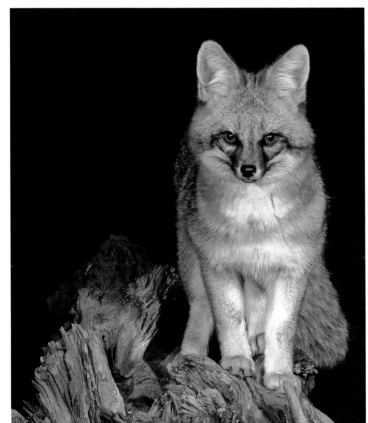

Night calling can increase customer satisfaction when calling to nocturnals such as bobcat, raccoon and ringtail cats and to switch hitters such as fox and coyote.

The ringtailed cat is ninety nine percent nocturnal but might occasionally come to a distress scream sounded during the crepuscular periods of dawn and dusk.

At about that time a cloud moved to release the moon, permitting a look at the creeper, a bushy-tailed wood rat looking for mesquite beans. I looked to the front and nearly lost it when I discovered an interested coyote delivering the bad eye from twenty yards. Ahhh, night calling. I love it. A hunter does not know what the night is likely to offer.

Night screaming to predators is exciting. The lack of light limits visibility, causing it to be difficult to see the customers; likewise it is difficult for the customers to see you. Perception usually comes as one big bright eye reaches out to illuminate two small bright eyes. Tension builds, then suddenly the customer looms up out of the night, often coming much closer than it would during daylight. It can be dandy.

The first question begging an answer is basic. Why in heck night hunt at all? Simply answered: There are critters to be called, animals that come reluctantly or not at all to day calls. About every land predator is most easily called at night. The raccoon is the most nocturnal of all. As noted within the chapter dealing with the masked bandit, screamers who do not work the night shift seldom see raccoon. Bobcat like the night shift but can be called during daylight if circumstances are precisely correct.

I am convinced many daytime customers of the cat kind slip in and slip out, avoiding discovery. This lack of discovery owes to two circumstances. One is the cat camouflage, a discrete fur that causes the Robert Kitty to be nearly invisible. The second circumstance has to do with bobcat hunting technique. The bob' is a sneak, using every bit of structure to creep close. Night cats are more easily discovered. Even though the camouflage stays constant, as does the hunt technique, the bright light causes the cat eyes to illuminate like a pair of miniature moons. Other land predators, dogs like coyote and foxes, are more of a switch hitter. Some, the coyote and the gray fox specifically, come dependably during the day but come most often during the night. The other fox, the red, does not. Those paranoid little boogers might respond to day calls when those day screams are heard in quiet land, places removed from habitation. Farm fox, the kind most often found within the Midwest and the East, disapprove of daytime activity, turning totally nocturnal, or nearly so. The littlest fox, sometimes called the kit and sometimes called the swift, stays one hundred percent nocturnal.

Another small predator works the night shift exclusively. I write of the critter sometimes called a cacomistle but most commonly called a ringtail cat. Even though cat-like in habit, this small predator is a 'coon cousin, sharing that family with the raccoon and with the coatimundi. The ringtail is common to parts of Mexico, to a half a handful of Southwestern states, and is uncommon within a few more.

Some states prohibit night hunting. Others prohibit the use of artificial lights, allowing a screaming as long as it takes place by moonlight. Some jurisdictions permit night hunting; permit lights, but limit gun caliber. Others, more enlightened, permit night hunting with minimal restriction. It is wise to check locally to learn the hunting regulations in the area you hope to hunt.

Night hunting can carry a responsibility. Darkness will hide the customer and that customer might come close before discovery. The shooting opportunity can be sudden, and just as suddenly evaporate. The gunner that shoots at a panicked predator

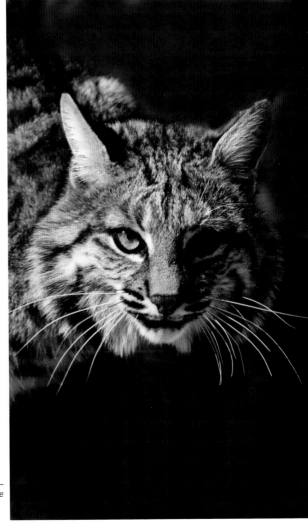

The moon-like eyes of the bobcat become beacons because of reflected light.

139

The kit fox is the little kid on the block and hunts the midnight to stay safe.

concentrates on the target and might not see background hazards. I write of livestock and such. The high power rifle round can travel far to do damage.

Even so, the night hunt can be safe, can be productive, and can cause one hell of a lot of hunting excitement. The animals I have night-called have owned varying attitudes to the light. The coyote is the most light shy of the ones I have called. Shine the bright part of the night light into a set of coyote eyes and be ready to shoot. My experience causes me to believe the coyote will allow a few seconds for the shot, then turn to make the retreat, most often at the gallop. Other predators are less light shy. The raccoon is an example. The 'coon I have called have stared straight into the light, not blinking, until they learn the circumstances of the screaming. Bobcat are nearly as focused. Fox? Some yes and some no. Depends on the fox and on the kind of country he claims.

Light technique can vary. Many night hunters, maybe even most, scan with the main light intensity held high, using the periphery of light to scan for eyes. Such provides a pair of assets. The low intensity of the peripheral light is not as likely to cause a customer to hang up, or retreat. Keeping the strong part of the beam high minimizes shadows, always a problem with light-shy critters like coyote. A low and bright light, one that moves to make the scan, cause brush and all other low structure to cast a shadow, a moving shadow. That sort of movement will often cause the customer to leave, or at the least to become too nervous to come close.

When eyes are sighted, when those eyes are close enough for the wet work, the light man lowers the brightest part of the beam, aiming for positive target identification and providing plenty of light for the shooter.

Some hunters place a red lens over the scanning light thinking the red light to be invisible to the predator. My experience causes me to think such is not so. The main function of the red lens is a reduction in light intensity. That reduction of light intensity likely causes the critter to be a bit more comfortable.

Shooting visibility decreases as light intensity decreases. The gunner might have more difficulty making absolute target identification. Range is substantially decreased. Using the red light causes a trade-off. The critter does not see you as well. On the flip side, the gunner does not see the critter as well.

Predator lights come in varying configurations. One such, a good one, is the cap light used by folks who spend a lot of time doing it in the dark, miners and other such. Their lights, much of the time, consist of a helmet light powered by a muscular battery pack carried on the belt. Those battery packs are rechargeable. I have used cap lights made and marketed by KW Oldham Caplight, Nite-Lite, and the Wheat Light by Koehler. All were damnfine.

Buying such a light necessitates also buying the charger. Proper care can cause both to deliver many years of service. A hand-held spotlight of varying candlepower is commonly used. I have seen some rated to 500,000 candlepower. As might be expected, that bunch of candles can generate a lot of heat, causing it to be necessary for the light handler to use caution to avoid the bad burn. All, or nearly all, are powered by a 12-volt system, the same system found within most automobile electrical systems. Some come with rechargeable motorcycle batteries. Plugging into the vehicle electrical system as the hunters travel from stand to stand can recharge some.

A subspecies of night light are the shooting lights that attach to the top of a one-inch telescope sight. Some can be easily attached to the barrel of a shotgun also. Lightforce offers one. Burnham Brothers offers several models, one being a compact little guy offering 20,000 candlepower output (SL-18), impressive considering its power comes from a pair of 9-volt batteries. A pressure switch, mounted to the forearm of the stock, provides easy accessibility. Lenses are available in clear, red, amber, orange and blue.

Burnham Game Calls, separate from Burnham Brothers, markets a dandy shooting light (SL-1) powered by four AA batteries. This lightweight model is easily detached and can be used as a flashlight.

Nite-Lite offers an excellent shooting light that comes as a part of their Nite-Lite kit. Their scope light plugs into the same belt-carried power source (6 volts) that feeds the scanning light, some models offering 13 hours of burn time.

Those who hanker for a shooting light with real muscle need to know about the NightBlaster lights offered by Optronics. These big boogers come with a six-volt or twelve-volt power supply. All models offer a stock-mounted switch and a selection of lens color.

What advantage does the gun-mounted light offer? A solo hunter is not

Raccoon seldom stray far from the den during daylight but can come in gangs during the dark.

required to operate the hand-held spotlight and shoot at the same time; difficult even for those who are coordinated. That solo can, instead, switch off the scanning light, lay it aside, and use the gun-mounted light for the wet work.

The gun-mounted light can work about as well during team hunts. The light man locates eyes. The shooter shoulders and sights, switching on the shooting light when ready. As mentioned, some states prohibit the use of lights during night hunts, saying, I suppose, "Sure, you can night hunt, Bubba. Just don't be using no light so-as you can see. Hee Hee."

Some night hunters take fur even though so handicapped. A bright moon (even a half bright moon) on snow can be dandy. So can that same moon upon fallow fields. Be aware that such conditions allow you to see the critter but lets the critter see you equally well, maybe better. Set up in the shade (yep, a bright moon casts shadows), sit still, and wear sensible clothing.

Those of us who skulk the midnight, the way I see it, have a special obligation to think safety. Visibility being limited to the scan of the light, we do not often need a gun that will shoot through three zip codes and throw fur for another couple. Centerfires should be sensible. I have used the .22 WRFM (for 'coon and fox), have used the .22 Hornet and have used the deuce. All did decently.

The shotgun does dandy as a night gun. Three-and-a-half-inch ten-gauge magnums like MooseDick are the biggest of the bangers available. The twelve-gauge chambered for the 3-1/2" fodder is good. So are the three-inch twelves. All such are basically short-range guns that minimize the obvious danger provided by the center fires. The shotguns I have used for night calling own a similar aspect. The bead sight of all has been painted with white fingernail polish to improve visibility.

Bill Del Monte with the Texas Department of Parks & Wildlife, uses a technique to call double dead 'coon and other night skulkers. Me and Ol' Bill made two calls high on the mesa but found that elevated aspect to be unproductive. The third call found us within the walls of a Texas-size canyon. Bill prepared for the screaming in a way that spoke of practice, I'm talking experience. We stood within the bed of the pickup truck (legal in Texas). Bill positioned a blanket and a pair of sandbags on the cab top to serve as shooting supports and readied the battery-powered caller and the light. I stayed ready with the flash-equipped 35mm. When all was ready Bill swung the light so as to cover a full 360° circle, doing so at a brisk pace. "Working within tight country," he whispered, "we have to swing fast. If not, a critter can run close and not be seen." The beam suddenly slammed on the brakes, then backed up. Bill slapped

my shoulder, telling he had eyes, those glowing coals being a hundred yards out. Bill kept the light moving, to cover twenty yards on each side of the eyeballs, keeping the main part of the beam high, illuminating the eyeballs using the lower intensity peripheral. "I don't know what the heck it is," he whispered. 'The spacing of the eyes and the height causes me to think 'coon." I nodded agreement and stayed excited. Seconds later the guess was verified. A big boar lumbered close, circled the truck a time or two, and posed as I worked the auto focus Canon, then left.

Coyote may come close at night but are often light shy and difficult to hit.

My relationship with the Texas raccoon turned ugly the next night. A neighboring rancher called to complain of raccoon depredation of his corncribs, asking that Bill and I attempt to convince the bandits to cease and desist. We said sure. We pulled the pickup into the 'Coon Canyon when it was decently dark. Bill readied and cranked up the raccoon fight tape. The dirty guys, according to the ranch foreman, were a pair of big bruisers, probably boars. I locked and loaded MooseDick and hunkered at the ready, staying low so Bill could swing the light.

The four eyeballs showed on the canyon wall almost immediately. "Looks like ringtail cat eyes to me," Bill muttered, then continued the swing. The eyeballs did not move during the next eight or ten sweeps, and then suddenly disappeared. Bill sent the scanner to search and discovered the eyeballs bobbing our way. "Those are raccoon," Bill judged. "Get ready." Hell, I was born ready and was ready then, but did not bother to say so.

The boars lumbered to 30 yards and slid to make a reconnoiter. Mistake. They mistook again when they stood shoulder to shoulder. I could not resist the temptation to show off. I placed the white barrel bead squarely between the heads and lit the fire. The boars rugged out like a couple of them Olympic swimmers that do that goofy synchronized swim. "AWESOME," Bill hollered, then began furious slapping of my shoulders (hurt like hell). He calmed down a little and said it again. "That was awesome," he says. "In all of my critter calling life I have not witnessed two critters killed with a single shot." I tried to be modest but did not have a lot of luck. "Nothing to it," I lied. "Out in Arizona I might double on critters two or three times on every hunt."

The Del Monte technique of night calling is sensible and effective. His light is a modified Nite-Lite hand-held spotlight that works from the 12-volt system of the truck. A pigtail at the rear of the cab allows easy hook up. The light has a flare guard, a protective tube extending several inches out from the glass, causing the beam to be more directional, preventing side light that can show the handler.

As mentioned, Bill likes a fast swing on setups that offer limited visibility. Swing too slowly and the customer can run in and run out between swings. The light scans more slowly in more open country.

The main beam of the red-lens light is kept high, letting the low intensity peripheral beam hunt for the eyes. "When eyes are sighted," Bill cautions, "take time to absolutely identify your target." The main beam of the light lowers to illuminate the critter, and when appropriate, the shot follows. Some new to the dark side of predator calling may think conditions to be too difficult. Even those, I am convinced, will change when they come in contact with the big-eyed critters that work the night shift. The coyote, the foxes, the cats, the snakes and all others; ahhh, night calls, how I love 'em.

Sunrise and sunset can be a productive time to call those who hunt the daylight and those who hunt the dark.

chapter 24

Tight Country Calls

Those who gun for fur are of two general types. There are those who use rifles and those who find an advantage to the shotgun. Some of those who use the rifle, it seems to me, shoot the centerfire for the same reason a coyote howls-it is their nature to do so. My friend George Oakey is one such. George has never hunted any animal or any bird with the shotgun, preferring to demonstrate his shooting skill using a Sako in .243 or .222. That precisely focused preference can be good news to those of us who see rifles and shotguns as tools specific to circumstance.

You want the truth? There are kinds of country able to chew up the best rifleman in the world and spit that purist out in chunk bait-size servings. That country is the thick hardwoods of the East, the Midwest and the South. That country is the chaparral and just plain brush of the West and Southwest. That kind of country, terrain where an eager customer might come so close you can smell his needs, and do so suddenly, is shotgun country.

Screaming the country I generically call the brush offers an obvious advantage. George and others like him do not call there. Those of us who do it in the bushes do so without the worry of extreme competition, at least not the kind of competition found in other more open areas. Critters found within the brush, some of the time, will be less pressured, less stressed, and more eager to cooperate in a screaming.

Even though I have commented a time or two on tight-country calling, doing so mainly within the chapter devoted to shotgunning, I feel it worthwhile to address the technique more specifically. There are different grades of brush. Put another way, all brush is not created equal. The brush of the low desert of the Southwest, as an example, is considerably different from the chaparral common to the transition woodlands. Both are different from the juniper forests found a bit higher within the transition woodlands. The ground cover and the hardwood overstory found to the East of the big river are different from all. Each type of terrain requires a slightly modified technique. A screamer in each must utilize the THINKING technique described in the chapter titled "Tough Calls." Experience and evaluation, much of the time, can cooperate to bring a sensible scheme. Here is an example to illustrate.

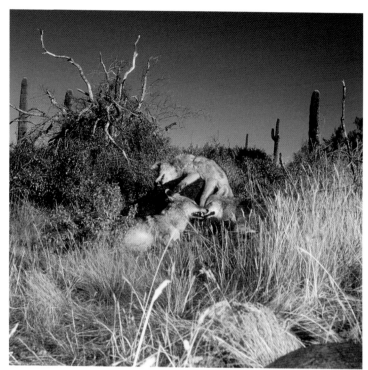

Chuck Spearman and I made the scream within a cluster of desert cover. Cholla, ocotillo, Joshuas, hohos, and greasewood competed. It was the kind of country nine out of ten hunters would sneer at. The setup where a hunter would be blind as soon as he sat down. The screamer who substituted the stand-up owned a better aspect, not much better but maybe enough.

The desert dog came at the gallop, made a desperate run-by that took him five yards to Chuck's right, and lined out for home and Mother. Chuck reacted, throwing a load of four buck at the disappearing customer. Bingo. I screamed the TallyHo to keep the stand-up alive. A littermate of the recently deceased showed within seconds, taking the usual paranoid reconnoiter then turning to retreat. A load of copper-plated BBs from MooseDick halted the escape. A third yodeler popped out of the brush and the Ithaca Mag-10 burped again. Total time elapsed? Maybe thirty seconds, making for fast shooting and fast fun. A cooperation often found within the brush.

Success during that stand-up came because we carried the right kind of gun, and because we modified our technique to respond to conditions. The most obvious change was the stand. A stander had his head high enough to own an overview that isolated the stingy spacing separating the structure. The sitter would be denied that aspect. A sitter would have his head on eye level with the greasewood and the hoho's, permitting a good look at the bush immediately to the front but little else.

Chuck and I sighted ten more coyote during that two-and-a-half day hunt and skinned half. Those eight coyote were not a two-and-a-half day total that would cause me to write home to Mother about, but were decent. More impressive when it is considered we tackled country too tough for most others.

The second obvious compromise made to accommodate the tight country screaming was the choice of guns, such being shotgun country. Experience suggests one of the class I call the big bangers. My own preference is for the biggest banger, the ten gauge chambered to take the three-and-a-half-inch hull. Those willing to accept the small handicap of reduced range can do well using a twelve-gauge chambered to take the three or three-and-half-inch shell. A full discussion of such will be found within the chapter dealing specifically with shotguns.

I often modify my setup style when calling tight country. Such cover, much of the time, will dampen the strength of the call to cause the screaming to be subdued. I compensate by shortening the distance between setups, maybe each half mile and maybe half that.

The scream is likewise modified. Experience suggests a series of desperate and choppy screams work best. The critters I have called out of the brush have come at a desperate run. I encourage that pace when I put desperation in those short duration screams, putting a drop of blood on each. I may call constantly,

Tight country bobcats are expert at using every available bit of cover to hide their approach, and at times, their departure.

or nearly so, when calling the brush, as a further encouragement to the critter that might come running. The TallyHo and other open reeds do fine when I place such to the corner of my mouth and breathe out the cadence.

Do not ignore the battery-powered caller when involved with the brush. Tubes require the cooperation of at least one hand if they are to work as good as can be. That means the shotgun must be held within the free hand. That posture adds seconds to the response. There will be times when those seconds allow the customer to retreat. The battery-powered caller can be caused to scream independently, leaving the hands free to keep the gun at ready.

There is a tendency in all of us, I think, to read an instruction and literally interpret each syllable. I refer specifically to instructions you may have read suggesting you place the caller or the speaker fifty feet or so out from the gun. Forget that sort of thing when calling the brush. I use the shoulder strap to suspend the battery-powered caller, keeping the speaker above the brush a bit to extend range. Controls are a hand movement away. Turning the body slightly causes the directional feature of the speaker to address new country. Best of all, hands are freed to manage the gun, and do so quickly.

Screaming in the hardwoods can cause obscured vision, just as tight cover calling does within other zip codes. I say so knowing that the over- and under-story are in the cold weather mode, leafless, for much of the prime fur time. Choosing an elevated set (or stand-up), maybe on the slope of a hill, can slightly improve aspect. Some screamers utilize blinds constructed to assist in the hunting of the wild turkey or white-tailed deer. Those elevated structures can provide a fine visibility. Many, maybe even most, are located in somewhat open areas, a good many adjacent to trails. I do not wish to insult the intelligence when I nag a bit about the danger inherent to the climbing of a tree carrying a loaded gun. I do feel compelled, as a friend, to make mention. Enough said.

The elevated aspect offered by the tree stand can cause a reconsideration of gun choice. Some such are likely to be open enough to permit the use of the rifle. Some might demand such. Use THINKING to decide. There will be times when the customer eschews the gallop to come at the sneak. Such, much of the time, will be heard and not seen — mostly as a rustling of the leaves or limbs. Close. There will be the temptation to begin a desperate screaming to cause the critter to show. Doing so does not get the job done, at least not often. I have found that screaming loud to a close critter has been counterproductive. Experience suggests a more low key approach. Use the Kiss of Death or another kind of close-in call (discussed fully within the chapter titled "Kisses and Other Close Calls"). I call little in such situations and call low, sending out a couple of low whines (using my voice) of two or three seconds each. I wait to see if that does the trick. If not, I play the ace, using the Kiss of Death. That "K of D," much of the time, will convince the bashful there is a trophy woodrat or cottontail nearby that is desperate to be eaten.

There is an important element to the calling of thick cover. That element involves the use of common sense. That sense of a common nature will tell you there are some brushy areas too thick to be screamed. Do not waste your time on such. Concentrate on areas offering a decent return for effort. There will be times when you will be able to set up to the edge of thick cover. Abandoned logging roads within thick cover can be dandy. Set up near to stream banks when those riparian areas offer a bit of visibility. A boat can be an asset along major waterways and lakes. The bottom line? Use THINKING to evaluate potential and select technique. Do that and you are likely to enjoy the excitement that comes with tight-country calling.

The Kiss of Death can cause a barely seen bit of fur to turn into a decent target.

Brushy terrain allows the gray fox to hunt successfully and to stay somewhat safe.

chapter 25

Teamwork

The coyote was not a virgin. I saw that immediately. He was a third of a mile out when first sighted, a barely-seen dot of fur in the distance. It took the paranoid a full five minutes to cover the next three hundred yards of pushdowns. Sometimes I could see him, sometimes not. I stayed patient and kept up the screaming. Lowering the volume of the TallyHo, blowing pitiful little screams, the kind bound to bring a tear to the eye of Hard Hearted Hanna from Butte, Montana.

My mind was made up. Even though I knew my limitations, knew that a 300-yard opportunity was not the kind of shot that fit my talents, I resolved to start the wet work the next time the yodeler paused for a reconnoiter. I shifted my eyeballs to slant sidewise, hoping to see how Joe Bob was reacting to the sight of his first called coyote. J.B. was not reacting at all. His uneducated eyes had not discovered the customer. "Just as well," I muttered to my mind, "if he can't see him, he can't spook him."

I thought wrong. Ten seconds later, at about the time I had worked through two pounds of the three pound trigger on the .22-250, perception occurred. "There comes one now," Joe Bob bellowed. He added insult when he leaped erect and laid into that 300-yard coyote with his twelve gauge. J. Bob would have been more correct if he had said, "There goes one now."

I sighed, gathered the junk, and headed for the truck. On the trudge back I amused Joe B. by telling him horror stories about the worst calling partners I had suffered through. Somewhere in that dialogue I thanked J.B. for providing the coyote with a good laugh, for allowing that same coyote to make the desperate run for home carrying the fifty-dollar hide I hankered for. Do coyote laugh? I'm not sure. If any do that one damn sure did, maybe at the sight of a hunter lobbing a load of four buck at an out-of-range target, or maybe because of the tears in my own eyes.

The worst calling partner I have hunted with was the one called the hummer. Vernon LaDuke (my stepdad) is dead now so there is no longer a reason to hide his identity. Duke was a fine hunting companion in many ways. He always did his share of the camp work, sometimes more than his share. He bragged on my cooking at about every meal. He did not mention, even one time, the time I missed a trotting coyote at 20 yards. Trouble was, Duke was a

The right kind of partner can cause a good hunt to become better. Gerry Blair and Raymond Branch.

compulsive hummer and would break into a tuneless hum at the least excuse. Duke hummed, I think, because he was nervous, and critter calling always made him nervous. He became particularly nervous when I had a critter nibbling at the bait. I recall one stand vividly. I had a pair of chargers coming from out of the stringbark, each hoping to be the first to get the rabbit. Duke hummed the pair clean out of the country. I regretfully ended the partnership. Whistlers, scratchers, and squirmers can be about as bad.

Screaming to predators is like other hunts in one respect. There is more fun to be found if you share the adventure and the excitement with a buddy. A pair of callers, if each is disciplined, dedicated, and use the right technique, can take more fur, more than either would take as a solo. Do not expect twice as much, however. A team of callers will fetch in about the same number of coyote likely to respond to a single caller. A hunter who knows where the coyote lifts his leg, and knows why is likely to take maybe sixty or seventy percent of those called critters. Buddy calling can cause a better percentage but it does not take a mathematical genius to figure there is not room for doubling.

One of my all time favorite screaming companions is George Oakey of Flagstaff, a man who has hunted predators for fifty years, since the mid-fifties. He has a talented touch on the tube (favoring an antique wood Circe in Trophy configuration) and is equally talented on the trigger, abilities that are in short supply among some calling companions. George and I have team hunted enough to develop a technique that maximizes our fur take. Here is the way it works.

Gun selection can be critical if a team is to take enough fur to keep the stretchers full. A solo hunter, much of the time, looks at the country and makes the choice between the shotgun and the centerfire. There will be times when the solo hunter guesses wrong. That hunter might choose a shotgun and have a bobcat hang up a hundred yards out to deliver the bad eye. That hunter might choose the centerfire and have a charger come from his back to cross his boot toes and disappear. George and I take away the guesswork. He carries a Sako, either in .243 (I keep telling him it's too damn much gun for fur) or in .222. I carry MooseDick, a junkyard dog kind of ten gauge that can cause a coyote to get dead at sixty yards. When a critter comes we let that critter come as close as they want to be, and at about then I lay into them with the load of copper-plated BBs. George cleans up on the escapees. Other times he surprises the bashful ones that dance around out of shotgun range.

We set up so that each watches an approach lane, not the same one. We do not set back to back as some early screamers advise. I usually cover the prime approach lane with the shotgun, most particularly if that approach involves trees and brush or both, where the critter must come close to see the rabbit. George sets up to one side so that he can cover the more long-distance approach.

If either discovers a customer, we lip squeak to put the partner on the alert. Two guns, we figure, are always better than one gun when a critter comes to call. That lip squeak (Kiss of Death), much of the time, is made when the customer is a ways out and not likely to notice. The "here comes one" signal has another benefit. Multiples are sometimes sighted. If each gunner is ready each can attend to one. How do we prevent shooting at the same critter? Easy. The shotgun guy takes the close customer. The rifleman takes the other. In the case of a double that are about equidistant, the hunter to the left takes the

Pre-arranged signals can alert hunting partners to seldom seen customers.

left-hand critter, the hunter to the right takes the right-hand critter.

I lost a critter, a good one, on one hunt because three good hunters didn't take the time to communicate. It happened this way. We were set up on a side hill below a rock rim, watching a juniper-choked canyon. Within that canyon a dirt dam caused a backwater stock tank. We were screaming to the gray fox and the bobcat we hoped would hear. Each of us carried shotguns because the tight nature of the setup caused visibility (shot opportunity) to be close range.

Mike Mell was the middleman and he was doing the calling, blowing deliciously on his plastic Circe. Twenty seconds of screams followed by a minute of silence. Repeat. I caught a flicker of movement at the ending of one series; a movement on the far side of the canyon and in a thick forest of string bark junipers. I looked until my eyeballs ached and finally found a bobcat face floating among the shadows. I looked at Mike and saw he had not made discovery. I placed my own Circe tube to my mouth and began a screaming. Mike got the message and searched until he discovered the cat. He relaxed then to let me finish the screaming. And I did. The bobcat moved out of the shadows and into the sun, showing he was a dandy blue-back worth a couple of hundred dollars within the current market. The cat looked at Mike and me and then moved across an open area of about twenty feet and then out of sight into the brush-choked drainage. We did not see that cat again for five minutes. Even so, I stayed patient and continued the scream.

Finally, the cat showed on our side of the drainage and stopped to look again. I gave him the "Kiss of Death" and he started my way at the trot, maybe sixty or seventy yards out. At about that time Mike and I heard the report from Little Gary's twelve-gauge, a hundred yards to Mike's left and a couple of hundred yards from the cat. The sound of the shotgun caused the cat to freeze in mid-stride. I panicked. Messed up. I figured the cat was bound to leave at the gallop any second. I laid into that cat with a load of four buck from the 3" twelve. The cat hit the ground, bounced erect, and disappeared into the canyon. Even though Mike and I gave chase we did not see that kitty again.

Little Gary had not shot at the cat, didn't even know it was there. His shot was at a fine silver coyote that had approached from his left, and he earned the evidence. How could we have done it differently? First, knowing then what I know now, I would not have shot at that long-distance bobcat. I now know that critters do not always spook at the sound of a shot. If I had kept on calling, continued with the lip squeak, it is likely the cat would have forgiven the shot to trot on in. Secondly, it is a good idea to develop a series of signals when team hunting. George and I use a system he used when he was involved in calling contests with Del Western during the early days. We blow a single scream if we have a fox on the hook, two screams for a coyote and three for a cat, bobcat or lion. Had we done so little Gary would likely have let the coyote walk, saved the action for the bobcat.

George and I use the call as a signal in another way. We'd take turns on the tube so that neither will develop the dreaded trombone lip. When the stand master (the screamer) is ready to call it quits he blows a single long blast, indicating his desire to abandon the setup. The second hunter answers with two screams indicating he has nothing in sight. Such a system avoids the embarrassment of standing while a customer is in sight. That sort of thing happened to me during 1995, while on a hunt with an Alaskan guide who had come to America (that's what they call the lower 48) to do a bit of cat screaming.

The Slammer and I were set up to call a brush choked canyon that was sort of fan shaped, the narrow end being close and the wide end maybe four hundred yards out. Gary was screaming his Tally-Ho and had done so for about fifteen minutes. Right about then I sighted movement at the top of the fan and looked to see a bob' trot an insignificant opening, headed our way. Our set-ups were too far apart to allow whispering. I hunkered down and hoped for the best. As often happens, I received the worst. Garry screamed for a couple of more minutes and then stood to leave. I started a desperate screaming, and when Gary looked I motioned him to sit. He did and I maintained the screaming for another thirty minutes, until dead dark. The bobcat never showed.

Double gunning at a screaming can double the fun found afield. When done right that double gunning can increase the fur take. A pair of hunters can share expenses to enjoy twice the hunts at a reduced price. For maximum fun, however, select the calling companion carefully. No hummers. When you find a good 'un, treat him or her right. They may be hard to replace.

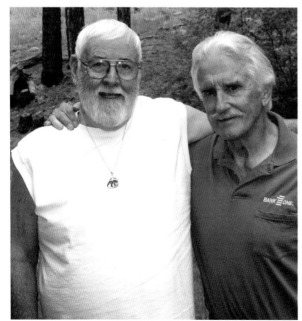

Calling pioneer George Oakey teamed with the hard hunting Del Western to shoot at heads and collect tails. (Beverly Blair Photo).

chapter 26

Double Trouble

I have mentioned in other chapters the asset to be found while calling after a kill, or after a missed opportunity. I repeat here, do so. If the country is good enough to give up one customer it might be good enough to give up a second. Some predators, dogs like the coyote and the fox particularly, pair for much of the year. Killing one, then calling to the other can be good business.

Those multiples that come to a single setup, but come within a somewhat separated time frame are not true doubles and not true triples, not the way I see it. Those that come to a screaming but come separately are simply two singles, each to be dealt with as such. Predators that come like grapes, in bunches, are a different matter. The screamer is confronted with double and triple excitement. Killing more than one of the gang requires THINKING.

Every screamer will have instances where he or she is challenged by multiples. Considering options before the hunt can help awfully when it comes time to consider options while in the big middle of the situation. If you customarily scream with a partner, I suggest you and the partner communicate to develop a scheme of action. Do so before the hunt. Doing so while critters are out front is seldom productive. An important question begging an answer can be basic, who shoots what? Having a pair of screamers double kill a

Calling and killing multiples can be a challenge not easily answered.

coyote while the neighbor runs can be depressing. Generally, if the critters are equidistant, the hunter to the right shoots the critter to the right. The hunter to the left shoots the left-hand customer.

Now, a bit more on the "keep on calling after the shot advice." There will be times when the first to respond hits the ground hard, but hits the ground so that the remains are out of sight, or maybe barely in sight. Sad experience has told me to quit the screaming right then to make the retrieve. Let me supply an example.

I was screaming the greasewoods with Chuck Spearman and his friend Gary Brittan (The Great Brittan, being the president of a Nebraska paper company). Knowing three to the screaming can be awkward; Gary and I dropped Chuck (drop & drive) a mile or so down the two-track, then continued on to select our own setup.

A minute or two into the screaming I sighted a customer of the coyote kind making a sneak from fifty yards out. The critter stopped and turned broadside, a body language that told me he had come as close as likely. I shouldered MooseDick, got down on the stock, sighted, and started the squeeze. All of that caused the coyote to become nervous. When I had tautened the trigger nearly enough to cause the ten-gauge to go bang, the critter left at the leap. I swung and continued the squeeze, causing the coyote to crash during mid-leap. The Great Brittan was impressed. Hell, I was impressed. I watched to discover a miraculous recovery.

I could not see the coyote. His tail would flag each half-minute or so, telling me he was still there. I returned to calling. Suddenly realizing I had not seen the tail in a while, I jumped up and advanced at a lumber. The coyote was gone. No blood trail. Nothing. We left, sad but wiser.

Common sense says you do not continue the call when a critter is downed but flopping, particularly if that flopping causes the critter to disappear from sight. Stop the screaming, cause the finish, and make the retrieve.

The Western coyote I have met have not been pack animals, except during the fall when pups and parents hunt as a family. Multiples that come are most often doubles — Ma and Pa. That does not mean gangs do not come to a single calling. I was with Chuck Spearman, calling on an Indian reservation where the coyote is considered to be a reincarnation of Granny, when we called and counted an even dozen coyote to a single screaming. All appeared as singles and doubles. The response caused us to shoot the auto focus Canons with a gleeful desperation.

After the shot, calling can be productive when the target is gray or red fox. Those little dogs are essentially miniature coyote, the way I see it, and respond coyote-like. Here's an example.

I was calling the Bagdad boulders during a winter and had completed three series when a pair of gray fox galloped close, then flared at about thirty-five yards. I made the easy shot on the close fox, and then swung the .222 to try for the trailer. Such, being no dummy, decided I was not the kind of neighbor worth visiting and disappeared into the rock jumble. I kept calling, staying hopeful, keeping one eye on the carcass. A couple of minutes later a second fox, maybe the same one that came as a half of the pair, peeked over a bug-sized (VW) boulder. I squared, shouldered, and shot. Staying with the scream had caused me to double the pleasure and double the fur. Do not expect a second customer to appear after every shot. It is not likely to happen. Even so, after-shot calling will work enough to make the practice worthwhile.

Shooting response to doubles and triples must be precise if the screamer is to take all that is offered. I cannot

Gray fox and other members of the wild dog family pair bond and remain so until one of the pair dies or loses vigor.

count the times I have taken the easy part of a double and then messed up to let the surviving half escape. Honesty causes me to confess to worse. There have been times the excitement of the double vision has caused me to mess up big time. I did such, nearly, on the pair of coyote called from windy winter pushdowns.

The coyotes let the forty mph crosswind cause them to be off course. Does the wind blow sound? Maybe. Those coyote thought so. Each came at the gallop but were headed wrong. I scrooched a bit behind the log, licked the call slobbers from my beard, and screamed, causing the duo to correct and come straight.

It was the winter of 1978. The pelts from that pair of high country primes would bring a hundred dollar bill, a significant sum to a recently retired highway patrol captain, struggling to supplement a stingy retirement. I watched the approach and hummed a mind song, don't mess up, don't mess up.

The positioning of the pair caused a complication. The front runner was fifty yards ahead of the trailer. If I used the three-inch twelve to do business with the leader, the trailer would likely veer to escape. Wanting both, needing both, I delayed the shot until the leader was nearly on me. I loomed from behind the log with the auto loader at the ready. Any decent coyote, I figured, would veer to avoid the danger out front, maybe provide a broadside opportunity.

This one did not. That sumbitch leaped. Leapt over the log, and over me. I caught a quick look at the coyote underside (it was a female) made the turn and tried the wing shot. Missed. Shot again, missed again. I returned to the front to see number two veering forty yards out. I got on target fast to send a load of four buck that way. The coyote was down, was up, and was escaping at the wobble-legged run. Out of shells, out of patience, I followed at the lumber, finally overtaking. I finished the job using the butt of the Model 1100 and strong language. Messy.

How could I have done differently? The same situation, if it occurred today, would see a differing response. I would keep as much Blair as practical behind the log, maybe have the barrel of the twelve gauge pointed toward the fur. When the lead coyote was forty yards out I would commence a fearful growling, maybe even cuss. Do all I could to cause the lead dog to stop to discover what the hell was behind that log. When he did so I would wait the seconds needed to let the trailer catch up to honor the point. I would shoot one half the double from ambush, then raise up as needed to take the second.

Some circumstances will cause one half of the double to be as safe as if within the den, sucking on momma. Screamers need to recognize such when they occur. They need to forget about the double and concentrate on the single. Doing so allows them to leave the stand carrying fur.

Can you stand one more? I once hunted the low country with Gordy "Gordo" Krahn at a time when he was the editor of *Trapper and Predator Caller* and I was a masthead author. During one screaming, the last made during a several day hunt, Gordo and I cooperated to call and kill a true triple. Having described that stand within a previous chapter I will not do so again.

Permit me to say, however, that such was damn fine.

No two doublings are identical. The country changes and the nature of the respondents change. I can give no good advice that will be constantly useful, excepting this. THINK on the subject of doubles. Train yourself to analyze each situation. Doing so as quickly as possible, and respond accordingly. Will that work every time? It doesn't for me and likely will not for you. The best we can hope for is an improved response.

Bonded coyote commonly cooperate during a call. One dies bravely as the mate runs desperately for her or his life,

chapter 27

Selecting the Setup

The country out front was as flat as a road-killed rabbit. Pushdown junipers to the rear. The kind of country Western coyote love. Plenty of open country to display the speed that can cause a jackrabbit to lose his wind. The piles of pushdowns are home to cotton-tailed rabbits, wood rats, white-footed deer mice, and a mind-boggling assortment of delectable critters. I had sighted pile after pile of coyote poop on the walk in. Each of those piles delivered an encouraging message. I was in coyote country. A proper screaming was likely to bring one or more to the gun. Optimism was high as I set out to find a setup.

I did not set up within the pushdowns. A coyote that came within the pushdowns would be hard to see, maybe not be seen at all before he tasted the wind to make the desperate run for home. I decided, instead, to set up outside the pushdowns, out in the open. I would scream the customer through the pushdowns and into the open, the kind of country best suited to the scope-sighted .22-250. Trouble was, there was not a good place to hide my extra-large frame. I hiked the perimeter of the pushdowns until I discovered a small grouping of leafless sagebrush. I gathered other sagebrush branches and finally had enough to form a hideout, a sort of a sagebrush overcoat. Seconds later I sent out the first notes of "The Dying Rabbit Blues."

The coyote came at the gallop when I was two minutes into the song. The critter stood panting, begging for the rabbit. Knowing the angle was bad for a shot, knowing I would almost surely miss if I did not square to the fur, I shifted slightly to start a scrooch. The coyote, obviously uncomfortable around moving sagebrush, lost his taste for rabbit and started the retreat. I lunged erect, taking parts of the sage overcoat with me, and laid into that amazed yodeler with the Ruger. I killed a rock with the first shot and insulted a pile of pushdown with the second. The coyote hoofed it out of the country, likely laughing his butt off at the big guy in the sagebrush overcoat. What the hell is the point? The point is, I did everything right on that stand except for one detail. I settled for a setup that did not offer the shooting advantage needed to collect the fur. A screamer who hopes to skin fur somewhat regularly must learn to recognize a good setup and a bad setup.

What does it take to cause a setup to be a good 'un? The setup must be

The most successful callers evaluate the terrain and decide upon a strategy that will offer an advantage to the gunner. Gordy Krahn with coyotes.

in country that houses a decent population of critters. The setup must offer visibility. I divide such into two categories: vision lanes and shooting lanes. I need to see the critter as he makes the approach, hopefully in plenty of time to get ready physically and emotionally. I need to have vision enough to keep the critter in sight as he makes his desperate escape. The setup should be somewhat open so that I can swing the gun and not have to force the barrel through brush and tree limbs. I carry a set of small size pruning shears in a belt holster to trim when need be. The setup should have some structure, at least enough to mute the outline of my camo-clad frame. The setup needs to be easy to get out of. A hunter needs to get unhid in a hurry sometimes, maybe to take a second shot at a missed critter, maybe to take a first shot at a critter that comes in awkward, or maybe to try for the second leg of a double that has spooked.

Finally, the setup must offer the advantage of safety. Not from the customers, as they seldom attack a 200-pound rabbit. Safety from (shudder) nasty snakes. Those who know me well know of my intolerance of snakes of every kind, particularly those that carry a noisemaker on their tail. Why am I a snake bigot? Don't know, I have been one ever since a five-foot western diamondback (coontail) laid a lip lock on the calf of my left leg.

Anyway, here in the West, those who call early in the season and late in the season need to know that snakes are out. And they need to know snakes love brush piles. I forgot all of that on one hunt and nearly paid the price. It happened this way.

I crawled into a cramped hole in a pile of pushdown during an October hunt, settled down, and started the music. A hungry coyote showed appreciation and came at the gallop. Trouble was, at about the same time I discovered a neighbor, a four-foot diamondback, the kind that finds pleasure scaring the scat out of snake-shy screamers.

The snake slithered close, tasted my smell using that black, forked tongue, and then coiled to assume the classic strike configuration. My options, as I saw them then, were few. I could fight my way free of the pushdown pile and make a run for it (a temptation I barely resisted). I could ignore the snake, pretend he wasn't coiled a couple of feet from my big butt, and concentrate on the customer, a coyote carrying about $50 worth of fur (1982 prices). Or, I could one-hand the twelve-gauge to point the barrel to the left rear (awkward), pull the trigger, and hope for good results. The snake started a hostile rattling as I moved the barrel his way. The load of four buck at the range of a foot or so spread snakeburger for yards. Even though I left that stand without fur, I left a happy man.

As stated, the ideal screaming setup will offer obvious advantages. Negatives will be few. Here are circumstances often overlooked by those new to screaming.

Even though fully camouflaged, set up in the shade when possible. A caller who sets in the sun can be obvious to a customer, particularly obvious when he or she makes a move. A shaded screamer is most difficult to see. Sun flash from the glass of the scope sight is less likely.

I pay particular attention to the wind. Experience and intuition can cooperate to help me sometime predict the avenue of approach. I set up so that the main vision area is upwind. I try to set up so that I have secondary vision lanes crosswind and maybe even downwind, knowing that the masking scent is likely to fool the critter's nose.

Calling crepuscular, calling the sunrise and the sunset, can be dandy. There is a danger to such. Pre-sunrise stands can be particularly risky. The screamer, much of the time, starts the stand before the sun has topped the horizon. Those who face east will pay a price. The sun WILL appear, and when it does, will shine directly into the screamer's eyes. This can cause irritation, can reduce visibility and can seriously hamper accuracy. Want an example?

I snuggled into a pile of pushdown on a first light screaming and did everything just right, sucking a nervous coyote to about fifty yards. The top half of the sun showed at about the same time. I could see nothing through the scope except sun flare. I tried a desperation shot, the kind of shot I seldom make. I didn't make that one either. I had trouble seeing the coyote leave. The sun was in my eyes. The moral? Set up so that the sun is in the customer's eyes, not in your own.

Calling the sunset can be nearly as bad. Sunset setups start with the sun already in position. Screamers who row with both oars in the water will see the obvious handicap and adjust the setup to compensate.

Sad experience has caused me to choose a setup that permits mobility. The critter might come at an awkward angle and you may need to move to make the shot. There may be more than one critter, and you may have to scrooch to take the trailer.

I make an effort to choose a setup that holds an open area that a critter must cross on his way to the rabbit. The more open the area, the better chance of putting a 52-grain chunk of copper-plated lead within his or her necessaries. Screaming at coyote, sad to say, can follow the doctrine of Murphy's Law: Anything that can go wrong will go wrong. Such is illustrated by relating a sad experience involving a canny coyote and one small and insignificant juniper bush, not even big enough to be a tree, for God's sake.

I was set up within the pocked aspect of a prairie dog (black-tailed) town in northern Arizona, a place coyote like to hang around even though I doubt they have a lot of luck dogging. Anyway, the area was mostly open, the dogs having eaten about everything alive, but had one small and insignificant (S&I) string bark juniper bush thirty feet out front. I saw that S&I stringbark when I set up in front of one just like it. I knew I should move but I did not. Three minutes into the screaming a big silver came at the lope, using the S&I juniper to cover his approach, took a quick peek around, and then turned tail to use the S&I stringbark as cover. I hate it when they do that.

I do my best to choose a setup that offers the comforts of home, or as many of those comforts as possible, knowing I will need to sit as still as a rock for at least 15 minutes and maybe more. That kind of marathon sitting demands some degree of comfort. I pick a spot free of thorns, spines, and scratchy leaves. I wriggle the backside to discover particularly obnoxious rocks and stubs, those that will cause big-time pain after about five minutes, and remove those suckers before I start the screaming. I avoid rotting logs, knowing such are often home to ants, those little black pests that can deliver a sting that will hurt until February. I pick dry ground (I sometimes kick at wet duff until I reach a dry layer) knowing that the discomfort of a frozen butt is not conducive to rifle accuracy. Finally, I almost always carry a square of camo-covered foam and use that as a cushion on the setup. No foam handy? Substitute a two-foot square of scrap carpet. Comfort, the way I see it, lets me sit still and sit longer without squirming.

While on the subject of comfort I might as well mention my favored setup position. Some new to screaming will sit with legs crossed and heels under the body, yoga-like. Such, to me, is somewhat comfortable for a minute or two. The legs then go to sleep. Not long after the pain begins. I like to sit with my backside firmly planted, a back support is dandy if available, and with my legs

Western hunters learn to look for health hazards like the western *diamondback* rattlesnake and the Gila Monster, each out and about during late spring, summer and early fall.

164

The San Carlos Apache Indian Reservation offers a plethora of brushy canyons interrupted by prickly pear covered hillsides, all such attractive to black bear during the fall of the year.

drawn up so that the knees are available as a brace for the elbows when it comes time to shoot. I can hold this position for fifteen minutes and not suffer. Rifle accuracy is enhanced. I have made setups (stand-ups when visibility requires), kneeling and laying on my belly. I have not made a setup where I stood on my head, not yet anyway, but might consider such if it will help me collect the critter. The point is, choose the position that is right for you and right for the country around the individual setup.

The careful consideration of stand assets should permit the sighting of the customer (or customers) as they make the approach. Most are running or at least moving and will be easily seen. Some, sad to say, make a discrete approach and are first seen as a coyote-like, fox-like, or bobcat-like blob standing to deliver the bad eye. Bobcat are the worst in the world for that sort of thing. The screamer can have trouble at identification, not knowing if it is a critter or a booger. You want the truth? I once shot a coyote-like bush, in front of a witness. Since, I have found it to be good practice to scan the area for boogers (critter look-alikes) and identify all such BEFORE starting the screaming.

I also recommend the screamer stay alert to the actions of wildlife within the vicinity of the screaming. I was screaming from a rocky rim in central Arizona on one hunt, hoping to interest a bobcat. When fifteen minutes of

A lip squeak caused this "Bird-dog" coyote to slow and look, allowing me to collect an unobstructed image.

screams did not provoke a customer, thinking I was whipping a dead horse, I considered calling it quits. Before I could quit, a covey of Gambel's quail, roosting in the brush below, began a nervous putting. Figuring they knew what they were talking about, I put away the tube and substituted the moaner. The quail continued to be nervous and eventually flushed. Twenty minutes of moaning caused me to sight a flash of fur within the brush fifty yards below. I put the little X of the six power duplex there and saw a suspicious eye surrounded by spotted fur. I centered on the eyeball, sucked in a breath, let half of it out, and stroked. The eye disappeared. Walking down I was elated to find a one-eyed and graveyard dead bobcat, a bailey, one of the pretty kinds. I muttered thanks to the quail, grabbed the fur, and hiked out.

On another hunt I was calling within standing junipers, armed with a 3" twelve (pre-MooseDick days). A half a handful of Herefords grazed the area as I set up. The whitefaces looked me over suspiciously when I sent out the first series of screams. It did not take them long to return to their hunt for gamma grass. Five minutes later a heifer turned her head to direct a hard stare to my rear. I scrooched slowly until I was able to see a pair of coyote that had come back door. I dumped one and peppered the rear of the second. The third shot took the survivor when he was forty yards out. I felt like kissing Ole Bossy for snitching off the sneakers, and probably would have if I could have caught her.

Selecting the setup is not that difficult. Use common sense to select one that offers concealment, favorable wind, no sun in the eyes, vision lanes, shooting lanes and comfort. Can't find a setup with all of that? Neither can I. Do as I do and do the best you can.

Even though this hunter is not skylined from a stand-up human aspect it is so from a coyote aspect.

The prone position offers concealment within open country but does not allow the shooter to swing and shoot as might be necessary.

chapter 28

Tube Technique

There is a tendency in all of us to turn something simple into something difficult. I know there is that in my own personality. Having pretty much mastered the basics of predator screaming, being able to use that boring and basic scream to fetch predators close, I find myself pushing that basic technique down the road in an effort to find improvement. Sometimes I do. And at times that improvement causes technique to improve, delivering more fur to the stretcher. Being honest, I have to say some "improvements" do not improve at all. In my collection of memories there are some that taught a sad lesson. Leaving the basics of critter calling can be a mistake. This chapter will deliver an encapsulation of the basics of the sport, tube-wise.

Some of the material contained here will be repeated in other chapters. Even so, I feel it to be important to have an overview of tubes and tube technique, allowing those new to the sport to see what screaming is about, doing so in a chapter rather than in a whole book. The distress scream technique takes advantage of the opportunistic nature of predators. All, at least all I have met, use their eyes and their nose to find groceries. Every hunter knows that to be true. Less well known, however, is the regular use of another sense. I am talking ears. Every predator uses that sense of sound to locate prey that might be beyond the scan of the eye and beyond the reach of the nose.

The distress scream is heard most often, I think, because a flying predator has swooped or stooped to capture the blue plate special. That capture, a part of the time, sees the collection of a cotton-tailed rabbit, a true hare, or the hare Westerners call a jackrabbit. The capture is affected using the talons to grasp the prey outside the chest cavity. Death is accomplished by compressing that chest cavity until suffocation occurs, a process that can use up a minute or more. All of that time, commonly, the prey screams piteously. What good does that do? Don't know. Maybe the critter feels compelled to do something. Not knowing what else to do, it screams.

Anyway, other predators, those that fly the air and walk the ground, hearing the action, know something good to eat is in trouble. They come at the gallop, hoping, I suppose, to steal the meal. Predator calls are designed to permit the duplication of that distress sound. Such calls are of basic design. A wood or plastic tube containing a stainless steel reed is one. Such calls are

Gerry Blair teaches B.jo how to kiss, saying such will cause coyote and other predators to pay attention.

easily mastered and do a decent job of producing the rabbit and hare distress (depending on the reed). Disadvantages? Each and all sound pretty much the same, even as they travel from mouth to mouth. Another disadvantage will be noticed during freezing weather. The moisture of the breath will collect on the thin metal reed and freeze there, causing a malfunction.

The second call type is also a tube, one that flaunts a thin shim of Mylar plastic exposed. This kind of call fits within the warmth of the mouth, does not freeze unless within a very cold mouth, and will consequently stay healthy during the coldest of weather. A second asset accrues because of call design. Moving the lips up or down on the plastic reed can cause a change of tone. Those who practice can use the plastic reed call (sometimes called the open reed) to scream out a rabbit distress, a hare distress, a fox distress, a pup distress, and even a coyote howl. Some will bugle. The plastic reed tube will change tone from mouth to mouth. The bad news? Not all that bad. The plastic reed call is a bit more difficult to master, not much of a disadvantage to a caller who is serious about the screaming. Not any that I can see anyway.

A third call type is the diaphragm call favored by many turkey hunters. This device is basically a section of latex held in an aluminum frame, covered with duct tape. These calls stay within the mouth when in use and are therefore freeze-proof. Some such are marketed as predator calls. Those are, I suspect,

Some callers reverse a reeded call and suck to make a realistic moan.

nothing more than a single- or double-reeded turkey diaphragm re-labeled. The diaphragm call demands practice. When mastered they do a decent job of screaming and whining. A second asset involves a lack of movement and that will translate to fewer spooked critters. No hands are needed, freeing the hands to do more important tasks, maybe shooting. The volume produced, to my ears, is less than that produced by either the metal or the plastic-reeded call. A second consideration is a lack of longevity. The latex used within the diaphragm call is light sensitive and will begin to deteriorate the day it is made. Spittle that collects within the latex can cause the dreaded slobber rot. I do not expect a used diaphragm call to last more than about a season. Even so, they are inexpensive and should be a part of every call collection. How much range can a hunter scream out of a diaphragm call? Don't know. I do know that I have called wild turkey from a quarter mile. And that is strange because a turkey has no ears! Not any I can see anyway.

The fourth call kind is the battery-powered caller that plays cassettes containing the recorded sounds of actual prey animals. Rabbits, hares, fox, birds, deer, and I don't know what all. Tapes containing howlings are also available. The tape players offer an advantage to callers who have not mastered the distress scream. The caller causes them to be immediately expert, at least as far as the screaming is concerned. Another asset comes because of the learning potential. Those new to the sport can listen to actual distress screams to learn sound and rhythm. Other assets also accrue, those to be covered within the chapter devoted to the battery-powered callers. Negatives? Not many. Mostly

The slow death provided by hawks, eagles and owls provokes a screaming that can cause about every predator to come at a gallop.

cost. The player and a starter tape collection will cost a couple of hundred dollars, maybe more.

A second kind of battery-powered caller retrieves sound from an electronic chip. Such commonly work from a four-chip board. The operator can change to any sound on that board by flicking a selection switch. Other sounds are available through the changing of the board. Neither the chip player nor the cassette player is compatible to the other. Put another way, you cannot play chips through a cassette caller; you cannot play cassettes through the chip player. A third type, the digital caller, does not need either tapes or chips.

The two most common calls, the metal-reeded tube and the plastic-reeded tube, will be discussed in depth. I cannot count the times I have been asked to describe a rabbit distress scream. Such is difficult, just as it is difficult to describe any sound without imitating that sound. Having said that, I will attempt such, saying first that some of the worst rabbit distress sounds I have heard have come from the throats of distressed rabbits. Some of the best I have heard came from the mouths of talented human screamers. Which sounds better to the customer? I am convinced the screaming from the prey animal is better. There are likely nuances, perhaps beyond the range of human hearing, that lend authenticity. An example follows.

Larry was taping footage for our *Masters' Secrets to Predator Calling* and had enlisted the efforts of a black-tailed jackrabbit to do so. The camcorder was on the tripod, set to wide angle. Larry was out front holding Jack. A squeeze of the chest caused the hare to holler. A minute or three into the holler

171

the sound of hoof and whuff announced the arrival of a small herd of collared peccary, some running to within a few feet of Jack and Larry. The cotton-tailed rabbit distress screams I have heard have been a constant and monotonous wah-wah-wah, repeated for twenty to forty seconds. Mostly of moderate volume. Even though I have not talked to coyote and cats on this, I am convinced the rhythm of the screams is as important (maybe more so) as the tonal quality. The tone of the screaming is pure, and no rasp is present. Some hares and all gray fox put rasp into their screaming, a hoarseness that is obtained by sending a maximum amount of air through the metal-reed call to cause the

Hawks such as this Harris often rule the day sky but leave the night sky to Great Horned Owls and associates.

reed to overload. That same effect can be coaxed from the plastic-reed call when the lips are placed to bottom of the exposed part of the reed, to the stop.

Now might be as good a time as any to tell my technique of screaming, using the plastic-reed call, the metal-reed call, and the diaphragm, starting with the plastic-reed call. The plastic-reed call I use most often is the TallyHo, a call that consists of a molded plastic call body fitted with a somewhat thick plastic reed. I have used others of a similar configuration, the Crit'RCall, Lohman's C-280, Johnny Stewart's PC-6, and too many more to mention. All are blown about the same. Blowing might be the wrong word. I do not blow into the call, even though doing so will produce a sound. The sound produced with the blow

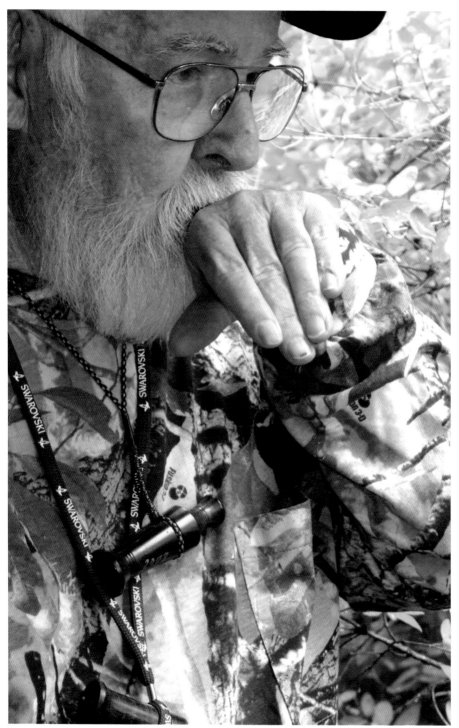

Gerry Blair uses the kiss of death and other close calls mainly as a means to stop a moving critter or to cause a hang-up to continue the approach.

is not a sound that can be easily controlled. It is better, in my experience, to breathe air out and into the call. The breathed sound can be modified as the breath is modified, permitting a selection of sound and volume.

I begin by placing the plastic-reeded call to the corner of my mouth, finding it to be comfortable there and finding I have good control. I place my lips to the stop of the call and breathe a series of moans. I cup one or both hands over the end of the tube to act as sound chambers. Opening the hand or hands as you breathe into the call causes a sound modification. Continue breathing out wahs, extending each wah to achieve a short, choppy series. If each wah is four beats long, insert a two beat pause between. Experiment until you find the rhythm that is comfortable, the rhythm that works for you.

Moving the lips toward the call tip can cause a change of tone. Generally, the farther toward the tip, the higher the tone. I like to position my lips to the bottom of the plastic reed when blowing jackrabbit distress. Placing the lips slightly beyond the stop can add gravel, the hoarse scream of some jackrabbit and of all gray fox. I position my lips about midway on the reed to provoke the cottontail scream. I move my mouth upward to about the first half-inch of plastic, bite down with my teeth, and breathe into the call to elicit the pup whine.

A jackrabbit–reeded predator call caused a sounder of irate javelina to come so close you could smell the ugly.

The plastic-reed tube can also be used as a howler. Some will work better than others. All, with practice, will produce a howl that can cause a coyote to howl back, maybe even come. I place the call to the center of my mouth, extending my lips to the stop, and blow to produce the howl. As the sound begins move the lips toward the tip until you find the spot that produces the best pitch.

Blowing the metal-reed call is easy. Place your lips to the call and breathe or blow to provoke screams. Even though mouth position is not as critical as with the plastic-reed call, habit causes me to be most comfortable when the call is to the corner of the mouth. Moderate air pressure will cause cottontail distress sounds. Maximum air pressure will cause hoarse/coarse jackrabbit and gray fox squalls.

The calling sequence stays somewhat constant no matter what kind of call you use. I like to start the stand blowing moderate volume screams. I blow a series of screams that continue for about 20 seconds. The length of the scream series is not critical. Blow a series for ten seconds, or blow a series for thirty seconds and you will likely do as well. Some callers I know blow continuously from start of stand to finish, and call critters.

I like to interrupt the screaming with periods of silence. That is the quiet time that offers the opportunity to stay as still as a rock to scan for customers. A coyote that comes during the silent period stays a bit confused as to the call source. That can cause a hesitation that can offer an advantage when it comes time to shoot.

I continue this call/quiet alternation for the life of the stand, usually about 10 minutes for grays and reds, 15 minutes for coyote, 30 minutes for bobcat, and maybe an hour or two for cougar and bear. As is the case with most critter calling truths, that truth is not a constant. Circumstances can cause a variation of technique to be good business. That fact is best illustrated by the telling of a tale, the tale of the super paranoid coyote.

By late September the dumbest coyote in the pushdowns east of town has been skinned. The coyote that remain are the super paranoids, Ph.D.s that have seen about all of the rodeo they can stand. I told all of that to Perry Shirley when he suggested we go there for a day of screaming. "Heck," he grinned, "as good as we are, I am betting we will do dandy." And we did, sort of. It was one of those foggy mornings when the mist hung tight, limiting visibility to about a hundred yards. Perry and I called coyote on the first two stands but the customers used the fog to stay discrete. No shot opportunity. Perry discovered a sneaker on the third stand and reached out to make the touch. Other successes followed. We were starting to feel pretty good about our averages when we came up against the paranoid.

I had screamed for 15 minutes when Perry discovered the sneaker, a speck of fur five hundred yards out, standing to deliver the long-distance bad eye. I lit into the screamer and the coyote showed his appreciation. He turned tail

Hunter howls work particularly well after a snowfall. Howling to tracks can be particularly successful. (Gordy Krahn Photo).

to trot away. I sent out a hoarse screaming that caused him to look over his tail, turn, and trot a few steps closer. I continued the screaming and the coyote moved our way a couple of hundred feet, and then hung up again. I moved my lips to the tip of the plastic-reed call and sent out a series of pup distress whines. The coyote moved closer.

I continued to mess with that coyote for a full forty minutes. Finally, as though he couldn't stand it any more, the paranoid gave up. He came straight in at a steady trot. Perry did the wet work with the .22-250 at fifty yards. A second experience illustrates further.

I was calling high plains with Chuck Spearman during a winter hunt when a long distance coyote made a lope by. Chuck did good, putting the critter down using fine and fancy shooting. We walked out to make the retrieve. Trouble was, we could not find the carcass. The long and indirect walkout, the lack of landmarks, caused us to become confused. We muddled around for 20 minutes or so looking for our fur. Suddenly, looking back to our setup, I saw a coyote make a lope by. That sucker had learned to wait a decent interval before coming to investigate a screaming. I returned on another day, called for ten minutes, stayed quiet for fifteen, and nailed that smart aleck as he made his cruise. Did we locate the carcass of the invisible coyote? Yep, walking out. The big female lay where she fell, maybe a hundred feet from the area of our search.

There is a proliferation of screamers currently available. I have used calls made by most manufacturers and have found all to be effective when properly used. The predator caller will almost surely find one or more within that offering that suits his or her needs. Having said that, it is also proper to say that some fine old-timey calls are no longer available. Two that come to mind are the wood Trophy Model Circe and the Wood Weems Wild Call. Each of those has become a valuable collector's item. Each of those, the way I see it, was as fine a metal-reeded call as any made. Some, those who hanker for one such, can measure an actual call and use a lathe and woodworking abilities to construct a replica. Hunters who have neither tools nor talent can prevail on a friend or ask a woodworker to do the job.

Some information is needed on call repair and it might as well appear here. First, it is bad business to fiddle with a sick call while a customer is on the hook. It is better to carry a couple of extra calls. When a screamer calls in sick, it is a simple matter to substitute one of the backups. After the dance is the proper time to do repairs.

Any mechanical device will malfunction. Predator calls are no exception. The most common malfunction to the plastic-reed call, within my experience, is a misalignment between reed and air channel. If the reed is not precisely centered the sound turns ugly. It is simple, much of the time, to use the fingernail to reposition the reed.

A second malfunction can occur when spittle causes a scummy build up along the reverse of the plastic reed. That sort of problem can be corrected. Remove the reed and wash it in warm soapy water. Use fine steel wool to scour away the scum when need be. Dry the reed and replace it. It should work as it did when new. All plastic-reed calls will develop slobber fatigue after a few seasons. No amount of effort will cause them to sound pristine. Replacement reeds are available and are easily installed. Refer to the information section at book's end.

Metal-reed calls also call in sick. They did so more so during the days when the metal reeds were of a galvanized stock. Slobber rot caused an oxidation. Current metal reeds are mostly stainless steel and do better. Even so, they do wear out. I have not had luck trying to retune a metal reed. It is best, I think, to replace them. Use a tool (usually a slotted rod) to push the old reed out, working from the end with the big hole. Work from the end with the little hole to position the replacement reed.

I like to call critters using either the plastic-reed call or the metal-reed call, finding satisfaction when I use such a simple device, coupled with calling skill, to bring a paranoid critter to the gun or the camera. Most screamers, I am convinced, feel likewise.

chapter 29

Kissing and Other Close Calls

Larry O. squirmed to square to the ghost, hoping to cause his eyeballs to make identification. No luck. The hundred yards of greasewood forest combined with low light to cause the animal-like part to stay discrete. Watching, sort of, Larry laid into the TallyHo one more time, sending delicious screams across the Arizona desert. The ghost remained as still as a rock. Larry gave up and returned to business.

Larry O. Gates, a "beastmaster," was screaming to coyote that hung around high dollar housing; residences scattered through the creosote bushes, the mesquite, and all other vegetation able to live and prosper on damn little water. The coyotes, a novelty when first discovered, became bad dogs when poodle hair and kitty fur started to appear in their poop. Larry was there for

Gray fox love brushy terrain and the edibles found therein. That kind of country causes this customer to be hard to see. A kiss or other close call can cause the gray to un-hide and offer a shot opportunity.

revenge. The first four or five calls of the day had fetched in a half a handful of coyote. Larry had helped all to get dead, using a three-inch twelve loaded with copper-plated BBs. No coyote had shown on this call. Larry was ready to call it quits after the usual fifteen minutes. Seeing a creosote trunk that looked to be critter-like caused him to continue. Five minutes later he was ready to say quit again and almost did. First, he figured, he would use the ultimate weapon. He pressed his lips together and sucked to produce the high pitched squeal we call the Kiss of Death. The leg-like stump exploded to action, coming to view attached to a big and hungry tom bobcat. The bob' was using all four of his legs to come straight at Larry, coming at the gallop. Larry had barely enough time to shoulder and shoot. The 25-pound bobcat rugged seven yards out. Trudging to the truck, Larry thought about the times he had used the Kiss of Death to cause a balky critter to come. No way to know how many. A hell of a lot, maybe more.

I have used the "K of D" other ways. I was on a dandy late fall hunt with Oakey; Thanksgiving-thirty or so, when the critters came like concords, in bunches. We were set up within the shadow of stringbarks when I sighted a shadow coming from long distance. I lip squeaked to let George know a customer was coming, maybe the first time I had done so, at least with Oakey. Oak turned his head slowly, looked my way, smiled, winked, and then kissed back. And after all of that turned to watch his assigned lane. Figuring there had been enough kissing for one stand, maybe more than enough, I returned to the screaming.

The coyote was making a gallop by sixty yards out, too far for the reach of the three-inch twelve. Not knowing what else to do I risked another kiss. A funny thing happened. Not so much funny as odd. That galloping coyote slammed on the anti-locks and skidded to a stop. Looking my way. Looking hungry. I was encouraged and kissed again. Even though George did not seem to be interested, the coyote sure was. He started a sneak on my hideout. When he was maybe thirty-five yards out I did the dirty deed. The Kiss of Death and other close-in calls can be a good friend to the screamer. There is something about the squeak and the low moan that causes the coyote, the cat, and the fox appetite alarm to sound.

Some experienced callers use some sort of close-in call to do about the same. I was working high desert down Texas way with Murry Burnham and was permitted a look at his Ace of Spades. We were set up within scrubby vegetation and Murry was blowing on a modified deer call (later marketed as the Black Beauty). Murry saw the coyote coming (we both did) from a somewhat long distance, coming slow, as a paranoid should. The Ph.D. hung a couple of hundred yards out, pretty much hid in the brush and at an awkward angle for either gun. Murry's mouth started the damnedest moany, groany sound I have heard and that sound caused the coyote to unhang, trotting in as if on a leash. Murry used the .222, causing the coyote to get dead. Later, after

Some hunters are convinced brush and weeds might cause a fast traveling chunk of copper plated lead to detour off course. Blair believes otherwise, having killed more than a few customers who wore a brushy bulletproof vest.

coaxing, he demonstrated. He makes the sound, he said, with lips drawn over teeth, and then making the suck that causes the moan.

I use mouth sounds to communicate to predators often, usually to articulate the Kiss of Death. Other good sounds for close customers are the whine and the growl. Each is easily done and each will increase the customer's interest. The growl and the whine are most often used to cause a running critter to pause, maybe used to cause a hid critter to unhide.

Those who might feel unsure about their ability to kiss, moan, growl, and whine might like to know there is a bunch of moaners and squeakers on the market, a subspecies of call marketed under the generic classification of close-in calls. Such will be of two or three general types. One is a rubber bulb of about walnut size containing a metal reed. Squeezing to force air through the reed causes a high-pitched squeal, a mouse-squeak sort of a sound. I have used Velcro to fasten one of the bulbs to the forearm of the gunstock so the little sucker could be compressed while the gun was in shooting position, a handy modification during some customer situations.

Another type of close-in call is the one I call the Moaner. All such consist of two slats of plastic, put together harmonica-like, with a rubber band (Burnham Brothers & Johnny Stewart) or a shim of metal (P. S. Olt) as a reed. The call is caused to moan as air is sent through. The sound produced is surprisingly Burnham-like, and is surprisingly effective. Some call companies have in the past (maybe still do) offered tube models that can be blown as a close-in call, some having devised a cunning tube that can be manipulated to sound close-in sounds as well as the generic scream.

How far can a keen-eared critter hear the K of D, the whine, the squeal, or the moan? Depends. The carry can be affected by structure and by wind. If the setup is in somewhat open country, if there is not enough wind to mention, I consider close-in calls to be effective out to a couple of hundred yards, maybe more. Those who permit the battery-powered cassette or chip player to do the calling will want to know about close-in options. Close-in sounds are available on both the cassette player and the chip player. Those who use the cassette player can obtain tapes containing baby cottontail distress squeals and bird distress chirpings, both dandies as close-in calls. About the same is available for the chip player, that device having a handy feature. A hunter wishing to shift from long-range screams to the close-in sound need only flick a switch to make the change. Likewise for the digital callers.

I do not use any of the close-in calls on every stand. Neither will you. The long-range scream gets the job done for me on most stands. There are times, however, when a kiss or other close-in calls cause a reluctant customer to turn eager. I urge all screamers to practice the kiss, the moan, the whine, and the growl, and urge all to include a couple of close-in calls within the collection.

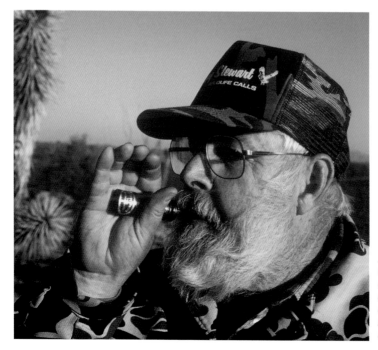

Gerry can be hard-core on moaners, doing so to encourage a customer to stop or continue to advance.

chapter 30

Tracks and Tracking

Every animal that walks the woods, the desert and maybe even the tundra, leaves evidence of passage. That evidence can be as obvious as a gallon or so of smooshy bear poop or can be as discreet as the partial track left by a light-footed cacomistle. I myself have used the tiny tracks of the dung beetle to facilitate the execution of a creature much larger. More about that later. The discovery and interpretation of animal tracks, animal offal, and other signs of passage can cause a good hunter to become a great hunter. How so? The most talented screamer cannot call critters if none are present to be called. And though the presence of sign does not guarantee a critter is close enough to hear the screams, the discovery of even stale sign tells the hunter he or she is in critter habitat. The discovery of fresh sign delivers a more encouraging message. The animal has been here recently and may still be close. Read on to discover examples where I used tracks, poop, and a prey carcass to find fur.

The weather front from the west had caused a wet storm to deposit a sifting of snow the night before the hunt. Knowing the wetted clay base caused an uncertain surface I drove the forest two-track using more than ordinary caution, headed for dry country to do a bit of screaming to coyote. The partial track was obscure, barely seen by the roadside. Pausing to investigate I was pleased to discover the track to be two toes and a partial heel pad, almost surely made by a bobcat; a big bobcat too, or at least a bobcat with one big foot. And even though the land beyond the track was juniper duff in the sun, causing a snowmelt that removed the tracks, the partial track told me the Robert Kitty had been by since the snow stopped, maybe within the past four hours. Toes and heel pad suggested direction of travel. I parked, grabbed my stuff, and set off in that direction.

Even though I did not find a second track I did find a brushy canyon containing rock overhangs along the rim, a dandy place for a bobcat to lie out the last of the storm. I made the setup and started the screaming. Ten minutes later I was walking to the truck carrying the carcass of a dandy baileyi bobcat.

I used coyote crap to cause me to enjoy a day of calling action while on a hunt with Chuck Spearman, a skilled screamer and at that time publisher of *Trapper & Predator Caller* magazine. Chuck and I had spent the day calling the foothills of the KOFA mountain range for coyote. Poor luck had caused us to relocate.

Even though Gerry Blair considers himself a tracker he had no luck with this one, such being too old, made about 160 million years ago by a dinosaur.

A study of this coyote track suggests the critter walked here recently, reveals direction of travel, was likely left by an adult male, about everything except sexual preference.

Even though towing the travel trailer at speed limit (perhaps a bit more) I was able to see unusual amounts of coyote scat along the roadside, all showing mesquite bean residue. I passed the area by to find a familiar camp and we called close to that camp the next day, having moderate luck. Early the next morning, well before daylight, I turned the 4x4 west, to Coyote Crap Acres.

"Where are we headed?" Chuck inquired. I smirked out an answer. "Chuck," I teased, "We are headed for my newest old time honey hole".

I do not recall how many coyote Chuck and I called that day. I know it was a hell of a lot, and maybe more. It is likely we might have ignored that ten-mile stretch of country alongside the U.S. highway if not for the roadside deposits. Can you stand one more?

Reading sign, knowing the kind of country coyote prefer, can cause a screamer to get lucky. (Gordy Krahn Photo).

I was hunting a PJ ridge within the North Kaibab National Forest for mule deer. It was the late hunt, the one that has big-racked mulie bucks down on the winter range where they become somewhat vulnerable. I was out early, just as I had been for the past several days, using the binoculars to investigate side hills. Walking to a new high point I came across sign of a drag, maybe a place where a hunter had drug a deer. I took a close look and found evidence of covering. The hunter had been a mountain lion. I followed the drag trail and counted three coverings. The last hid the remains of a decent buck. I searched out a setup and started a screaming. The female lion came as a tan ghost that materialized eighty yards out. She weighed 95 pounds, middling big for a pussy lion on the Kaibab.

Even though I have written on tracks and other sign in the individual chapters on species, I consider it to be proper to write more, covering tracks and tracking from a more general aspect. Critter tracks vary in size as the age and body size of the animal varies. The track of an adult bobcat, as an example, might be about two inches across. The track left by an immature bobcat might be obviously less. The point is, do not expect every track found to be exactly the same as the last. Hell, some critters, most notably members of the dog family, have fore feet larger than the rear feet. All of the bear feet

I have I have examined show a difference in size and a difference in aspect between front and rear feet.

Track identification would be less difficult if all tracks were on level ground and imprinted on dust, mud, or snow, and were fresh. And offered a series of tracks so that gait could be determined, offered the advantage found when tracks left by the front feet could be compared to tracks left by the rear feet. Common sense says such is not so. Some tracks are partials found on ground that resists imprinting. Some, as was the case with the roadside bobcat track, consist of a single partial. A single track, even a single partial, can show an overlapping of rear foot over front foot, causing further difficulty. A tracker who hopes to read all the track offers must be astute during discovery and reasonable during interpretation.

Multiple tracks offer a lot of information. A string of tracks, to the eyes of an experienced tracker, offer information on definite direction of travel, whether the animal is hunting or traveling, showing if the animal was at the walk, the trot, or the run, and even offering a determination of age (adult or sub-adult) and sometimes sex.

The widely distributed black bear, being larger than all of the U.S. land predators except the uncommon grizzly and some uncommon humans, is a fine example of a critter that leaves a lot of evidence; tracks, trashings, clawings, and the always impressive crappings. Even though the bear is mostly nocturnal, and may select exceedingly private habitat causing them to be seldom seen,

Bigfoot camped at a desert water tank and gobbled down $30,000.00 worth of transplanted desert bighorn sheep.

Collared Peccary (Javelina) print

Front
L = 1½"
W = 1"

Rear
L = 1¼"
W = 1"

Walking

Mountain Lion print

Front
L = 3"
W = 3½"

Rear
L = 3"
W = 3"

Double Print

Red Fox print

Front
L = 2½"
W = 2"

Rear
L = 2"
W = 1½"

Double Print

Raccoon print

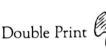

Front
L = 2¼"
W = 1½"

Rear
L = 3¼"
W = 1½"

Double Print

Black Bear print	Bobcat print

Black Bear print

Front
L = 4½"
W = 3½"

Rear
L = 7"
W = 3½"

Double Print

Bobcat print

Front
L = 2"
W = 3¼"

Rear
L = 2¼"
W = 2"

Double Print

Coyote print	Gray Fox print

Coyote print

Front
L = 2½"
W = 2"

Rear
L = 2¼"
W = 1½"

Double Print

Gray Fox print

Front
L = 1½"
W = 1¼"

Rear
L = 1¼"
W = 1"

Double Print

the hunter who looks will find evidence of bear presence. That evidence can tell a lot to those willing to look and learn.

The track left by the hind foot of a bear is somewhat similar to the shape of the human foot. The track left by the front foot of the bear is a lot like the looks of a partially clenched human hand. A bear track, or series of tracks, can show the usual: how long ago the bear stood, walked or ran there; direction of travel; whether the bear was traveling or feeding; and even supply good evidence of bear size. How so size? Biologic inquiry has suggested an informal formula. A front foot track measuring 4-1/4" or more was likely made by a mature black bear. A hind foot track measuring 7-1/2" or more was likely made by a mature black bear.

Other bear track trivia follows: The bear is a plantigrade, just as we are. What in hell does that mean? Bear and folks like us walk on the flat of their feet, putting the weight of the body on the entire foot. The pad of the foot shows an elongated triangle fronted by oval toe-prints. The large toe on a bear, unlike the large toe on a human foot, lays to the outside of the foot. The marks left by the toes will be fronted by indentations left by the non-retractable claws. The placement of the claw marks can be an indicator to species. Some habitat has the black bear sharing the range with the grizzly bear. Even though some grizzly are larger than some black bear, all are not, causing track size alone to be an undependable identifier. The griz has much longer and more massive claws. Grizzly tracks, much of the time, have a significant gap between toe and claw

Want more? The walking gait (pace) of the black bear will show the hind foot imprint slightly forward of the front. The imprints left by front and rear feet will at times overlap. The inside toe might or might not register when the track is imprinted in dust or shallow mud, causing the track to show only four toes. Tracks left by a galloping bear are distinctive. The hind feet are brought of the fore feet at every step. CAUTION: If the galloping bear is after you do not pause to examine the tracks.

Black bear are like most other land predators in their hunting and travel habits. Bear use well-established trails. The trail used might take the bear from their feeding grounds to their bedding grounds. At times there is not a difference between the two. Fresh bear tracks found within an area that shows recent feeding activity should be an encouragement. Chances are good the bear is nearby. A feeding bear leaves evidence of such. Fruit, acorns, and other masts are stripped from branches in the messiest manner. Rotting logs, those containing grubs, ants, and other edibles, are trashed. Boulders are rolled to expose edibles on the moist underside. Plops, in cattle country, will be turned for the same reason. Raccoon, skunks, crows, and ravens, and even the wild turkey are also ploppers. Finding a turned plop without supporting evidence is not enough to determine bear presence.

The generic bear has an urge to bite, claw, and rub. Trees are the main targets but wooden signs receive a fair share of attention. This trashing of trees and signs is often territorial behavior. Bear scat is distinctive and can say a lot about the bear that made the deposit. The size and shape of the offal causes the deposit to be bear-specific. Contents can cause current feeding habits to be obvious. The bear that dines on meat or carrion might deposit a black and odoriferous goo containing hair. A bear that has dined on insects retrieved from a rotting log might leave scat containing minor amounts of wood. A bear feeding on nuts or berries will leave scat containing nut hulls, or maybe leaves and seeds from a berry bush. Bear crap might be formed or formless. Stools may have a diameter of a couple of inches but are usually less. The formless deposit can be of impressive size. Dinner plate big. Maybe bigger.

The inquiry and evidence written about bear sign applies almost equally to the sign left by every other animal. A careful reading of the writings devoted to the sign left by specific species, to be found in the chapters describing the hunting of that species, is encouraged.

Finally, it is not this book's intent to offer a complete dissertation on tracks and tracking. The information I have included might motivate the curious to search out texts specifically addressed to those subjects. Such texts almost always include information on many interesting aspects of the creatures discussed, even a discussion of their crap. It would be fair, I suppose, to say these authors really know their shit.

Blair has hunted bare many times, often becoming so cold he must return to camp to put his clothes on. Ha Ha!

Bill Rice and Michael McCasland of Tucson like to set tall when they hunt the brush.

chapter 31

Tough Calls

A discussion of why animals come to the call appeared in an earlier chapter. A following chapter investigated the circumstances that might elicit non-response. In both chapters I mentioned the Case of the Ph.D. Critter. Ph.D.s are animals that have seen a rodeo or two and have decided dying rabbits are not for them. The earning of the doctorate comes, most often, when an animal owning a set of virgin ears comes at the gallop to find a welcome of hot lead waiting. Such, repeated a time or two, could cause the most cooperative of critters to turn to a more healthful diet. Inept callers, or unlucky ones, can beat up on a chunk of critter habitat to cause all within to become tough calls.

There will be times when a critter becomes educated because of the nature of the hunter. One such, a person who will not be named, found fun when he called a coyote kind of customer close and shot a .224" diameter hole through one ear. Why? He could not compel himself to kill such an intelligent and noble creature, he has said. To his credit, I have not heard or witnessed one instance where this pervert (sic) re-called and re-holed the opposite ear. Way to go, Rich, you be a real humanitarian.

Even though such customers become paranoid to the tenth power, a screamer who uses the correct technique can scream at a paranoid individual, can scream within a heavily-called area, can compensate in other ways to find calling excitement and maybe collect a bit of fur. The technique that permits all is one I call THINKING. The tool required is basic. Those who use the THINKING technique must have a brain. Many of the critter callers I have met (maybe even most) have had such.

My honest nature causes me to say I have not used THINKING to solve tough call problems for my entire critter-calling career. There was a time, at first, when I had learned the basics needed to bring a critter close somewhat regularly, when I repeated those basics on every stand and did not concern myself with those super smarts. I figured, I guess, there were plenty of dumb ones to be called. Why waste time working the Ph.D.s when two or three sophomores could be called with about the same effort?

Somewhere along the way, I am not sure just when, the critter calling turned tough. Screamers within the writing racket, guys like me, hunted hard, hunted successfully, and then wrote about both for nationally distributed publications. Interest and hunting pressure increased. The dummies disappeared early, leaving only the tough calls. When I tired of being whipped I broke out the old brain and invented THINKING.

My years of THINKING have caused me to subdivide the technique to best respond to specific problems. One such is a category I call TARGETING. What is TARGETING? How can you use such to increase your screaming success? It works this way. Targeting is a technique that causes the screamer to carefully consider the goals of each hunt. While thinking along that path, the screamer identifies the circumstances that will most affect that goal-directed hunt, positives and negatives. An analysis of each will suggest ways to maximize results. The THINKING/TARGETING technique is best explained using an actual example.

Gary "Slammer" Hull is a big fish guide on the Kenai Peninsula during much of the summer. He also works as big a game guide, guiding hunters to caribou, moose, goat, sheep, and even griz, all such, for much of the winter. A few years or so ago the Slammer wrote to offer a trade hunt. He would host me and the other Beastmaster during a big game hunt or a big fish hunt in Alaska. As payback, he asked to come to America (that is what Alaskans call the land within the lower 48) to have the Beastmasters provide a series of screaming, particularly aimed at one of the cats, maybe bob and maybe cougar. Larry and I said sure. The fall of 1994 found us on the Iliamna Barren Grounds hunting for a trophy bull.

The hunt was interesting. We were within a tent camp for eight days. It rained every day but one. On that day it snowed. The wind blew at fifty mph for every day but one. On that day the wind blew at sixty mph. Caribou, cows, calves, dink bulls, and trophy bulls were conspicuous by their absence. Hard hunting, perseverance, and luck caused each of us to take damn fine bulls. At the same time we had the opportunity to scream at a good part of Alaska.

The first payback hunt took place during February. Why then? THINKING and TARGETING mainly. Knowing Gary hoped for a cat we chose a time when the cats are roaming the land in an effort to shake the sugar tree. And dependent on the degree of desperation present, each was likely to make the look both night and day. Those who know their pussies might tell me that cats do not always have a locked-in breeding season, saying that circumstances might cause a romance about any time of year. My response? Hell, I know that. I also know that cats most often breed during early spring. Meanwhile, back at the ranch.

Knowing the target was of the cat kind, we hunted cat country. We drove the 4x4s to the end of the road and walked to the roughest and toughest country we could find. Not the kind of country likely to hold a lot of coyote, and that means we were in country that did not offer a lot of action. The action, when it happened, was apt to be of the kitty kind.

A fawn distress scream caused this Barren Grounds Caribou to walk a mile or more to meet the bullet. Gary Hull and Gerry Blair.

THINKING/TARGETING also suggested we scream out cat calls. Long moans, mostly, the kind most likely to interest a cat of the cougar kind, and also the bob'. The kind of screams most often heard from the scream box of a deer or some other such. T/T further advised to stay on the stand to give the cat customer plenty of time. Most screaming continued for a minimum of thirty minutes. Some were longer.

Gary Hull came to America three times during the paybacks. On one of those trips he was able to gun down a close-range bobcat. On another hunt he was there when Larry gunned down a cougar. The Slammer also participated in wet work involving gray fox and more coyote than I care to mention. The T/T technique made it all possible. A second example that shows T/T to good advantage follows.

The desert subdivision was high dollar housing. The folks living there were lovers. They loved every hog, every burro, and every coyote. They did, that is, before the poodles and the kitties started to disappear. Some looked suspiciously at the coyote that patrolled between the houses on a somewhat regular basis. Indoctrinated in the American concept of jurisprudence, however, many refused to make a harsh judgment as long as there remained a reasonable doubt. That reasonable doubt diminished when an examination of coyote turds showed poodle hair and kitty fur. The residents turned ugly. Some

Gary Hull came to America three times to take bobcat, gray fox, coyote and watch as Larryo put the hurt to a hungry lion.

became berserk. Some (I am not making this up) collected turds, sorted them out according to the color of the evidence, and conducted a service. Right after the ceremony they called 911 and 911 called me.

Screaming to subdivision coyote can be a challenge. There is always a neophyte screamer within who has messed with the coyotes' minds enough to cause paranoia. Larry and I packed up the junk and headed there with wet work on our mind. Nearly all calls took place close to the paved highway that led into and led from the luxury subdivision or close to one of the secondary roads that circled. Larry and I parked close to the road and made a walkabout to call the coyote, and we did call a few. Trouble was, the survivors turned into tough customers. Some were paranoid because of the screaming done by the tyro. Others became paranoid because of Larry and me. It did not take long for them to connect the slowing cadence of a combustion engine, the sound of a truck parking to the screaming sticks that go boom.

What to do? We "T & T'ed." We thunk on it, identified problems, struggled mightily, and gave birth to the drop and drive technique. One Beastmaster slowed enough to allow the second to make the dismount and then drove on. The gunner would walk a decent distance, set up, wait a decent interval and scream away from the road. Considerable wet work followed. Enough, at least, to provide a measure of revenge to the bereaved. Enough to cause the sighting of a coyote to be somewhat unusual.

The Beastmasters refined the DROP & DRIVE during a hunt involving Gordy Krahn, at the time editor of *Trapper & Predator Caller* magazine. It was day three of a three-day hunt, a hunt where circumstances had caused Gordo to miss a bunch of coyote. Gordo said his scope sighted centerfire had been mishandled by the airline, causing a misalignment (now there's an alibi for you). Anyway, Larry slowed the Dodge diesel to make the drop. Gordy and I walked.

Even though the setup was in hard-hit country, close enough to the interstate to hear the rumble of the nineteen wheelers (we count the spare), we called two coyote on that setup. Not taking a chance that Gordo might embarrass himself further; I shot both, earning the new nickname of "Quickdraw." We used the DRIVE-DROP-DRIVE TECHNIQUE, modified, to hunt another bunch of uncallable land. Much of the country in northern Arizona is high plains, flat land, some with gently rolling hills, short grass prairie. Much of that country is favored fawning area for antelope, and within the ridgeline junipers, for deer, and for elk. The coyote know this and hit those areas hard, particularly during early summer when fawning takes place. The plains were hard to hunt. No place to hide the truck. No place to hide the hunter. A perfect place for drive and drop. One Beastmaster would dismount while the second drove away. The hunter half would find a likely looking place and lay flat on the back to stare at the sky, to scream at the pale daytime moon. The screamer would pause often to listen for the sound of galloping paws. When that happened he would rise up out of the grass to do business. Ahhh, the look on those coyote kissers.

Want another? Sure, why the hell not. We were headed for the boulder jumbles that decorate a part of central Arizona, a kind of country friendly to gangs of gray fox, clusters of cats, more than a few coyote and

The Drop & Drive can cause a Ph.D. coyote to dumb up.

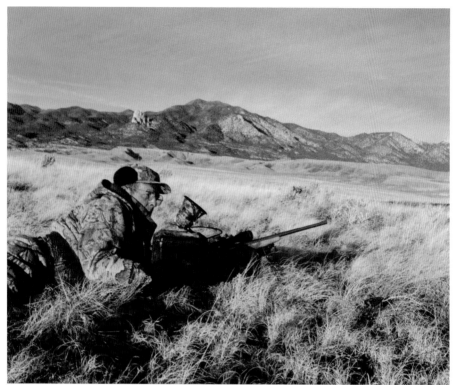

The D&D works wonderfully well within open prairie where truck hide outs are seldom seen. Bill Countess from Colorado.

even the occasional cougar. That's the good news. The bad news? We were not the only screamers who knew of this critter heaven. Screamers of every shape and size, every nationality, came to the boulders for early season screamings. The dumb coyotes turned dead. Those that survived turned paranoid. A lack of action would cause many of the screamers to move on, searching for a new honey hole. After a bit of rest some of the educated critters would become somewhat trusting. A few would sneak in for a sly look at a scream, sometimes providing a shot opportunity. Knowing there was a hell of a lot of critters (maybe more) within the boulders, Larry and I whipped out the THINKING technique.

The problem, as we saw it, was one of association. The fox, the bobcat, the coyote, even the somewhat learning-challenged cougar, had come to associate the sound of the rabbit distress scream with pain and emotional trauma. What to do? This one is easy. Change the sound. We did and enjoyed moderate success. We needed to do more. We moved the THINKING technique a step further, and thus was born the infamous DOUBLE SCREAM to DOUBLE YOUR PLEASURE technique.

Knowing that all gray fox, all mountain lion and all coyote enjoy the sound

Recording multiple sounds on a single tape can cause a smorgasbord of screams guaranteed to assault the eardrums and maybe call a coyote. (Gordy Krahn Photo).

of a gray fox in pain, we chose that somewhat coarse complaint to be leg one of the double call. Larry would play the gray fox distress scream. At the same time I would sound cottontail rabbit distress screams on the TallyHo. Did it work? Hell, yes, it worked. I shot the Moose at so many fox that my shoulder hurt for a week. Later, hoping to improve, we modified. We took the gray fox distress and a cottontail rabbit distress and married those two sounds within one tape. That may have worked even better. Other options exist. The Gray Fox Distress and the Yellowhammer Woodpecker Distress. Baby Cottontail Distress and Gray Fox Distress. Gray Fox and Canine Puppies. Others. Such couplings offer a couple of advantages. A new sound is one. A sound that stays somewhat new is the other. Making your own combinations causes you to carry a unique sound, one not available to the generic screamer. Can you stand one more? Much of the country Larry and I call is desert covered with creosote bushes, a more-than head-high shrub sometimes called greasewood. Such country can be dandy for shot gunners when the greasewood is spaced to permit vision and shooting lanes. Trouble is, much of the greasewood country is so thick a screamer cannot find such. Most callers drive on by to find country friendlier. Those uncalled areas turned into a coyote sanctuary, offering the kind of challenge any Beastmaster worth the name must respond to.

Some of the crowded creosote country was interrupted by knobs of rock and cactus rising above the highest creosote, enough to provide a vision down into the meager spacing between the creosote. Staying high, we figured, would allow us to look down on the coyote, maybe see enough to cause them to get dead. Calling from on high was not that successful. The coyote would come, stay within the thickest of the greasewood, and pause long enough to look up at the source of the screams. When they did not see the rabbit, saw instead four hundred pounds of hunters, they made the retreat. Back to THINKING.

A main part of the problem came about because the coyote looked high on that barren hill to reconnoiter the source of the sound. Causing the sound to stay low while we Beastmasters stayed high seemed sensible. We taped a couple of minutes of silence onto the start of a jackrabbit distress tape. How did we do that? Easy. We put tape into a recorder, rewound, and then hit the record button. Didn't talk. Did not sneeze or even pass gas. We recorded the sound of silence. The tape was removed after a couple of minutes.

We took the tape player to the greasewoods to hide it within a particularly thick part, one that had small openings around. We hit the GO button and made the stroll to half-way up the hill. The two minutes of silence permitted a leisurely setup. The coyotes, when they came, galloped or trotted close and then started a stalk. None even glanced to the hill. We had plenty of opportunity to shoulder, sight, and shoot. And even though the shots were somewhat long range (averaging about 200 yards), shooting .22-250s across the steady support offered by a Harris BiPod (or the knees) caused hits to be routine.

Finally uno mas. This will be the last covered within this chapter. You have my word on it. I include it mainly because this description comes from a recent hunt, not one of those long gone sort of hunts that took place when the coyote were plentiful and all so dumb their butt hurt. As some of the young turks like to believe.

Placing the player on the flats and the shooter upon a hill allowed Gerald Stewart to collect this Congress Crummy.

Rich Higgins is truly rich. Rich in coyote knowledge and rich in coyote hunting know how. His twenty-one year son Tyler is nearly as wealthy, having hunted with Dad from about the time he stopped pooping his pants. Rich and Tyler combine their talents to become a coyote's worst nightmare. Our hunt took place within mid-November 2006 and took place wthin an area hard hit by about every one of the thousands of screamers who read this book and about all else they can find within a critter calling format. You talk about tough calling. Tougher than Hard Hearted Hannah from Butte Montana.

My first surprise came when I was allowed a look at the calling country. Many of us screamers head for the boon-docks to do our thing. Rich and Tyler took me to an area surrounded by farms. Conventional wisdom suggests we make one stand in about every square mile. My-own-self and the Higgins army of two completed five set-ups within an area of about one square mile.

We called and killed coyote during three of the five. A suspicious adult male answered to screaming number four but left quickly before offering a shot opportunity. No worry. We moved a quarter of a mile down wind and Tyler called Big Dog back. I did the dirty deed with the Sako at a paced 225 yards. Impressive? Nah, maybe I got lucky, making up for all of the easy ones I have missed for the past half a hundred years. Stay tuned for an example of creative thinking that produced creative calling.

Knowing the educated and evil nature of the potential customers Rich and Tyler gave them something other than the generic scream of a troubled rabbit. Sure, they screamed but offered variety, articulating moans, groans, quavers and growls of infinite variety. Interspersed within were dominance howls, female invitation howls, pup distress yips, maybe even an up-yours howl. All such being awesome to the tenth power.

Another variation was timing. Ignoring the conventional wisdom that suggests calls to coyote be limited to about ten or fifteen minutes the Higgins Guys took as long as need be. The first coyote called back-doored Tyler at 27 minutes into the screaming and was .243-ed at a paced ten steps. PHD coyote, sad to say, can be a slow sell.

The second kill took place when a reluctant came to the call after eighteen minutes of cajoling. Rich shot this bashful at about twenty yards. I shot he third at a paced 225 yards.

All here might wonder why so many coyote assembled within this particular square mile. Aha, I exclaim, that is the final lesson. The square mile is infested with field after field of melons, everything from a honey dew to a casabah. The coyote became fat by murdering melons. The area offered coyote inducements. Multiple groves of mesquite to offer a sanctuary as needed. A soft alluvial soil that permitted an easy dig to burrowers such as 'Roo rats, antelope ground squirrel and other protein sources. A decent population of the rabbit called conntontail and the lagomorph called jackrabbit. Desert mule deer. Javalina. Thinking on it causes me to wish to be a coyote. It does so until I think about Rich and Tyler. No thanks!

I do not intend to whine but do feel compelled to mention that screaming is a lot tougher now than it was when I first screamed for fun and funds, such being long ago, about the middle of the last century. I freely admit my own mea culpa. I have written about screaming successes for about all of that time. Others have done likewise. At the present time (November of 2006) a number of publications are partially or totally devoted to the art, science and excitement to be found within the sport of predator hunting. Even so, as the coyote has become more intelligent, hard hunters such as Rich and the son of a Rich have evolved also.

THINKING will work in about any kind of country. Even though the techniques described above might not exactly fit the situations of the kind of country you hunt, the essence of the technique of THINKING surely will.

chapter 32

Lessons Learned

Some might say that Gerry Blair has learned about all that can be learned about the sometimes exciting sport of screaming to predators. To those (both of you) I say thanks a heap and a half. I also say "not so." Even though I freely confess to having lived seventy six years, and likewise admit I have screamed for much (I was actually born screaming) of that time, I do not claim to have seen all and am certainly not a know all. You ready for the truth? Gerry Blair and all similar should learn a new predator calling truth or relearn a predator calling truth, each and every time they toot the tube. I know that I do and my recent hunt with Tucson's own Bill Rice proves my point.

Bill is a screamer of the first water, being inclined to scream, howl, moan or groan at every opportunity. Lulu Rice is not basically a screamer (unless unduly provoked) but I love her anyway. All such explains (sort of) how Bill and Lulu happened to be at my Flagstaff diggings during December of 2006.

Bill and I traveled west from Flagstaff during a cloudless and windless pre-dawn and were set up and screaming during that crepuscular period some folks call dawn.

The trustful coyote stared at the 200 pound rabbit carrying the bang stick.

The stand site had almost everything. We parked my Ford Diesel to the side of a pair of power line ruts, closed each door gently, gathered our tricas trocus and climbed the hill crest to become discrete among scattered and scrubby second growth pinion/ juniper pushdowns. I do not recall who did the screaming but either way it should have been bloody enough to fool a coyote. Nada. Nothing. Not even a raven.

As mentioned the stand site had about everything. Everything but coyote. We walked and drove in an effort to discover set-up two. And then a funny thing happened. Not funny ha-ha but funny strange. The gate upon every ranch road we passed was decorated with an amazing collection of Stay Away signs. Even locks. Maybe even booby trapped, although I did not spend a lot of time inquiring. The message varied from sign to sign but all such told a similar tale. My favorite message was succinct. "Trespassers will be shot. Survivors will be shot again." We motored on to discover a plethora of trailer houses and huts. Civilization had moved onto one of my favored honey holes. Lesson learned? The passage of time can seriously affect calling conditions.

Day two was better. Not perfect but better than nothing. We were on Hopi land east of Flagstaff doing our thing) upon short grass (sometimes no grass) prairie land decorated with moderate push down scarred hills. We were considerably encouraged when we sighted a pair of coyote crossing the two track (Arizona Freeway) ahead of the truck. We drove out of sight and I stopped to let Bill off. He stalked the pair, and was able to snap a shot at a galloper at an estimated two hundred yards. Close but no cigar.

We returned to the truck to discover more bad news. The left rear tire on the diesel was flatter than a freeway fox. I watched and amused Bill as I commented humorously as he demonstrated his tire changing skills.

During the next set-up Bill screamed as I shivered and held onto my hat. We were on a sidehill that overlooked a mud tank and a long drainage filled with sage and other such. We abandoned the set-up fifteen or twenty minutes later. "Did you see them?" Bill asked as we walked to the truck. I nodded a no and he explained. "Four coyote came to look near the end of the screaming," he said. "Maybe six hundred yards out. Couldn't cause them to come closer".

I screamed during our next set-up, Blowing a Rhino, and sending out the usual cast of characters. Slow paced and pathetic groans and moans, each and all resembling the articulations emitted by a rabbit or hare who has misery on his mind. Those screams, to my way of thinking, were really bad. Bad in a good way. Bad enough to cause tears of compassion to flow from Saddam Hussein's eyes, maybe causing him to join the catholic church and light a candle.

Some might need to know the elements I considered as I evaluated the assets and the deficits of the set up.

I was within the time tribulated arms of a stringbark juniper, such doing a decent job of subduing my silhouette. A five strand barbed wire fence was twenty or thirty feet to my back. A moderate south wind traveled from a juniper decorated drainage to the front, bringing the pleasant scent of juniper woodlands and the somewhat pleasant smell of cow crap. Logic birthed by experience suggested the customer was likely to be laid up within the less windy junipers situated within the less windy drainage during a moderately windy mid-day and would therefore be likely to travel to meet the bullet with the wind at his back and the wind into my face.

Ten minutes into the screaming intuition advised of a presence to my rear. I turned my head nearly 180 degrees (looking somewhat like a swivel necked great horned owl) and eyeballed a curious coyote standing a hundred yards out.

I butt scooted to achieve a slightly improved angle, shouldered the .22-250 Sako, and attempted an awkward offhand shot. I was not surprised when I scored a clean miss. The coyote ignored the 52-grain Sierra hollowpoint that tickled his ear hair and continued to watch the rabbit while the bang stick watched him.

A few seconds later the coyote wandered off, obviously disappointed. With the customer out of sight I butt scooted again, this time until I was completely facing the place recently vacated by the coyote. I replaced the Rhino in my mouth and delivered one more blow job.

The coyote reappeared within seconds and stood within the precise place he had been a minute or so ago.

I shouldered the Sako, centered the small x of the duplex variable (set at 3X) to the rear of the shoulder bone, drew in a breath, partially exhaled, and squeezed the three pound trigger. The moderate recoil of the Varminter

caused me to miss seeing the moment of truth but the satisfying thump of air leaving the lung cavity was encouraging. I continued to scream for another few minutes, hoping for a bonus, and when nothing showed, unhid, slithered beneath the bottom strand of the five wire fence, and began the search.

The ranch roads were gated, signed and maybe booby trapped.

Blair butt scooted square to the target and recalled the coyote.

It took Bill and I several minutes to locate the recently deceased. A fresh dead coyote resting among same colored grass can be discrete. We did accomplish discovery, however, and noticed the hollow point had entered precisely on target, leaving a .224 inch entry hole. As is somewhat customary, the fast traveling (3750 fps muzzle) fifty-two grainer had exploded within the chest cavity. There was not an exit. All such causing the skinning to be minimally messy. All such causing the pelt to be pretty much pristine.

Our hunt was essentially ended. We used up an hour or two obtaining images of me and the coyote, Bill and the coyote, and images of the coyote by himself looking all dead.

Later, during the drive out, we discussed the circumstances of the hunt and the lessons learned.

Lesson number one had to do with traditional thinking about coyote nature. Some have said that a coyote will always circle to taste the wind before munching the rabbit. Such was obviously not so during this instance. I cannot count the times a coyote kind of customer has walked, trotted, creeped or galloped to taste a rabbit that smelled disgustingly like Gerry Blair, doing so with the wind directly in his nose.

Lesson number two had to do with traditional thinking concerning coyote behavior after the shot. My experience once caused me to believe that "shot at and missed coyote" will often run as if all the demons within hell were hot on their heels, which they are. And further, that such customers will not return to the scene of the crime even though you may beg. I say horse pucky to that and to all such dogmatic statements made by those who believe themselves to be the ultimate authority on coyote behavior and all else within this wondrous world. The truth, as I see it now, is less precise. Just because coyote "A" behaves in a certain way on a certain day does not justify the assumption that coyote "B" will behave precisely the same way. It would be equally wrong to assume that coyote "A" will behave exactly the same way tomorrow, next week or next year. DernaMitey, there is no guarantee coyote "A" will behave precisely the same fifteen minutes later. The truth is, Rule Number One about coyote and coyote behavior is as follows: "There ain't no rules."

Please stay with me as I present a for instance. My-own-self, Michael McCasland and Bill Rice ganged up on coyote during the HuntMaster camp-out held near Picacho Peak (Arizona) during late October of 2006. We three hunted hard and screamed enthusiastically for nearly all of one day and did not sight a hair or a hare. Bill and Michael even used their secret weapon, sitting tall upon a ladder to no avail. A couple of dozen other screamers also did poorly.

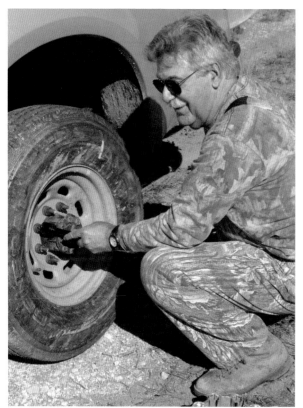

Recently, Michael returned to the exact same area and screamed during an afternoon that allowed six stands. Six stands, called coyote at five of the stands and "harvested" all five. What was different? Not much. Same coyote and same country. Same screams. Different day. Go figure.

Gerry amused Bill Rice by uttering humorous remarks as Bill changed the flat.

To summarize, I suggest you learn all you can learn about the nature of coyote, fox, bobcat, lion and bear. Ponder that information and structure your hunting strategy around what the customer is most likely to do. Tailor your technique to be effective within the terrain you hunt and on the customer being hunted. Having said that, allow me to say also that you should not be surprised when the customer does precisely the opposite. It is possible, the way I see it, the customer does not read the same articles and books, view the same videos and CD's, as we hunters do. Maybe not even read articles by the old guy called Gerry Blair.

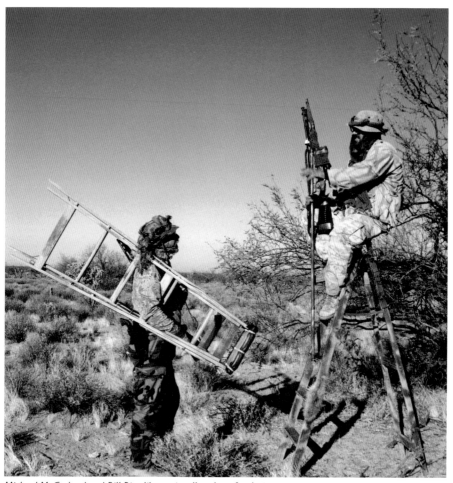

Michael McCasland and Bill Rice like to sit tall and see far during a screaming.

chapter 33

Calling Bear

We glassed the bear at about daylight, while the air was cool, before the sun heated the cactus-covered ridges to cause the air to be choked with heat waves. The critter was an insignificant black speck in the prickly pear at an estimated three-mile distance. Mike Mell cased the spotting scope with the 20X lens. "That bear will be bedding as soon as the sun shows," he mused, "and I am betting it will bed close to the feed grounds." Even though my own knowledge did not match that of my wife's cousin, a licensed big game guide, his assessment made sense. Why would the bear travel far away from the sweet and juicy fruit of the prickly pear cactus to find a bed? We gathered up

Some black bear are red, some are brown and others are black. The name refers to a species and not a color.

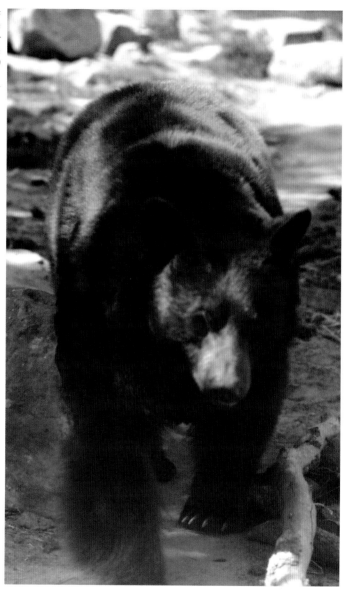

our junk and returned to our open-air camp. Later, after a leisurely breakfast, we loaded the daypack and the packing frames, and were on our way to the feed grounds.

I started the screaming at about 4 p.m., using a Trophy Model Circe fitted with a jackrabbit reed. I called as I almost always call to bear, blowing hard to add a hoarseness to the screams, and blowing so that the individual screams were drawn out. I did my best to cause the screaming to simulate the agony of a larger prey animal, perhaps an immature or adult deer. The bear showed thirty minutes into the call, appearing upon the back of a distant ridge, pausing to make the reconnoiter. I stayed still. When the bear started the move to descend the ridge to head for the prickly pear patch, I screamed again, reducing volume somewhat, hoping the bear would hear. He heard. The bear started to lumber our way, paused to back its butt to a boulder to enjoy a scratch, and then came again. I took the shot when the 175-pound sow was a hundred yards out. We did the dirty work and made the pack out. It was near midnight when we arrived at camp.

Even though that hunt on the San Carlos Apache Indian Reservation took place many years ago, the technique of glass, stalk, and scream is as good now as it was then. Fall bear in the West often feed upon open and semi-open hillsides, permitting long distance discovery. Stalking close to such-sighted bear to make a screaming causes success to come more often.

Black bear can be found in good numbers throughout Alaska and Canada. Blacks can also be found in the mountainous areas of most of the continental United States, in the hardwood forests of the East, and in the swamps of some Southern states. North central Mexico has a fair number. Some jurisdictions do not have a handle on total bear population. My home state of Arizona did not before a game and fish biologist used foot snares to capture and collar bear of a rough mountain range called the Mazatzals. Only adult bear were collared, for two good reasons. Placing a collar on an immature bear could cause that bear to suffocate as it matured, as the neck increased in size. Reason two had to do with territoriality. The study was aimed to determine the number of bear territories within the range. Adult bear are territorial; immature bear are not.

The study provided surprising information. The seven-year study suggested a territorial bear density within the Mazatzals (pronounced Mat-ah-zals, don't ask me why) of about one territorial bear to the square mile. The chaparral-covered canyons and ridges offer all a bear needed to prosper. Thick high brush to cover movement. A primitive area with few roads, keeping out most of the humans. Plenty of fruits and mast to keep his big belly full. And an almost complete lack of houndsmen. The high and thick chaparral causes difficulty for the hounds and for horseback houndsmen. The Mazatzal study, and other studies, caused Arizona wildlife professionals to estimate a population of 2,000-3,000 on non-Indian lands. Substantial bear populations can be found within the boundaries of the White Mountain Apache, the San Carlos Apache, and some parts of the Navajo Indian reservations. Adding such to the Arizona estimate causes that total to increase. All permit bear hunting by non-Indians who have paid the proper fees.

Black bear do not live exclusively in the Arizona chaparral. Populations can be found in the mountains and in the canyons that traverse those mountains, about every part of the state, actually, excepting the low deserts.

The black bear, it should be mentioned, refers to a species and not to a color.

The black bear species might be black but might also be brown, cinnamon, or red. All color phases. The brown bear, sometimes used to describe the brown phase of the black bear, is correctly used to describe a subspecies of grizzly bear. Bear mate in early summer. The mating period might last for a month. Male and female caress during that time and engage in much moaning and bawling. When the love affair ends the two go their separate ways; they do not even remain good friends. The male returns to his territory and the female to hers. The cubs are born the following winter when the sow is denned in the fitful sleep sometimes called hibernation. The one to four cubs are born small but grow rapidly on their diet of Momma's milk. They will be about a foot and a half long when they follow the sow out of the den at the starting of spring.

Bear spend the summer and fall building fat so that they might survive the winter. Yearling cubs return to the den with the sow. The bear "hibernation" is a fitful sleep interrupted by periods of fitful wakefulness. The bear does not eat during this period nor does it defecate. A grass fecal plug has jammed the bowels.

Territorial bear are the biggest and baddest of the bear. And they are the smartest, the most difficult to hunt. Young bear are tolerated until they reach about two years of age. The female is tired of fooling with them then, and she is ready to breed again. Those too hardheaded to leave to find a territory of their own might be killed. The young bear so displaced, having low survival skills, are apt to wander about until they come upon a hunter. I said in the chapter dealing with tracks and tracking that bear preferred wild and remote country. That is true. Some bear, particularly the wanderers, will do the opposite. Such become "nuisance" bear when they hang around campgrounds or close to human housing. The sentence for such behavior, much of the time, is death.

Black bear that develop a taste for beef can also be sentenced to death. A hungry bear, one coming out of hibernation with an empty belly or one headed for hibernation and hoping to do so with a reserve of fat, will find it difficult to resist the sight of a frisky and vulnerable calf. Black bear also eat carrion. Livestock that die of natural causes, even unnatural causes not bear related, often end up in a bear's belly. Such bear, much of the time, are guilty of nothing more serious than stealing a buzzard's supper. The main meal of the bear, through much of his range, is berries, fruits, and nuts. Insects. Garbage. Bear are opportunistic feeders. They take what the country has to offer.

I presented a comprehensive discussion on bear tracks and other sign within the chapter on tracks and tracking. There is no good reason to repeat that information here. It is proper, I think, to write a bit about bear, bear habits, and bear habitats.

Black bear can vary greatly in size. Many hunters have trouble estimating the trophy potential of the bear they see. Here is a simple way to recognize a fully adult bear, one with trophy potential. A bear has ears that are five inches long, true of both mature and immature bear. A bear that has ears that seem

Investigation in-dicated the big boar climbed the poles, selected from the menu, and left to dine alone.

too big for the head is likely to be an immature. A bear that has ears that are widely separated by the skull, ears that seem to be insignificant in relation to head size, is likely to be a fully mature bear. A trophy.

Some idea of bear size can be determined from the track. A front foot track that measures more than 4-1/4" from heel to toe and more than 4-1/4" wide was likely left by an adult male, a boar. A hind foot track that is more than 7-1/2" long and more than 4" wide was likely made by an adult male. A really big boar bear is likely to leave a front foot track that measures more than 5-1/2" and a hind foot track that measures more than 9". Such a track is likely to have been left by a bear weighing 300 pounds or more.

As mentioned earlier in this chapter, I like a call that is on the coarse or hoarse side for a bear screaming. I prefer the sound of a series of long and drawn out screams rather than the short and choppy series I sometimes use for coyote or fox. The sound I send imitates the distress scream of a fawn deer. Might such a sound interest a bear? A wildlife professional working within bear country on the sprawling Navajo Indian Reservation says yes. Pat Ryan and Kathleen McCoy conducted a study to determine the cause of mortality among mule deer fawns. They had captured and collared a particularly vocal fawn and had left to return to the truck when they heard the fawn repeating the bleating. They returned just in time to see an adult bear leaving, with the fawn in mouth. Pat gave chase but lost the race. He returned to the truck, grabbed the antennae, and followed the beeps, eventually catching up with the fawn-loving bear. Pat used sticks, stones, and strong language to cause the bear to give up the still living fawn. No happy ending, however. Trauma, bear slobbers, maybe human handling, caused the doe to abandon the fawn. Death came a day later.

Some Navajo consider the bear to be one of a class of witches (called Skinwalkers) capable of changing from animal to human form. That belief provokes a fear that causes the Navajo to avoid the bear when possible. No

The glass, hike and scream technique can be effective within open or semi-open country, here used by Tim Barrachough of Raton, NM and author, Gerry Blair.

killing, even when a bear shows he or she is a bad neighbor. Under those circumstances the Navajo wildlife people call in a non-Indian hunter to do the wet work. Larry and I hunted such a bear when the critter climbed within an aspen pole corral to select a sheep, and did so on a mighty regular basis.

The mutton-lover hung out in a rough country basin choked with Gambel's oak, and those oak were loaded with acorns. Even so, apparently, the bear tired of an all acorn diet, hankering for a bit of mutton.

Larry hunted the basin, surrounded by bear sign in the form of acorn husks and even a bit of wool. Larry used a Lohman C-280 open reed (plastic reed) call to blow out a series of desperate screams. The bear came during one such screaming and was .30-06-ed. The red-brown female weighed an estimated 150 pounds. How can we be sure the bear Larry shot was the mutton lover? I could be cute and say the bear had a sheepish look about her. I will not. I say instead, there is no sure way. The bear Larry called and killed was of the same color and about the same size as the one seen raiding the corral. To the Navajo, and to Larry, that is close enough.

Prime time for bear calling is dawn and dusk. I like dawn best, sometimes starting the call before daylight, but no shooting until legal light arrives. Dusk can be nearly as good but carries a disadvantage. A slow bear, at times, will show after legal shooting light ends. The nature of the bear body causes him to be a tough kill. The hide is thick and hairy. That hide covers a layer of fat that can be inches thick. Under the fat is massive muscle and stout bone. A good bear gun should push out enough lead to get the critter's attention. The right kind of cartridge will not cause the bullet to move so fast it will explode within the hide, the fat or the muscle. Controlled expansion is best, permitting the bullet to penetrate to the necessaries.

Even under the best of circumstances screaming to a bear can be slow work. The mutton-eater Larry called in the Navajo highlands took 25 minutes to respond, even though Larry was set up close. Bear do not respond to the call dependably. Only the bear know why. I have had bear start a hard run upon hearing the first scream, running away from the screams. Others, maybe even the same bear on a different day, will run to the call. The nature of the bear, much of the time, causes it to come at the stroll. I recommend plenty of time on the bear stand, a couple of hours are not too much if encouragement is present.

A hunter might scream at a dozen setups and not call a bear. And then, unexpectedly, a big black shape (or brown, red, maybe even white) will loom up. The excitement created by that response causes all of the hard work to be worthwhile. Expert bear hunter Mike Mell has guided hunters to a couple of dozen bear, one a 430-pound (estimated weight) red carrying a silky coat. "Most of the bear I have called came out of brushy canyons," Mike says. That brush, much of the time, is scrub oak and manzanita, both shrubs that produce bear groceries. Mike calls most of his bear during the months of September and

October, at about the beginning of the Arizona bear season. He recommends using the spotting scope to locate a feeding bear (as we did on the San Carlos hunt) and then stalking close to take the shot or make the call.

Mike Mell verifies that bear do not respond to the screaming dependably. Mike and a hunter watched a bear go into a brushy canyon during one hunt and figured he had bedded. They stalked close, to the canyon rim, and watched for nearly an hour, hoping to sight the bedded bear. No luck. Why didn't they drop off into the canyon to make an effort to flush the bear? Not a good idea, according to Mike. Too often the bear will slip away and not be seen.

After an hour of scanning Mike used the varmint call (a Trophy Model Circe) to start a screaming. Still nothing. Mike eventually threw a chunk of log down into the canyon and the bear ambled out.

Bear guide Riney Maxwell hunts rough country along the Arizona-New Mexico border. Rough country is the key to successful bear calling, according to Riney. "Rough country is where the bear stay," Riney says. "I have called dozens of bear out of that kind of country. The rougher the better." Riney screamed country that was a bit too rough during one hunt. A bear was downed within the steep bottom of a double rough canyon and Riney led his horse, following a sorry game trail, hoping to get somewhat close. The horse miss-stepped and fell to the bottom. The horse, a good one, was dead before he hit the bottom.

Maxwell has his best luck calling to bear early in the morning and late in the evening. He seldom calls after 10 a.m., and does not start again until about 3 p.m. Riney uses a wood Circe and prefers the jackrabbit reed, blowing loud for the first thirty-second series. He pauses then to glass. Another series follows after a couple of minutes. The scream-glass cooperation continues for about thirty minutes.

"You need to give a bear plenty of time to show," Maxwell says. "The bear does not race to the call and is further slowed within rough country. Too many hunters give up too soon and walk away when a bear is on the way."

The Blue Wilderness area Maxwell hunts is some of the roughest in the state, in any state. Maxwell rides horseback to make a camp away from roads and within area too rough to interest many other hunters. On one memorable day he sighted seventeen head of bear. That is the kind of country bear hunters love. Some of that crowd of bear will almost certainly appreciate a well executed screaming. The pack out? That's another story.

Those who know me well know I am the sort of hunter who enjoys talking about his hunts. I am sometimes invited to speak to various groups. About every kind of group except the Defenders of Wildlife. Why me? Mainly, I suspect, because I work cheap. I frequently begin the talk by telling a joke. "Have I told you about the time I hunted bare?" I ask. "I walked a mile or more beyond camp and became so cold I had to return to camp and put some clothes on".

chapter 34

Calling Bobcat

There is a hell of a lot of bobcat (maybe more) in the wilds of the West. The state of Arizona, as an example, reports a harvest of about eight thousand bobs (trapping, calling, and opportunistic taking) year after year. Arizona biologists have estimated an adult population of about 40,000 bobcats. Impressive? Not really. Not when you consider that the neighboring state of California is home to an estimated 74,700 with an annual harvest of 15,000. The estimated populations for the eleven Western states that are the bobcats' favored habitat totals about a quarter of a million, give or take a bobcat or two. Add the generous populations found within the Lone Star State, and in Dixie, and that total is considerably increased.

Knowing all of that, knowing of the number of bobcat around, one wonders why the bobcat and bobcat nature are so poorly understood. That lack of understanding can cause screamers to have a difficult time while hunting the bobcat.

Bobcat size is a good example. The long-legged nature of the bobcat, coupled with his furry aspect, causes hunters to be a poor judge of bobcat size. The 40- or 50-pound trophy (estimated weight) can shrink to about half that when the weight is verified on honest scales. You want the truth? I have called and killed and trapped and killed a bunch of bobcat during the last half century. Nearly all were weighed on honest scales. The largest was a tom called to the ten-gauge while on a high country hunt (Arizona) with George Oakey. That big blue back weighed 26 pounds. Conversations with other honest trappers and callers cause them say about the same.

I do not say no bobcat can be bigger. Oscar Cronk of Wiscasset, Maine, and a bluetick hound named Emerson took a 35-pounder from Maine's Allagash during 1984. A 55-pound bobcat came out of Lake County, Ohio, a few years back. Neither of those husky Roberts came close to the all-time fat cat; that honor likely goes to a 69-pound cat-and-a-half that came out of Colorado many years ago. Those fat cats, in my view, are freaks of nature, about as rare as a 600-pound human at a convention of nudists. Each is a sight not often seen but one that is remembered for one hell of a long time.

Other aspects of the bobcat nature are often as obscure. The hunter who hopes to scream a bobcat close on a regular basis cannot permit that poor

Even though the bobcat is primarily nocturnal, a bob' with the hungries might hunt day and night.

perception. Knowing about bobcat habitat and bobcat habits can cause increased success. Bobcat can be found from southern Canada to South America and from coast to coast within the continental United States. Color can vary as geography varies. Cats of the Northwest typically show a chocolate tinting. Southwestern bobcat range from light gray to almost silver. The color of bobcat everywhere is a mixture of browns, buffs, and whites. Body fur is almost always spotted but the spots can be inconspicuous. The belly is snow-white, showing contrasting black spots. The tail is insignificant. Ears are usually tufted on fully adult bobcat.

Bobcats mostly work the night shift but will hunt night and day when so provoked by weather or hunger. Even so, screamers who do it in the dark have the best chance of fetching in a bobcat. Day callers who work the crepuscular periods of dawn and dusk will also do well. Dead noon callers will do least well.

An Arizona study caused the scat contents of 176 bobcats to be examined. The study showed the bobcat that left the scat lived mainly on the cottontail rabbit with substantial amounts of other rodents present. The rodent diet was supplemented by minor amounts of snakes, birds, lizards, fox, fish, and insects. Big bobcat eat little bobcat. Mature bobcat will take the young of antelope and deer when available and have been known to kill and consume adult deer, particularly when that adult deer is winter-stressed or is yarded. The bobcat can trot atop crusted snow and the deer cannot, causing the deer to be vulnerable.

The hunting technique of the bobcat is essentially the same as that of the mountain lion and essentially the same as the hunting technique of the feral house cat. All locate prey using excellent eyesight or a poorly developed sense of smell. The cats stalk when the prey has its head down feeding, will freeze when the head comes up, and will continue the sneak when the head goes down again. When the sneaker is close he makes a rush to take the prey, pinning small animals with razor sharp claws until the jaws can make the kill.

A hunting bobcat might cover five to eight miles during a night of hunting. The bob' will follow about the same pattern on each trip through his hunting territory, at times placing his foot at precisely the place traveled during the last trip through. The bobcat will pause at significant (to the bobcat) points within his territory to deposit scat, urine, and at times, a yellow paste from the anal glands. Territorial markings. The bobcat territory will vary as geographic conditions vary. A generous prey base coupled with huntable habitat can cause the bobcat to hunt and defend a territory as small as a few square miles. Territory size increases as available prey decreases. The territory of the male is almost always larger than that of the female. Even though a male and a female territory may overlap, the two avoid face-to-face meetings, except during late winter when it comes time to shake the sugar tree.

A bobcat mating is a mixture of aggression and submission. The mating is

almost always noisy. The passionate caterwauling can be heard for a long distance. The males will leave their territories to seek out females. When one is found, the tom announces his needs, using a series of growls, snarls, and moans. The female crouches to show she is interested. After an hour or so of noisy foreplay the female shows her willingness by joining the caterwauling.

A bobcat den may be in a jumble of boulders, in a cave, in a dugout,

An examination of stomach content and an examination of scat has indicated the main prey of bobcat is the cottontail rabbit. (Larry Gates Photo).

or within an abandoned mine tunnel, any place away from the weather. The litter is born about two months after the mating. There may be as many as seven kittens (the average is much less), all born blind and helpless. The female must leave the kittens to hunt and that causes them to be vulnerable, particularly to the appetite of the male bobcat. A tom that finds the den will almost surely kill and eat the kittens, causing the milk of the female to dry up and affecting her return to estrus.

Summer is a time of learning. The young travel with the female on night hunts, learning hunting and survival skills. The young will stay with the female until cold weather hits. When the food supply diminishes the female encourages the young to get the hell gone. If prey is plentiful, if the cottontail rabbit population is at a high cycle, many will survive.

As the coyote is a dog the bobcat is a cat. What the hell does that mean? Each is within a single species. Joinings between the sub-species can occur. Though uncommon, breeding between bobcat and domestic cat have produced offspring. I know of a successful mating between a bobcat and a black domestic cat. Four of the litter produced were black, resembling the domestic. The remaining three within the litter had bobtails, tufted ears, and were light gray. All of the kittens had feet obviously larger than those of domestic cat. All had bobcat-like legs.

Fifteen years appears to be a long life for a bobcat in the wild. A bobcat in captivity lived for 32 years. The main enemy of the bobcat, aside from man, is the largest of the flying predators; other bobcat and large land predators like

Bobcat can be efficient wild turkey predators, killing vocal mature toms during the spring mating cycle.

The Congress Cat dined on poodles and allowed vocal local coyote to be blamed.

the mountain lion and the coyote.

Bobcat scat can be fox size but is usually larger. The offal is segmented (I call it the Tootsie Roll effect) so that breakage occurs at sharp right angles. When first deposited the bobcat scat is a shiny black. Exposure to arid air causes a crusting but the color stays black. Continued exposure causes the scat to turn gray and then to white. The scat, much of the time, consists of cottontail rabbit hair, sometimes including small fragments of undigested bone. Toilets are sometimes found, places where a bunch of bobcat scat shows repeated visits, often from more than one bobcat. Some bobcat will dig out a bowl to hold the scat. Bowl deposits may be covered or uncovered. A covered deposit indicates scat left by a territorial cat.

The bobcat track is typical of all cat tracks. Look for a somewhat round two-inch diameter track showing the characteristic heel pad, bi-lobed at the front and tri-lobed at the rear. Four toes, no claw marks. Bobcats are not a really tough call, not in the same sense a mountain lion is a tough call. As noted, there are a bunch of bobcat around, particularly within the West and the Southwest. As is the case with most predators, the bobcat must be opportunistic to prosper. A hungry bobcat (most stay so) that hears the advertisement is compelled to investigate, sometimes at the trot and sometimes at the creep. The inconspicuous nature of the bobcat, sad to say, can let him creep in and creep out without being seen. My experience causes me to think many (maybe even most) called bobcat do exactly that. The kitty-eating cat of Congress illustrates.

The Congress (central Arizona) cat was an oversize tom that hung around a cluster of luxury homes scattered among the high desert, a country containing forests of creosote brush (greasewood) and with mesquite, desert ironwood, and foothills Palo Verde within the washes. It did not take the tom long to discover the domestic cats and small dogs who patrolled the properties, and the tom developed an appetite for all, causing the residents to become cranky. Coyote, being somewhat plentiful and always obvious because of their howling, were the clear suspects. One resident called on Beastmaster Larry O. Gates, and asked that he do a screaming.

The first half-dozen setups caused three coyote to come. Larry used the three-inch twelve to send all to that big gut pile in the sky. During a midmorning screaming Larry looked through a greasewood to see a single critter leg, or at least something that looked somewhat like a critter leg, maybe sixty yards out. Interested, Larry continued to look and scream. The leg look-alike did not respond. Screaming continued. Minutes later, when Larry's aching eyeballs had convinced him there REALLY was a critter hiding within the greasewood, he played the ace. He compressed his lips and sucked, sending out a squeaking the Beastmasters call the Kiss of Death. The leg unhid and, attached to a big bobcat body, came at the charge. Larry did the wet work when the Robert was 20 feet out, still coming. A less observant hunter might not have discovered

Bobcat climb mainly to stay safe but may climb to visit a tough turkey or fat porcupine. (Charlie Rhodes Photo).

The Canon Cat learned to love the hum of my autowind camera and came depressingly close.

the leg, might not have kissed, and might have abandoned the stand to leave the tom undiscovered. An isolated incident? I don't think so. The same has happened too many times.

The bobcat that comes to the night call, the way I see it, is more likely to be discovered. The bobcat eyes illuminate like a pair of miniature moons when hit with the light, drawing attention to the obscure body. Some hunters, particularly those screaming to coyote, do not call bobcat because they stay within open or semi-open country, good habitat for coyote but not the best habitat for bobs'. The bobcat is not fond of open country. Those I have met prefer somewhat thick cover. The brush, the kind of country a bobcat can hunt successfully, is where the groceries are found. The brush and woods, finally, offer a sanctuary when it comes time to make the desperate run away from a lion, a couple of coyote or a bigger bobcat.

A lack of hunter patience can cause the bobcat to keep his hide. Some hunters, particularly those who call to coyote or fox, abandon the stand after ten or fifteen minutes. Even though some bobcat will come during that time frame, most will not. Bobcat will travel a surprising distance to investigate a screaming but will do so at his own deliberate pace. I suggest a minimum of thirty minutes on the stand when the target is bobcat, or when the hunter suspects a bobcat might be within range of the screams. Unlike some coyote, the bobcat does not become call-shy, at least not in the same sense an experienced coyote becomes call shy. The bob' does not seem to associate the screaming and the human hiding in the brush holding the banger. A cat that is called and escapes is likely to come again, maybe even on the very next day. The Beastmaster experience with the Piggyback Cat of the Harcuvars shows this aspect of the bobcat nature.

Larry and I were on the tip-top of Pete Smith Peak in the Harcuvar Range, taping action for *The Master's Secrets to Predator Calling*. The late afternoon screaming had me hid within a clump of beargrass, singing the "Dying Rabbit

Blues" through the TallyHo. Larry stood a hundred feet or so to the rear, aiming the camcorder.

Ten minutes into the call Larry started an urgent slip squeaking. Knowing I carried the only gun, I unhid and responded at the lumber. Larry pointed downhill. Looking, I saw a bobcat leaving in a hurry. The cat, Larry said, had come to stand at his side, somewhat like a dog at heel, during the screaming, so close such could be touched.

Larry called the same area not long after, while on a muzzleloader hunt for mule deer. He made the screaming hoping to attract a rutting buck. A sense of danger caused him to look to the rear. Imagine his excitement when he saw a big bobcat, maybe the same cat that had come to heel, launch from ten feet out. Perceiving a mistake while in midair, the cat sheathed the claws, hit Larry's shoulder, and bounced off. Larry turned to square to the target and did his best to have a shot opportunity with the front stuffer. Too late. The attack cat disappeared within the boulders.

Even though bobcat do not often wear name tags, Larry and I are convinced that same cat responded one more time. We were in the Harcuvar foothills with the camcorder when a bobcat showed atop a boulder a hundred yards out. Larry did the wet work with the .22-250. I taped. The cat was the same coloration and the same size as the cat called in the area on the two previous occasions, a female weighing 21 pounds.

Stand selection can be crucial when the target is bobcat, maybe more so than with any other screaming excepting those addressed to cougar. The hunter must discover a habitat that is bobcat friendly. An evaluation of that habitat should cause clues that suggest where the bobcat might be at that time of day (or night). If it is dark, early morning, or late evening, the bobcat is likely to be hungry and hunting. Look for him within heavy brush that may

The distress cry of the red shafted flicker can cause cats to come close.

border fields. If the call is at midday it is likely the cat will be bedded. If the day is warm the cat is most likely to be bedded on the shady side of the hill, probably half way or higher on a hillside. Cold calls will find the cat on the sunny side. Thick brush, natural caves and the gaps within a rock jumble are preferred layups.

An ideal bobcat setup will have enough cover to hide the hunter and enough to cause the cat to feel comfortable during the approach. The cover must not be so thick as to significantly diminish vision lanes and shooting opportunity. Bobcats are not constant as they react to the call. I have called cats that stopped far out to reconnoiter (as did the Kitty Eating Cat), sometimes refusing to come one step closer, even when invited by the Kiss of Death. Others come too close, and come at the gallop, as did the Piggy Back Pussy. I called a tom to thirty feet on one hunt and was busy firing the shutter of an auto-focus Canon. Something about the click of the shutter and the hum of the rewind made it happen for the bobcat. The cat went into the classic crouch and creep. I became nervous when the cat was ten feet out and invited that sumbitch to get the hell gone.

Bobcat will respond to a surprising variety of distress sounds. Cottontail screams are always popular. So are the hoarser hollers from the hare called the jackrabbit, or from any other hare. Bird distress calls work about as well. I have called bobs' using nearly all of the tube calls, plastic reed and metal reed, and using many sounds played through the battery-powered caller. I begin a bobcat screaming making low moans on a mouth call or playing a battery powered caller at about half volume. I seldom call for more than about fifteen seconds, pausing then to let the customer (if there is one about) consider. After a minute I repeat with another series. If a customer does not show within a couple of minutes or so, I crank up the volume, striving for distance, continuing such for thirty minutes or until I end the setup.

A hunter who calls a cat that remains out of sight can sometimes guess the whereabouts because of the presence of birds. A bobcat presence causes nearby birds to become paranoid. Those birds might squawk, scream, and hurl the vilest profanities. Birds will, at times, make swoops in an effort to drive the cat away. A hunter who witnesses such, even though he does not see a cat, is advised to keep calling.

Those who have trigger fingers that might become nervous under stress, as mine sometimes does, might find they miss a bobcat at embarrassingly close range. The cats I have missed seldom spook at the sound of a close miss. The hunter, much of the time, has ample time to reload and fire. A cat screamed close usually would stay close until he gets the rabbit. More information on cat calling will be found within the chapter on night calling.

chapter 35

Calling Coyote

There was a time when the coyote was a critter of the western wastelands, actually, about all western lands. Canis latrans (barking dog) was not much seen before Merriwether Lewis took time out from the Lewis and Clark march to write this in his journal on May 5, 1805. "The burrowing dog of the West has large and erect ears, the head being pointed like a fox. The beast associates in bands of ten or twelve and is seldom seen singly, being unable to singly attack the deer and the antelope."

Even though he was succinct, Merriwether Lewis did a decent job of describing the critter he sometimes called the "prairie wolf." It was, as a fact, the best-written description to that date. Another explorer, one who traveled to the West nearly twenty years later, closely examined a specimen of coyote collected near the present day site of Blair, Nebraska. (I am not making this up.) Thomas Say, traveling with Long's 1823 expedition to the Rocky Mountains, called the critter Canis latrans. The word coyote came from the Mexicans, being a modification of the Aztec word coyotl.

I do not know if there were Blairs around Blair, Nebraska, during those days. If so, I am betting the Blairs and the coyote had fun together, the Blairs having more fun than the coyote. Two years past the Long Expedition, the coyote started to get on the neighbors' nerves. Folks in the Missouri legislature passed a bill encouraging counties to pay a bounty on coyote ears. The man/coyote relationship was all downhill forever after. Over the years the folks who knew the coyote best, the country folk, devised a mind-boggling assortment of desperate technique to cause old Mutton Breath to get dead. Not wishing to offend the sensibilities of those who might have a nervous stomach, I will not go into the specifics. I don't mind mentioning, however, general technique: traps, snares, strychnine, cyanide, Compound 1080, chasing with greyhounds, denning, air strikes, and so forth. Do not forget a predator screaming followed by a load of four buck in the butt. All such, it should be noted, were during the days before it became politically correct to love every wolf, every coyote, and every buck-toothed gopher on God's green earth. The coyote, to his credit, took all of this bad luck in stride, kept focused on the big picture: making more coyote, eating mutton, deer and antelope, and scratching away at fleas. The coyote, to the dismay of some, showed true grit.

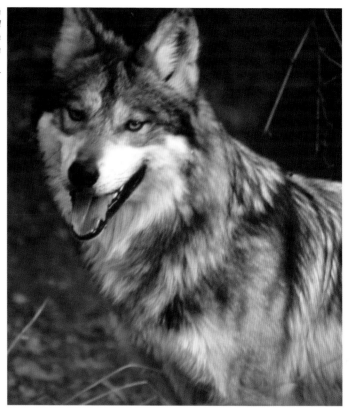

The seldom seen Mexican gray wolf can be called and camara-ed within the Blue Wilderness area of eastern Arizona.

A few Westerners and a hell of a lot of Easterners, suffering from the God's Dog mentality, professed a profound love for the poorly understood coyote. The critter, they whined, had every right to eat sheep, feed a flea that can kill a human (bubonic plague), and spread rabies. The coyote problem is not now limited to the country to the west of the big river. Coyote have extended their range to include the Midwest, the Mideast, the East, and even the South, Hell, maybe even Mars, bringing western problems to all of those areas, and more. The coyote has moved to the East, taking along problems such as livestock and poultry predation, big and small game predation, rabies, and plague. Heck, in some areas, places where deep snow and extremely cold temperatures cause the whitetail deer to become winter-stressed and to yard up, the coyote pads across the crust to kill at will. Gangs of coyote have seriously impacted whitetail deer survival in those areas.

The coyote is better adapted to survive than many other land predators. Many of those are somewhat specific in diet. The lion eats the deer and the bobcat eats the rabbit. The fox eats little critters and eats vegetables and fruits. The coyote eats all of that and more, the more usually being carrion ripe enough to cause a buzzard to toss his waffles, attacking with a gusto so great it might turn a skunk trapper's stomach. Coyote have been known to hang around cattle fields to slurp up the milk-rich plops passed by the calves. And of course, the coyote will slurp up the calves also, if given a decent opportunity.

Had enough? OK, just so you know. I finish off the listing of coyote chow with a few in-offensives. Juniper berries, fruit from the prickly pear cactus, mesquite beans, manzanita berries. The list would be less long if I listed the things a coyote WOULD NOT eat. The coyote is a mammal owning a western weight of about thirty pounds for the male and maybe five or ten pounds less for the fat female. Exceptions occur. Gerry Blair once called and killed a half handful of coyote that hogged out within a grove of screwbean mesquite that averaged forty pounds; the coyote, not the beans. Hard hunter Tyler Higgins offed a carrion eating 'yote that scaled forty-three pounds.

Weight changes radically as the zip code changes. Obeying Bergstrom's Law (actually more of a constant) coyote to the north own bigger bodies and shorter legs (in relation to body size) as a heat conservation mechanism. Coyote in the Mideast and the far East own genes that permit super size. Locally called brush wolves, fully mature examples of these extra-large yodelers might weigh more than fifty pounds.

Predators as a class own uncommon intelligence. The coyote is near the top of the predator intelligence scale. Some are so smart they hunt the highway, patrolling two lane and four lane roads to collect the rabbit splats, and anything else that becomes mashed. The coyote has eyes that can discern a mouse at a hundred yards during a half moon night. His hearing is acute. The long nose is home to a bunch of sensors, causing the coyote to smell a piece of meat (alive or dead) at a quarter of a mile.

Color variation is common among coyote. Pups in a single litter might show radical color variation, but are not likely to. A coyote is commonly brown but may be roan, red, or silver. An ole timey trapper told me he once hooked a snow-white coyote. Maybe an albino? He says no. The critter did not display the pink eyes. The coyote commonly shows a black-tipped tail. Some I have collected have had white tipped tails. Such, it seems to me, occur in pockets, such suggesting a gene pool origin.

Prices paid for coyote fur vary according to fashion (demand) and amount of pelts available, as is the case with all fur. An extra large Montana Pale is usually at the top of the line. These big Northerns have a finely textured fur of a desirable silver gray color. The Southwestern grading is at the other end of the scale. The fur on this utility is usually blah brown, having a coarse texture to the under fur and an absence of guard hair. Size is generally small to peewee. Southwesterns are most commonly found in the Southwest (no surprise there), usually in one of the deserts. You want to hear something strange? Even in the habitat of the Southwest the pups of the year can be decent. These mostly grown teenagers have never shed. The hair is almost always finer and is almost always of a better color. Go figure.

Proper fur handling can cause a pelt to accrue beauty and value, demonstrated by John Spearman of Sutton, NE.

Many coyote are night hunters, just as about all land predators are. The coyote prey is most active then and hunting effort is likely to be rewarded. Such might not be critically important to the spring and summer 'yote, a time when groceries are generously available. Such can be the difference between life and death during a tough winter when coyote walk a thin line between survival and starvation. Having said that, it is also proper to say a hungry coyote will hunt night and day. And that same hungry coyote will eat what is most available. A coyote that hangs around populated areas is likely to visit garbage dumps, garbage cans, and even pet food pans containing the Purina or the table scraps. Those same coyote, when opportunity allows, will also eat the pet if that pet is the least bit smaller than Bruto the Rotweiller.

A short list of favored coyote foods appeared earlier in this chapter. Add to those ground nesting birds, large and small mammals, grasshoppers, snakes, lizards, watermelon, cantaloupe, vegetables and grass. Too much more to mention.

Southwestern coyote mate during late winter, usually during January and February. The litter is birthed about two months later (60-65 days). Litter size averages between five and ten. There are exceptions. A den found in Utah held 19 pups. A den found in Modoc County California held 14 pups.

The coyote den might be in a small natural cave, an enlarged badger hole, in a gap in a rock jumble, under an old building, or in a dugout den that extends to beneath a large boulder, maybe the roots of a tree. In the Southwest, where den sites are difficult to locate, the female coyote may dig a tunnel into the soft bank of a sand wash.

Pup care is a function of both male and female. The pair bonds for the season and likely bonds until one dies or loses dominance. The latter is most common. The female nurses the pups, supplying a rich milk. That mother's milk is supplemented by offerings of regurgitated food, mainly meat. The meat is offered whole as the pups age. When the young are able, they travel with the adults to learn hunting and survival skills. Those who do not learn well are not likely to survive.

The coyote family remains a unit throughout the summer. They do not always hunt as one pack, separating at times into hunting groups that keep

Coyote pups are fed a diet of mothers milk and regurgitated meat. (Duane Rubink Photo).

in contact through yips and howls. When the leaves turn in the fall, the unit will dissolve. Dispersal occurs. The fall dispersal can be a fine time to be a screamer. The teenage coyote, most owning limited hunting and survival skill, can be an easy target for the distress scream.

Mated coyote, as noted, remain together until one loses dominance or dies. The survivor howls to advertise for a new mate. The newlyweds defend the territory with the same vigor displayed by the oldweds. Most coyote respect territorial boundaries. Those that do not will be in for a fight. Some non-territorial coyote are allowed within to serve as a sort of a tolerated guest, most commonly young from a previous litter. These tolerated coyote will be constantly reminded of their low status. They will be nipped upon the hips by the terrirorials and must demonstrate their unworthiness constantly. This consists of a laying upon the back with tail between the legs, legs in the air, an avoidance of eye contact and a pitiful whining. When groceries become scarce the tolerated coyote will be attacked and forced to leave. Those that resist are killed.

Territorial boundaries are verified by howl points and scent posts. The home size varies as the kind of country varies, as food supply varies. A study of collared coyote in a Northern Arizona habitat showed a typical range of 8.1 square miles. The study also suggested the coyote within the territory would move seasonally, the winter and summer range being in different parts of the territory.

Game and Fish guys watched as a coyote killed this pronghorn fawn during the Anderson Mesa Study. (Don Neff Photo).

Coyote can answer eagerly at seasons' start but survivors smart up quickly.

Now might be a good time to comment on a point of coyote behavior. I have studied papers prepared by wildlife professionals and see where they write as though the coyote in their study area typify every coyote in the world, an error called extrapolation. One such publication stated the primary diet of the coyote was the jackrabbit; it further stated the coyote would not turn to other foods unless a serious shortage of jackrabbit existed. Such might be true in the study area (Idaho) where there exists (at times) tons of jackrabbit per square mile. Such is not true here in Arizona where we do not have enough jackrabbit to feed a small percentage of the coyote. The main prey of the coyote, in Northern Arizona, is the juniper berry during the winter, antelope and other big game fawn during the spring, and mice and voles during the summer. The coyote is like all other folks; many are individualists who modify their behavior to respond to the demands of habitat.

The coyote has a few friends, a few enemies, and a bunch of folks who ride the fence. I am in the latter group. I admire the critter for his ability to survive against serious threats. I consider the coyote to be a worthy adversary. I do not let that respect and admiration cloud good judgment when it comes time to control the coyote.

The coyote probably kills more big and small game than all other predators combined. This is mainly due to the number and nature of the critter. The Anderson Mesa Antelope Study (mentioned previously) showed a survival rate of about ten percent. What in hell does that mean? It means that only about ten percent of fawns born in the study area survived. Evidence suggested the coyote to be the dirty guy. Game and fish studies in a second area showed the coyote to be a major predator of the mule deer fawn. Biologists have estimated that half of the offspring of ground nesters like pheasant, quail, and grouse survive predation. The coyote seems to be constantly hungry. That coyote, mostly, is an opportunistic feeder, gorging, whether hungry or not, when opportunity allows. That is good news for us screamers. The coyote is likely to answer a scream even if not particularly hungry. As has been mentioned, the coyote is by nature a night feeder. Even so, the coyote will come to the call day or night, coming best at night, next best during the crepuscular periods of dawn and dusk, and least best during the day. The effect an approaching storm or a departing storm has on coyote appetite has been well covered in the chapter on weather. I see no reason to repeat all of that here, except to emphasize. Coyote often go on a feeding frenzy as a major storm approaches. Some will lay up during the worst of the storm to return to the hunt on the first clear day after the storm. Screaming at such a time can be dandy.

I am convinced the phase of the moon can influence coyote feeding habits. Tom Britt, a wildlife biologist and a regional manager for the Arizona Game & Fish Department (now retired), once participated in a night study of white-tailed deer populations in a Southern state. The researchers used spotlights to conduct the census. They made few sightings during the dark phases of the moon. They saw few deer, few rabbits, and few predators. Such knowledge can be helpful to those of us who hide in the brush to make a sound like a coyote's supper. A predator that does not hunt during the dark of the moon is likely to hunt the following day.

It is best to ignore frustration howlers. Continuing to call can attract another coyote, maybe even the howler.

Coyote prime at the start of winter, the precise priming dependent on weather, latitude and photosynthetic stimulation. The fur stays prime until the sun of spring causes a loss of prime and causes other obvious degradation. The first change noted is called rubbing. This is apparent on hips, showing about March. As weather warms the fur will thin and shed, causing further degradation. The hair of the back will curl (called singeing). The fur turns patchy and uneven. Any such degradation should cause the fur hunter to put away the screamers. Fur from such critters will not be salable.

Coyote come to the call in different ways. The response will be influenced by previous experience. A young coyote, one with virgin ears, will often come at full gallop, anxious to taste the rabbit. Multiple young will at times involve themselves in a desperate race, each hoping to be the first to claim the prize. I have had such come to five feet before deciding 200 pounds is a bit big for a rabbit. Others, older and wiser, will come at the sneak. A coyote that has hoped for rabbit but tasted hot lead loses much of his gusto for rabbit. That coyote might come but will do so the same way porcupines make love, very carefully.

The hunter who makes a minor mistake will likely lose this coyote. Take your shot at the first decent opportunity. Learn to read coyote body language so as to tell his thinking. A coyote that stops facing you is likely to come closer. A coyote that stops broadside is not likely to come on in. That coyote, when he moves, is likely to make a circle to taste the wind. A coyote that turns his tail to you, looks at you over his back, is a coyote about to leave.

The coyote I called from across a brushy canyon showed paranoid behavior. I watched the coyote come for a quarter of a mile. The country had been hard hit. It was obvious the customer was not coming to his first rodeo. The critter used every rock and every bush to make the sneak. It took him fifteen minutes to come to shooting range. He stopped each hundred feet or so to taste the wind to reconnoiter, finally stopping two hundred yards out. The hang-up was in high grass that covered all but the coyote head. I put the crosshairs on the grass, at a place where his chest should have been, and stroked. I missed, of course, and the coyote took thirty seconds to cover the quarter of a mile approach route. That coyote, I am convinced, will not trust a dying rabbit ever again.

Educated coyote will sometimes make a circle around the screaming in an effort to taste the wind, hoping to find a taste of rabbit. If that rabbit tastes like after-shave, the coyote is gone. Masking scent will sometimes fool these nose hunters. Take your shot at a circler at the first decent opportunity. Nothing really good is likely to be offered. Some educated coyote hang up a few hundred yards out to howl out insults. They will not often come an inch even when you beg. Some writers have speculated that the howling is an effort to warn other coyote. I do not believe that to be true. The coyote I have met have not cared scat about other coyote, seeing them as competitors and not as chums. Some

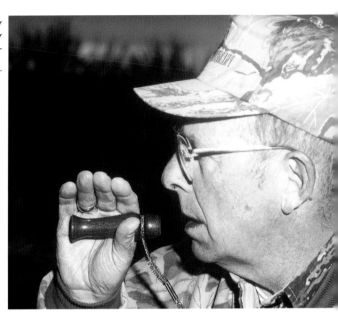

Continuing to call after a kill (or after a miss) can double the fur and double the fun. Bill Countess of Mancos, CO.

howl, I think, to voice a frustration. They want to come but are afraid to come. Experience and observation have caused me to consider a second hypothesis. The howler may be hung up because of a territorial boundary. He or she may be howling hoping to get a non-response from the territorial resident. The bottom line? A hung up coyote may howl because of a multiplicity of factors. Only the coyote knows precisely.

A hunter can do a number of things to respond to the frustration howler. The best course of action is to ignore the howler and continue with the call. I have called in other coyote while the howler complained. When you near the end of the setup, if you want to try for the howler, reduce the volume and the frequency of the calling. Then shut up. Sit tight and stay quiet for another ten minutes or so. Sometimes the howler will come at the sneak.

Sometimes I give the howler a taste of his own medicine, howling at him (or her), saying the same. That howling, at times, can cause the coyote to come on in. A pair of callers or a caller using a battery-powered caller can sometimes make a sneak on a howling coyote. Not often, but once in a while. If with a partner, have him or her stay at the setup to continue the call. Circle so as to approach the howler or howlers from the side. Take the shot at the first opportunity. If solo, leave the battery powered caller going, and then make the sneak, also from the side. I once snuck up on a coyote that was sneaking up on the rabbit (Gerry Blair). We met unexpectedly within a gap in the greasewood. MooseDick reacted a second or so before the coyote.

The squeezing of the rabbit was covered in the chapter on tubes and the chapter on battery-powered callers. I will say a bit more, however, on calls specific to the coyote. I prefer the rabbit or the jackrabbit distress scream for coyote. Those critters, through much of the coyote range, are a primary food source. Either of the two can be broadcast from the metal reed tube or from the plastic reed tube. I call to coyote in two general ways. One way is the short and choppy distress scream. Short duration screams with not a lot of pause between. The second screaming causes the screams to be longer, more of a moaning with a definite separation between screams, more typical of the deer family than the rabbit, but still hare-like. Which is better? Don't know. Each will work some of the time; neither will work all of the time.

I start the coyote screaming using moderate volume calls, beginning with a short series, maybe only ten seconds followed by a minute or so of silence. If that effort does not provoke response I start the hard sell. Full volume screams aimed at the coyote standing at the county line. I lengthen the series to twenty or thirty seconds, maybe more. Then follow with a minute or two of quiet.

A part of the screaming I do to coyote has a lot of rasp, a hoarseness reminiscent of some jackrabbit and all gray fox. Such, it seems to me, tells the coyote there is a substantial meal behind that scream, a meal worth walking the mile for. Electronic callers can be dandy for coyote. I mentioned a use or two in the chapter titled "Tough Calls." I say here that the gray fox distress tape is a good sound for coyote. So is the bird distress, the one sometimes called the Yellowhammer Woodpecker Distress and sometimes called the Flicker Distress. Heck Fahr, I have killed more than a few coyote using the canine pup distress,

The ability to change calling sounds, to sort through the tape or stick collection to find a sound that the critters love on that particular day, is the main asset of the battery powered caller. I generally let the tape run continuously when calling to coyote. I start the stand using moderate volume screams. After a couple of minutes of such I crank to full volume and sometimes hold the speaker high to turn it in a 360-degree circle, focusing the sound to all areas.

When tube calling, when I have a coyote in sight, I stay quiet. A critter moving your way is as good as it gets. Calling while he comes will not cause him to come faster. Calling then might cause the critter to become suspicious. At the least, calling while a critter comes will provide that critter with a one hundred percent lock on your hideout. Perception is likely.

I sometimes flutter my lips as I blow the tube and flutter my hands at tube end to provoke a tremulous varying to the screaming. Such works particularly well on coyote. I almost always assess the potential of the calling stand before starting the music. I check for vision and shooting lanes. I check for obscurements. I check out ghosts, boogers that might be critter-like at some point into the call. A coyote coming to the call can be easy to see if that coyote comes from the front and comes at the run. When shotgun hunting I let the critter come to sure-kill range, shoulder, sight and shoot. The critter will be on the move but that does not matter to MooseDick. When rifle hunting I stop the coyote when he is fifty yards or so out, knowing that a too close coyote can be difficult to hit with a rifle. How do I stop that coyote? I lip squeak (Kiss of Death), growl or cuss. About any new sound will cause the coyote to pause to make a reconnoiter. The pause will not last forever. Before making the announcement, have your gun at the shoulder, ready to shoot.

I have said it is proper to stay on the stand for at least 15 minutes when calling to coyote. Honesty causes me to say I do not always do so. There are times, usually in brushy country, when I abandon a stand after ten minutes, figuring any coyote in hearing has had enough time to show. Some stands, those where I receive encouragement, might have me staying considerably longer. There is no hard and fast rule on stand length, for coyote or any other critter. Evaluate each stand to decide what is right.

Calling pressure will almost always cause critter response to slow. Late in the calling season I almost always stay longer on the stand. Some screamers abandon a stand as soon as they take a shot. Hit or miss, they figure, it is time to move on. Those screamers are making a big time mistake. The sound of a shot does not always cause a customer to spook. I am not talking about coyote in sight, those will almost always spook. I write of critters that may be on the way but out of sight. The bang, to them, might sound like thunder or sound like the noise produced when a jet breaks the sound barrier. I always continue the call after a kill or a miss. That effort is rewarded, much of the time, by the showing of a second customer. I illustrate.

George and I hunted a miserably cold dawn a week after Christmas. A fog bank reduced visibility to about a hundred feet. The wet air diffused the sound, making the screams delicious, coming from everywhere and nowhere. A pair of shadowy figures half-materialized in the fog. One came and the second disappeared back into the fog. The one plodded close and George Oakey placed a hundred grainer through his ribs. I continued the screaming. A minute or so later a second coyote came from hard right, at the gallop. I dumped him at thirty yards. Continuing the call had doubled our pleasure and doubled our fur.

I could tell stories of second kills until you would cry for mercy. I will not. Be convinced, however, that all critters, especially the coyote, will continue to come after a shot. A good hunter stays alert as he abandons the setup. I have sighted several coyote on the walk back to the truck. On one hunt I made it to the truck and spotted a big silver standing two hundred yards out. I exited the truck, as law requires, and caused the coyote to attempt escape at the gallop. Even though offhand shots at two-hundred-yard galloping coyote are not my specialty, I got lucky. Staying alert added to the fur collection.

Running coyote are easily missed, most often because of insufficient lead. A coyote that is serious about speed can cover ground at about thirty miles an hour. That translates to 43 feet per second. A bullet having a muzzle velocity of 3,500 FPS will take about a fifth of a second to reach a two-hundred-yard coyote. That coyote can cover about eight feet during that time. Too much lead? Not in my book.

Where you place the bullet will affect kill and affect pelt damage. I aim for the ribs, behind the shoulder and midway between back and brisket, when shooting at broadside coyote. A properly loaded round will enter, causing a .224 (with the .22-250) diameter entry hole. The bullet that behaves will explode in the necessaries. There will not be an exit wound.

Coyote that face the gun offer a reduced target. I aim for the center of the chest, below the joining of the neck to the body. Again, the .224 entry and no exit. When aiming at a running coyote, tough shots for me, I aim at the part of the coyote easiest to hit. I would rather have a damaged pelt, I figure, than have no pelt at all. Calling the roads can be a decent way to take coyote. I like road calling particularly well after a snow. Tracks are fresh and indicate coyote presence and movement. Parking to find a setup to call to the coyote that made the tracks always improves response. The same technique, sort of, can be used after a rain or even during dry weather when dust is present. I look for scat and fresh tracks.

Sighting a coyote while driving can be exciting. There is always the tendency to jam on the brakes and light into that sucker as he heads for Chicago. Trouble is, much of the time such is illegal. And too, at least for me, seldom productive. It is better, I think, to ignore the coyote, drive out of sight and out of sound, park, then make the setup and the scream. That coyote, much of the time, will come as though you had a rope around his neck.

The coyote is the main screaming target through the West and the Southwest, even in some parts of the Midwest and the East. He is a worthy opponent. Here's to him (gulp). Long may he come to our screaming.

chapter 36

Calling Gray Fox

Every gray fox I have met has had the heart of a lion. All who earn a look into the heart of this small wild dog must admire the grit within. When I set up to scream at the gray, on a moonless midnight, in that crepuscular period the gray loves so well, or even at precisely noon thirty, I often consider the nature of the gray and thank the fox maker. Thanks for what? Thanks, buddy, for not making that little sumbitch as big as a St. Bernard.

The gray fox nature causes him to be a dandy target for the scream. Most come to the scream with an enthusiasm that staggers the karma. Nearly all I have called have responded at the run (or at least at the trot) and have come with eyes alert, ears erect, and tail at attention. Ahhh, what a sight. The gray that Chuck and I Canon-ed along a desert wash is a good example.

Chuck Spearman, as anyone with scents knows, was once publisher of *Trapper & Predator Caller* magazine, a friend and a predator-calling fanatic. Chuck and I had purchased a pair of toys, identical Canon EOS-620 Auto Focus Auto Wind 35mm cameras. And each of those smart boxes carried a dandy 300 mm telephoto lens. We headed for the winter desert, hoping to find fun. We set up within a moderately big desert dry wash, the kind that runs like a river when it rains but stays as dry as a popcorn fart the rest of the time. The banks were lined with mesquite and blue Palo Verde, and there was greasewood beyond that. Good country for critters.

As we usually do when calling to the camera, we set the Johnny Stewart MS-512 battery-powered cassette caller thirty feet out, hit the go button, and got a little bit excited as the tape sent out damn fine recordings of a cottontail rabbit distress scream. The gray came early into the call, maybe no more than a minute or two. The critter was about as handsome as a December fox gets. A lush winter coat and a particularly fine tail, the back fur being the typical salt and pepper with a rim of orange on the chest and belly, and then, stark white. The salt and pepper tail carried the typical black stripe. The texture of the fur was exceedingly fine; the kind buyers call the western silky.

The fox came on Chuck's side of the stand-up (we were erect to permit visibility), placing Chuck's big body between the fox and my own big body. No opportunity for me to photograph. I relaxed to watch. Chuck rocked and rolled with his autofocus. The gray ran close to the bush hiding the caller, circled a time or two, and wheeled to whirl away, but didn't. He paused 30 feet out, looked longingly at the sound (is such possible?) and returned at the charge. That maneuver was repeated and repeated again, the repeats continuing for the fifteen minutes of the screaming. The fox watched forlornly as Chuck and I gathered the junk to leave, figuring, I guess, we were running off with his rabbit. The fox did not follow us to the truck. Knowing gray fox as I do, I would not have been surprised if it had. That aggressive behavior might have surprised someone who does not understand the gray. Some, knowing the gray to be the little guy within the woods, knowing the gray is not at the top of the food chain, knowing the gray must spend a good deal of time worrying (WORST NIGHTMARE: A close encounter of the coyote, bobcat, or cougar kind), those might presume the gray to be a bit more low key. Not true. The gray doesn't give a scat about all of that. A screaming, to the gray, means there is a rabbit around somewhere, and the gray is twitching to get that rabbit.

Even though the gray is the common fox of the West and the somewhat common fox of the Midwest and the East, he is not commonly understood. A predator screamer needs extraordinary knowledge if he or she is to gain a full measure of fun from this ordinary critter.

The gray fox is common to most of the continental United States and is particularly plentiful in the Desert Southwest, a place where a generous prey base, little critters like cottontails, wood rats, 'roo rats and all such, causes the gray to live long and prosper. Gray fox are found in good numbers south of the border, down in Old Mexico. You will not find many gray (maybe none) in the high plains states, the northern Rockies, the northern parts of the Great Basin Desert, and the coastal rain forests found within Washington and Oregon.

Some gray fox range overlaps the range of the red fox. The shared habitat causes few problems. The gray follows his nature and works the brush. The red follows his nature and works the fields. As mentioned, the gray does dandy in the Southwest. The little critter thrives within the chaparral midlands and is equally at home in the high and low desert. I have screamed in grays within the ponderosa pine belt, at an elevation of eight and nine thousand feet.

I look for gray fox in rough country interrupted by many small canyons, many of them brush choked. The gray needs that kind of country to make his hunt. Unlike some members of the dog family this fox makes his living by stalking prey to get close, and then pouncing, cat-like. The presence of trees causes such habitat to be even more desirable. The gray is the only fox that is a tree climber. The gray climbs a tree often, not just when he HAS to, but when he WANTS to. Again, cat-like.

The gray also does well within boulder jumbles, within thick oak brush and manzanita, the kind the cowboys call chaparral. The gray, being nimble, can use such to stay somewhat safe. The cat-like nature of the gray has caused some to consider him to be more cat than dog. An old time trapper (aren't they all?) shared my camp one winter. During one campfire we huddled together

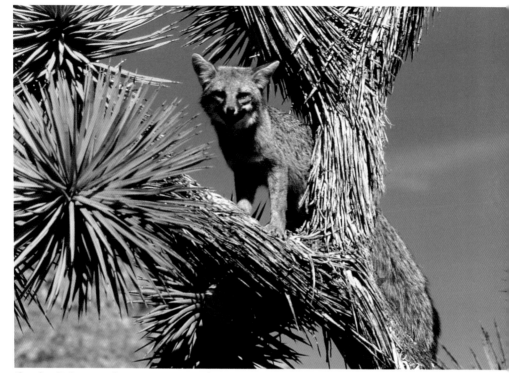

Gray fox climb trees and even cactus to stay safe, a valuable talent within coyote country.

and began philosophical discussions. "The gray fox," Stanley Pike said with a great deal of conviction, "is not a fox at all. That critter is a cat. Look at the way he hunts. Look at the retractable claws. Look at the gray's ability to climb a tree." I disagreed mildly, using logic. Stan finally compromised, saying he now considered the gray to be a cross between a dog and a cat.

Fox fur price is determined by fashion trends and by the amount of fox fur available to the trade. The fur of the gray fox, actually the hair, is not as fine or full as the fur of the red fox. Even so, the market for gray fox fur stays strong much of the time. I have sold collections of grays for a $60.00 average and I have sold collections for an $18.00 average.

The average gray will be about a yard long from nose tip to tail tip. A third of that length will be the bushy tail. Large adult fox will weigh about ten pounds, maybe more. Eastern grays, much of the time, are larger than Western grays. Gray fox fur is salt and pepper gray on the top of the back and on the tail. The under-fur is buff. The fur turns a red brown, actually an orange, on parts of the throat, the chest, and the belly. Other parts of those areas turn to snow white. The tail is decorated with a stripe of black that extends from hips to tail tip. That tail tip is characteristically black. Even so, I have called and killed a few grays that showed a white-tipped tail.

The gray fox is mainly nocturnal, just as are other land predators. Even though that is true, the gray is easily called during daylight, particularly during the crepuscular periods following daybreak and preceding dark. The secretive nature of the gray causes him to be seldom seen. Few non-hunters come across grays causing many of those to be convinced the gray is in short supply. Campers and others who may be about at night have likely heard the barking and yapping of the gray and failed to recognize the source.

Gray fox are territorial. The home range is determined by the lay of the land and by prey density. The gray fox territory may extend to a few square miles in stingy country. What does the gray mainly eat? Being omnivorous (eating both meat and vegetable) the gray eats what is available to eat. Prey animals include the cottontail rabbit, and at times, a jackrabbit that may be nearly as big as the gray. They also take birds, ground squirrels, mice, rats, bugs, lizards, and some snakes. Along waterways the gray will work the shore to find crawfish and frogs. Preferred fruits are juniper and manzanita berries, all other berries, and the fruits of most cacti.

Where coyote and gray fox range overlap, the coyote can be an important gray fox predator. So can the bobcat and the cougar. So are screamers like Gerry Blair, Larry 0. Gates, Gordo Krahn, and all such.

The gray fox is monestrous, coming into season during January and February. Like other dogs, the pups are born a couple of months later. Litters average four or five. The pups are born fully furred and blind. The pups are attended by both male and female, the two more or less bonding for the healthy life of each.

The gray fox den might be located in an abandoned badger den, in a dugout beneath a brush pile, in one of the openings of a rock jumble, or in a natural cave. Maybe an abandoned mine tunnel. About any place the fox can find privacy and protection. The pups stay in the den until about five weeks old. Short trips to the area just outside the den begin. Those forays continue until the pups are ready to hunt. By mid-summer all are trotting along with male and female to learn the hunting skills needed to survive on their own. If it is a poor year for groceries, the young fox will be forced to leave the territory when cold weather comes. Those that leave during those tough times, particularly those having poor survival skills, are not likely to live long. When food is plentiful the litter may stay within the territory to share with Mom and Pop.

Fox are mostly monogamous. The males stay with the females to help raise the offspring. I have called fox pairs during the fall and the winter, non-breeding times, and am convinced the two bond somewhat permanently.

As noted, fox hunt mainly at night. A hungry fox throws away the clock, however, and may hunt both day and night. If your state allows night calling you will find the gray responds best during the dark. You will call more fox and will find that those fox come close to the screams.

The vixen gray becomes receptive during March and April and delivers a couple of months later.

Where night hunting is not allowed screamers will have the best luck calling crepuscular, an hour or so after first light and an hour or so before last light. The fox seem to be on their feet and thinking of food during those times. Do not give up on daytime fox. They can be called then but do not often come as enthusiastically and might not make the close approach. My home state (Arizona) does not permit night hunting. I can't count the number of grays I have called during dead daylight. I know it has been one hell of a lot, maybe more.

I look for fox in brushy basins, canyons, and in mesquite-lined (yep, the gray eats mesquite beans) washes. I look for grays about any place there is an adequate prey base or an adequate supply of fruits and berries.

The gray fox must also have cover. The best food supply in the world will not sustain the gray if he does not have the kind of country needed to keep his butt safe from cousin coyote and from the other named fox lovers. The fox does not have the legs or the lungs to run a long distance and must rely on his ability to hide, maneuver, and climb.

Even so, some fox will be found in country that looks to be open. Look at that country close and you will discover fox sanctuaries, patches of brush, clusters of trees, or rocky outcrops. Gray fox love the desert. You want the truth? The desert habitat is the kind of country where gray fox (and their little cousin the Kit) do best. Cactus offers sweet fruits and offers maneuvering room to escape the less agile coyote. That same desert is home to a plenitude of tasty little rodents. Brush is almost always present. Look to the north side of hills and look within drainages. Where in hell is all of this desert and where can you get your share? Look to the southwest within the U.S. Look to parts of Southern California. Look to Nevada. Look to Arizona and look to Texas, parts of New Mexico. Look to Old Mexico. Find the desert and you will find the Western gray fox.

Eastern and Midwestern screamers are not likely to find much in the way of desert. They need to look within woodlands that border fields and look within brush-choked drainages that traverse fields. Fence lines graced by weeds and brush can be good. So can overgrown fallow fields, places where rodent density is high.

Those who scream to the east of the big rivers will find the gray to be a lot like the red and the coyote in one respect. Daytime activity can cause the gray to turn nocturnal. Call the gray during the dark if you can. The grays I have met have not been fussy about the kind of song I sing. I have called grays using open reed calls such as the TallyHo, the Crit'RCall, the Lohman C-280 and other such. I have also called grays using metal-reed calls like the Johnny Stewart PC-1 and the old Weems WildCall. About any metal reed tube will do as well. Those metal reeds, as has been mentioned, are likely to freeze during really cold weather. One of the plastic reed calls is best then.

I have also called more than a few gray fox by playing the yellow hammer woodpecker distress or the cottontail rabbit distress through a battery powered caller. I play at moderate volume and shorten the distance between setups to compensate. The gray (and any red within the area) seems to feel less threatened.

Mike Mell, a licensed guide and dandy predator caller, sucks at a piece of grass or a section of leaf to produce a sound gray fox find delightful. Mike offers a tip, "Screamers should keep on calling after they call and shoot a fox. Many times a year I call a second fox after I have called and killed the first. On one stand I called four fox and killed three of the four." Other tips follow.

Do not avoid legal hunting areas that might be close to towns, villages and houses. If you can obtain the proper permission and can hunt there safely, such areas can hold significant fox populations and are often overlooked by other hunters. When night hunting, secure permission ahead of time, midnight is a poor time to ask. Scout night calling areas during the day to learn the lay of the land, so you can select the setup that offers the most advantage. Use that day scout to identify potential shooting hazards, some such not readily apparent at night.

Gray fox can be killed with about any caliber of centerfire rifle, most shotguns and some rimfires. Options are reduced if you hope to sell or save the fur. The fox is a small-bodied critter (obviously so when you see him naked), not much bigger than a black-tailed jackrabbit. The fox frame, being fragile, will not tolerate too much trauma. My thoughts on good, bad and ugly fox guns follow.

I give the .22 rimfire an ugly rating as a fox gun. I have shot gray fox with the rimfire, using the .22 Long Rifle Hollow Point and using the Long Rifle Hollow Point in one of the souped up configurations, and have had inconsistent results. A few of the fox drop graveyard dead. Other fox have been inconsiderate, maybe going down, getting up, and running wobble legged to the nearest hole. They likely die but die slowly. I am thinking we owe a quick and humane death. I do not recommend the .22 rimfire as a fox gun.

I hold an improved opinion on the .22 Winchester Rim Fire Magnum (WRFM). I have shot more than a few grays with such and have had generally good luck out to about 100 yards or so. My favorite in that caliber is the Model 700 H&R Auto-Loader. That dandy gun was marketed between 1977-1985, offered with a five shot clip but with a ten shot clip available as an option. Those who crave to have one might like to know used models are available at moderate price. Look for a publication called *Gun Digest*, published by Krause Publications, 700 East State Street, Iola, WI 54990.

What makes the WRFM better? Velocity. The 40-grain pill leaves the muzzle at about 2000 FPS and maintains good velocity and good punch out to about 100 yards.

The occasional bobcat that comes to the fox call can be offed handily at about that range. Customers of the coyote kind, sad to say, are too much critter for the WRFM, particularly when that coyote critter is one of the big brush wolves that hang to the east of the big rivers. I top the WRFM with a big guy scope, one of the one-inch models recommended for the centerfires. I have fitted the gun with a sling also. I sometimes carry a lot of junk to a screaming and need all of the hands I can find.

Some of the fast shooting .224 centerfires will do a decent job on fox if bullet and powder cooperate to produce a medium fast loading, pushing a non-explosive bullet. Legendary caller Murry Burnham uses a .222 loading so slow it has been passed by VW Bugs on upgrades. Murry figures that his slow loading is good out to about 100 yards. That somewhat short range is okay with Murry. Much of his fox calling takes place at night. Fox come so close you can smell the rabbit on their breath.

I like the .22 Hornet as a fox gun. Ruger modified their Model 77/22 WRFM to accept the Hornet cartridge during 1994. This clip fed bolt action is dandy for little critters like the fox, even some critters that are substantially larger.

How about shooting a Full Metal Jacketed (FMJ) bullet at fox? Maybe yes and maybe no. An FMJ loaded hot will kill the fox deader than need be. Reloaders can slow the FMJ down to achieve a decent fox load. Trouble is, slowing the bullet down takes away long-range muscle.

In the right kind of country the shotgun can be dandy for fox. Stay away from somewhat open country where the fox (or any other customer) can reconnoiter from a rock a hundred yards out. Stick to tight country where the critters must come closer to get a look at the rabbit. The shotgun gets on the critter fast and throws lot of lead. The famed Morton Burnham (Murry's dad) used a shotgun almost exclusively. His choice of birdshot instead of BBs was logical for the kind of country he hunted. I prefer the BBs. Even though such might not be needed on fox, they sure come in handy when a coyote volunteers. I recommend one of the three-inch twelves and have a preference for the auto loaders. The ten-gauge, for those who have the shoulder for it, also does well.

Do not give up on shotgunning fox if your bird gun happens to be a twelve-gauge chambered for the 2-3/4" chamber. Range is reduced a bit. Shooting the so called "Standard Magnum" loads in copper plated BBs, the gun will rug out a fox out to about 30 yards. Lighter gauges do less well but can do the job if the shooter stays shot selective.

There is no such gun as the "best" fox gun. Every choice can be a trade-off. The screamer should evaluate the kind of country he or she calls most of the time, and make a guess as to which gun will do the best job there, most of the time.

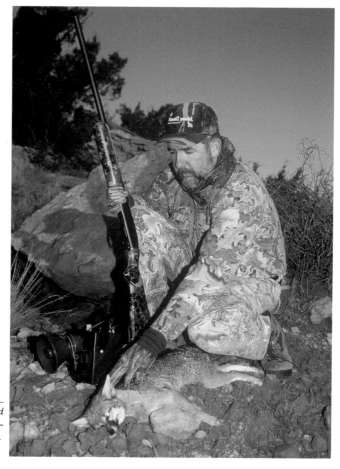

Texas hunters like Gerald Stewart call gray fox regularly. (Gordy Krahn Photo).

246

chapter 37

Calling Lion

The mountain lion is not often seen to the east of the Missouri and Mississippi rivers. Those Midwestern, Mideastern, and eastern states having remnant populations almost always prohibit the hunting or the killing of those few lion hardy enough to exist in habitat degraded (from the lion view) by population and ruralization. The scarcity of lion groceries, namely the white-tailed deer during the somewhat recent past, caused further difficulty. Even though enlightened game management has restored the whitetail in nearly all of the original range, the lion has not returned.

The western population of mountain lion in the eleven western states that is the main current range has stayed constant, and in some cases that population has prospered. A lion specialist for the Arizona Game & Fish Department has estimated a population of 2,000 adult lion in that state. That is a lot of lion. That many lion can and do eat a significant number of deer, elk, and livestock including cattle that roam to graze the Arizona wild country contained in mostly public lands: National Forest lands, Bureau of Land Management (BLM) lands, and State Trust lands. The Arizona biologist has conducted studies that suggest an adult lion must make a major kill every eight days: a deer, an elk, a cow, or less frequently, a sheep or goat. It does not require much in the way of mathematical talent to discover that each of those 2,000 adult lion in the state kills a big bodied animal (usually a deer) fifty times each year.

Under certain circumstances a small population of lion, or even a single lion, can seriously impact, and sometimes extirpate, pockets of game animals. The $30,000.00 lion was one such. The $30,000.00 (1985 dollars) lion probably thought he had died and gone to heaven when the Arizona Game & Fish Department transplanted the 22 desert bighorn sheep into the Tres Alamos (Three Cottonwoods) Range (Central Arizona) at an estimated cost of $2,000.00 per sheep. Before the transplant the big tom ranged the Tres Alamos, the Harcuvar Range, and, most likely, the Harquahala Range, looking for the scattered mule deer that hung out on the mountains, in the canyons, and on the desert floor. The deer diet was supplemented, when opportunity permitted, with javelina, a critter common to all of that range. The transplant changed all of that. Dropping a herd of sheep into a water poor area caused

A solitary tom camped near a desert water hole and feasted on a desert bighorn sheep transplant.

those sheep to cluster around one of the few sources of constant water, a trick tank in one of the Tres Alamos drainages. It did not take the lion long to learn about his new neighbors. Eight of the 22 sheep carried radio collars containing a mortality feature-if the sheep did not move his or her head for an hour or two, that lack of movement would cause the collar to say so.

Ewe #981 was the first collared sheep to bite the dust. An investigative, team found the remains of the carcass in a dense thicket of Palo Verde, prickly pear cacti, and galleta grass. The carcass had been moved and covered at least two times, as a lion is likely to do with one. Tooth punctures in the hide that had covered the throat showed the lion was an adult.

More bad news followed. All of the collared sheep and most of the uncollared sheep went to feed the lion. The sheep transplant failed, because of one or two hungry lions. Why didn't the Game and Fish guys get rid of the lion or lions so that the sheep would have the opportunity to establish? Don't know. Probably because it was not politically correct to do so.

Congress, Arizona, hunter and trapper Larry O. Gates, a Beastmaster, had no such hesitation. While in the Tres Alamos to check traps on a fox and bobcat line, Larry sighted one of the remaining sheep, maybe the only remaining sheep, a young ram. The next day, checking traps again as Arizona law required, Larry found fresh sheep tracks that showed the sheep was on the run. Fresh mountain lion tracks were atop the sheep tracks. A skilled predator caller, Larry set up to make a series of calls in the area, blowing an open reed model called the TallyHo.

Seconds into the second stand a small herd of desert mule deer broke and ran from a brushy wash. Twenty minutes later Larry sighted a flash of fur, maybe one of the mule deer sneaking back for a look. More calling caused the critter to come somewhat close, but always in the brush so that identification was difficult. Larry called for ten minutes more, decided that thirty minutes was enough, and prepared to move on. Before doing so, however, he made a final scan. The lion stood in the shade of a mesquite eighty yards out. The Tres Alamos tom weighed 132 pounds on certified scales, mighty big for a desert lion.

The nocturnal nature of the mountain lion, its tendency to travel long patterns, and the beast's secretive nature cause the lion to be seldom seen and poorly perceived. Lion country can be about any kind of country. The Arizona low desert is home to a subspecies humorously called the Yuma Puma. That same state has catamounts (from the Mexican Gato del Monte, or cat of the mountain) roaming in the state's highest mountain ranges, those having elevations that approach 14,000 feet.

A favored lion habitat is the transition woodlands, a country chopped by tough canyons and covered with scrub oak, Gambels Oak, Turbinella Oak, manzanita and other brushes, the kind the cowboys call chaparral. Such country offers groceries to mule deer and whitetail, both lion edibles. The ground cover is made to order for lion hunting technique, a technique that has the lion sneaking close to the prey, and when close enough, the blinding burst of speed to make the assault.

Felis concolor is Latin for cat of the same color. That color, almost always, is a light brown, about the color of tanned leather. The adult lion will measure about five feet from nose to the rear of the hips. The slender tail will extend for another three feet. Fully-grown lions weigh from eighty to about two-hundred pounds. The adult male is almost always larger than the adult female.

Lion kittens can be born at any time of the year but are most likely to be born during late spring or early summer, coinciding with the birthing of prey animals like deer and elk. The kittens are spotted for the first few months of life. The birthing, feeding, and protection of the kittens is strictly a female function. Most of the present population of mountain lion is in the western United States, all of Mexico, and parts of Canada. Other states have minor populations with some eastern and southern states reporting increased sightings. It is not known if populations are actually on the increase. The increased sightings might be because of a more sophisticated census.

Western lion seem to prefer rimrock country in the Transition Life Zone, characterized by pinion/juniper woodlands, land interrupted by steep canyons and rocky rims. The main food of the lion is the deer; most often the big bodied mule deer of the West. Many populations of such deer are migratory, staying high during the summer and then retreating to lower elevation ahead of winter snows. The lion, almost always, follows.

A biologist for the Arizona Game Department has estimated an adult lion will make a kill each eight days and that kill is most often a deer. If deer are not plentiful the kill may be an elk, a feral burro, a bighorn sheep, or livestock. Cattle depredation seems to be greatest in the states of Arizona, New Mexico and Texas, most often in areas where calves are born in lion habitat. Stock killing increases when deer densities are low.

Blind calling to mountain lion, that is, setting out to call lion habitat indiscriminately, is not likely to produce a lot of action. The wide-ranging habits of the lion and the low lion density can cooperate to cause it to be unlikely a lion will be near enough to hear the screaming. Many of the lion I have called have come while I was screaming to other ears, most often coyote or bobcat. The lions that came to a screaming in the Kinnikinik Indian Ruins are typical.

It was late in the season to be calling for fur. Under ordinary circumstances I would not be perched atop the rubble of this ancient Indian village playing

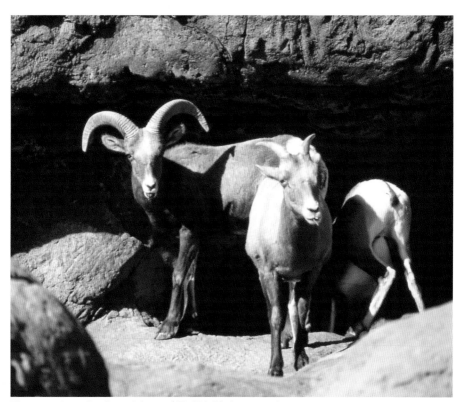

The mutton loving lion hogged down a $30,000.00 sheep transplant.

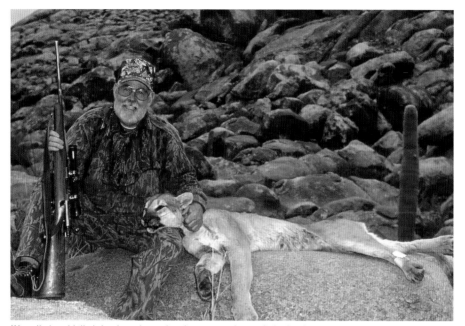
We called and killed the sheep loving lion but was too late to help the sheep.

the "Dying Rabbit Blues" to a pair of game biologists. I was there because of coyote predation of antelope, a predation that threatened the existence of an historic antelope herd. Knowing that the antelope were due to drop their twin fawns soon, and knowing that gangs of hungry coyote would go on the hunt almost immediately, we were there to remove some of the antelope eaters from the habitat.

The ruin stand was the third screaming made that morning. The first two were duds. Not so much as a raven. Knowing the target was coyote and that fifteen minutes can be plenty of time to allow a coyote to respond, I had terminated both screamings at about that time. The ruin call took place at the junction of two major drainages. Canyons. Kinnikinick and Grapevine. Each of them brush choked and rimmed by pinion pine and juniper. PJ in forest service language. The kind of country favored by lion succulents such as mule deer and Rocky Mountain elk.

I slobbered into the screaming with enthusiasm, ready for action. The two Game and Fish guys were also ready. Ten minutes into the call I saw movement sixty yards out. Thinking it might be a tawny coyote I squared to the flash of fur, shouldered the .22-250 and readied myself for some wet work. Imagine my surprise when the small x of the duplex six centered on a lion head. I moved the crosshairs down to touch the lion throat and begin the squeeze that would cause the three-pound trigger on the Ruger 77 to release the sear. Halfway there I paused to wonder if my wallet contained a lion tag.

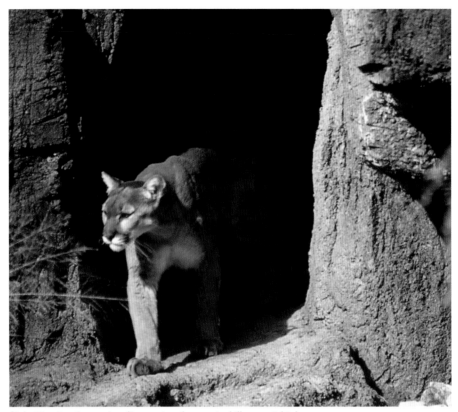
Biologists estimate a mature lion must make a major kill every eight days.

Knowing it was a poor time to gamble, having two Game and Fish guys sitting near, I released the pressure on the trigger, unshouldered the gun, and made a search of the wallet. No tag. All of this time the lion stayed still and stayed interested. Finally, whispering hoarsely, I asked Don and Norm if they might have a lion tag. Neither did. We let that lion walk and let another lion walk that came up to the rear of Don, maybe fifteen feet close. Damn. Calling a double on lion and not a two-dollar tag among the three of us. Two days later, the rancher who leased grazing rights to the area found a cow elk and calf killed and partially eaten by a pair of lions.

Elk are a common prey of the mountain lion in areas where range overlaps. The target, much of the time, is a cow or a calf. Mature bulls are oversize and can be more than just a mouthful. The same is not true of deer. Radio transmitting collars and tracking devices have caused biologists to discount the fallacy that the lion takes only the old and the sick. Lions, studies suggest, take the deer that is most easily killed. Probably pregnant does during the spring, fawns during the summer, and mature bucks during the rut, when a swollen neck and swollen testicles cause the breeding buck to become careless. Do lion also kill the old and the sick? Sure they do. The lion is an equal opportunity killer.

As mentioned, the lion grabs his groceries using a technique that sees cooperation between sneak and run. A hungry lion stays alert as he or she patrols the territory. When a prey animal is sighted, the lion begins a slow and stealthy stalk. If the intended is a mule deer or a white-tailed deer, as it often is, the lion will advance when the deer's head is down. When the head is up the lion will turn to stone, at times pausing in midstride. The head goes down and the lion sneaks. When the lion is close enough, and the lion almost always knows, he turns to a blurred streak of tawny lightning, making a leap that puts him atop the deer's back. Razor sharp claws dig into the shoulders. Massive jaw muscles cause the substantial canine teeth to bite through neck muscles to search for the vertebrae. Small deer go to the ground almost immediately. Large deer, small elk, and livestock almost always make a run for it, hoping to end the deadly embrace. That effort is seldom successful.

The lion will eat his fill of the fresh kill and cover the leftovers with leaves and sticks, maybe snow or dirt-whatever is available. That lion will return to the kill when his appetite alarm sounds once again. The remains will be dragged to a somewhat clean place and the lion will feed, covering the carcass when through. When the weather is cold, keeping the meat somewhat fresh, the lion may feed from a carcass for as long as two weeks. One lion, observed during an Idaho study, fed from the carcass of an elk for nineteen days.

This aspect of the lion nature can cause a benefit to the predator caller. Screamers who find an active kill, those who set up to make a series of screamings in the area, have an excellent chance at success.

Adult male lion are loners. Mature toms get together with the ladies when it comes time to shake the sugar tree, but leave abruptly when the fun and games end. The mating might continue for several days and is almost always accomplished to the tune of much moaning, groaning, snarling, growling, and caterwauling. The female selects a den site located in any natural shelter, perhaps a cave or the overhang of a rim. A pregnant female may or may not use that same sanctuary when it comes time to deliver another litter but will usually return to the same general area. The female delivers a litter only once each two or three years. That litter can come at any time of the year but is most often delivered during the summer, a time when the young of prey ungulates offer easy hunting.

The litter of cubs, averaging three, is totally dependent on the female for the first months of life and need total protection, even from the mature tom who may have sired them. Male mountain lion, when opportunity allows, will kill and eat the cubs. That loss can cause the female to return to estrus and the male has one more chance to shake the sugar tree. The cubs stay somewhat dependent for the first year of life. The Parissawampits Lady ran with a female offspring that was nearly two years old and was about as big as Momma. How do I know that? Hell, I was there. It happened this way.

The radio-collared adult female lion ran a rough piece of real estate called Parissawampits Canyon, a brush choked gash that began atop the North Kaibab Plateau and fed off into the dismal depths below the North Rim of the Grand Canyon. The batteries of the radio collar at her neck began to weaken and it was time for recapture and recollar, a function most often accomplished using a pack of precisely trained hounds. Trouble was the Lady ran country too rough for the hounds, or at least too rough for the hunters to follow. I was asked to help, asked to make a screaming that would cause the Lady to come out of her wilderness sanctuary.

I did and she did. The game guy sitting beside me during the screaming held an antenna that monitored movement. The lady came to about two hundred yards, out of sight in the brush, and that was close enough. Harley used the radio to call in the hounds.

The chase was short but exciting. A lion was treed in less than a mile. Trouble was, the lion was not The Lady. The lion halfway up the 150-foot-tall ponderosa pine was an eighteen-month-old uncollared female, probably the nearly adult offspring of The Lady. What did we do? What could we do? We used a modified Thompson Contender to shoot a dart into that ponderosa

Gerry Blair screamed the Parrisawampits lion close to recharge her batteries.

Lion toilets can be obvious or discrete, dependent upon the persona of the pooper.

pussy, climbed to her, attached a rope, and lowered her gently to the ground. A radio collar fitted with a two-year supply of batteries was attached to HER neck. And then back into the mystery of her territory in Parissawampits Canyon.

All lion are motivated to be territorial. Adult lion who have their own territory are at the top of the pecking order. Those who patrol and defend a territory that offers the most to the lion survival are the best of the best. Territorial lion adapt to the nature of their territory. Lion in the Spider Ranch Study (chaparral of west-central Arizona) showed little variation between summer and winter range. Lion in a North Kaibab Study (at considerably higher elevation) showed a preference for summer and winter territories that were some distance apart. The cause, most likely, was due to the migratory nature of the mule deer that is the lion's main source of groceries on the Kaibab.

Lion territory can vary as the sex of the lion and the wealth of the territory varies. Female lion on the Spider Ranch had home areas that varied from ten to almost seventy square miles. Adult toms in the same area had home areas that averaged fifty-nine square miles. Studies in northern states have established home areas much larger.

Lion sign is most often discreet, that is, not easily discovered during a casual investigation. Those who have learned to look, however, will find ample evidence of lion wanderings. The sign most often seen is an oversize cat track in dust, mud, or snow. Tracks left by large dogs can somewhat resemble lion tracks, at least in size. A close inspection will make positive identification possible. The heel pad of the lion is like the heel pad of all cats, that is, bi-lobed at the front and tri-lobed at the rear. (See sketch page 186.) Dog tracks show a heel pad characteristic of the dog family, triangular in shape, coming to a point at the front, and bi-lobed at the rear. The tracks left by dogs almost always show toenail marks; tracks left by lion seldom do. Finally, the lion is a most efficient traveler. Unless pursued or on the chase for groceries, the lion does not move at more than a deliberate walk. Feet are firmly placed, leaving no disturbance outside of the track itself. Drag marks left by feet and by tail are often visible in deep snow.

Lion tracks left on level ground show that the print left by the rear foot will partially or totally overlap that left by the front foot. Tracks by members of the dog family, by comparison, are most often left when the dog is at a trot. Dirt and gravel around the imprint is often disturbed. Dogs also have a tendency to move with the body at a slight angle to the line of travel, causing an offset in the front and hind feet so that overlap is avoided.

Lion scratches are sometimes found, showing where the lion urinated or defecated to mark territory. Look along rocky rims, in major drainages, in saddles and along trails. Such are most apt to be found when the territory of adult males overlap. The scratch will be seen as a series of long furrows. Scat may or may not be present. Dung heaps are an aspect of lion territoriality. Such may be made by both male and female. Some, left near a kill site, might act as an aid to rediscovery of the carcass, or might be left there to establish ownership of the remains. Others, most likely, are territorial markings, pure and simple. Mounds are constructed markings most likely made by females, particularly by females who have litters close by. Look for a dome of pine needles or other debris about five feet in diameter; somewhat resembling a covered kill but containing no animal remains.

A kill site, when fresh, can be positive evidence a lion is nearby. Members of the cat family and the grizzly bear are the only U.S. predators who commonly cover a kill. A kill not covered might also be a lion kill, as they do not always cover. Drag marks will show the number of visits.

Screaming a lion track after a new snow can cause a bingo. Shown here, Mike Forrest of Flagstaff, AZ.

As noted, blind calling for lion can be a tough way to take a lion. Most lion killed by screamers are taken opportunistically as the lion comes to a scream directed at a coyote or a bobcat. Even so, experience has convinced me a dedicated hunter can use certain circumstances to increase his or her chance of calling in the second largest of the North American cats, the jaguar being the largest.

I have said random calling does not often cause a lion to come. I say also that certain techniques of screaming will increase the likelihood of calling a lion. Calling over or near a fresh and still active kill is the technique that offers the best opportunity to succeed. How does a hunter discover the presence of such? Develop contacts with those who spend a lot of their time in the wild country. Field folks employed by the U.S. Forest Service. The same in the State Game Managers. Become friendly with ranchers, a group almost always eager to cooperate in the killing of a stock-killing lion. Any and all others who know a lion kill when they see one.

Calling in an area that shows fresh lion sign can also be dandy. Fresh tracks, fresh scat, or a fresh scratch shows a lion was close by in the recent past. Driving forest roads on the morning after a night snow can be effective. Lion tracks found then are absolutely fresh, made since the snow stopped. Following those tracks to pause and scream at selected sites can produce. Larry and I have used each and all of those listed techniques to call and kill lion, random calling in lion habitat, having a lion come while calling to other species, calling a kill, calling a fresh track, and calling the snow. Each will work some of the time. None will work all of the time.

I call to lion about as I do to other animals, modifying technique to suit the lion nature. I prefer to use an open reed call (Crit'RCall, TallyHo, or Lohman C280) and blow that call so as to produce a scream that is more deep-toned and having some rasp to it. A lion, the way I see it, is more likely to walk a mile to find a deer dinner than to walk a mile to gobble down a cottontail rabbit. I blow loud and strive for a rhythm that approximates the rhythm sounded by a deer fawn in distress. I scream for 30 seconds or so and rest my lip for a minute, then blow another 30-second series, repeating for the length of the stand. How long do I scream to a lion? Depends upon the circumstances. If I am screaming over a kill or over fresh sign I scream until the lion shows, almost. Larry and I screamed a boulder jumble for more than an hour after finding a smoking hot track in the sand of a desert dry wash. The 135-pound tom showed near the end of legal light. I have, more than once, continued the screaming for more than two hours. On the average, given moderate encouragement, I deliver no less than one-half hour of screams.

Every lion I have killed, every lion Larry has killed, fell to a .224" diameter bullet sent from the bore of a .22-250 at about 3700 fps muzzle velocity. Any caliber larger will do as well. Calibers lower become iffy. Even though a proper hit on a lion will cause that lion to get dead, every hit is not precise. I would worry about wounding when using calibers to the low end of the centerfire range. There are a lot of lion in the West, more than most realize. The hunter who spends a lot of time at the screaming, those who deliver the right technique, will eventually call lion. Doing so can be the highlight of any predator calling career.

chapter 38

Calling Raccoons

I have heard it said, "God must have loved the common man because he made so many of them." The same must be true of raccoons. You want the truth? In some parts of the country, maybe even most parts, there are a hell of a lot of raccoon (maybe more) skulking the midnight. That midnight skulk delivers mischief much of the time. That aspect of the raccoon personality can be a benefit to those of us who hide among the hardwoods, or the corn, to make a noise like a raccoon's supper. Landowners, even those cold-eyed ones who turn ugly when the question of access is asked, become emotional and chummy when they learn you are there to call and kill 'coon. The circumstances surrounding the wet work involving the Ms. Sadie situation illustrates the point.

Ms. Sadie was the kind of critter who loved every gopher and every sewer rat in this wide world. Didn't love 'em physically, of course, but loved them because they were "wild things," as she loved the rabbits, the chickens, the ducks, and the geese that roamed her property.

Sadie's collection of cluckers and quackers caused a lot of interest among the wildlife that roamed the adjoining national forest. The coyote, the bobcat, the gray fox, and the raccoon saw Sadie's loved ones as groceries. The mysterious disappearance of a part of the goose flock caused concern. On a moonless midnight Sadie was jolted awake. One of the remaining geese was honking piteously. Sadie grabbed a light and went to the rescue too late. She arrived in time to see the final phase of a messy struggle between the goose and a big boar 'coon. Sadie did not have the decency to wait until daylight to call me.

Having my sleep disturbed, particularly by a bunny hugger, causes a change of personality. My eyes narrow to bloodshot slits. Frown wrinkles cover my forehead. I am not a nice person. I had no cage traps big enough to hold a big boar 'coon; I lied to Sadie. The only help I could offer involved the ultimate sanction, wet work. It was that or kiss the rest of her geese (and probably the chickens and the rabbits) adios. Sadie gulped a couple of times and did just as any animal lover would do when confronted by a situation where something that belonged to her was threatened by something that did not belong to her. She did not come right out and say, "kill every one of those miserable scumbags," but she nodded a go ahead. And I did.

Some southwestern raccoon live far from water but will almost always wash their feet when circumstances allow.

The same sort of thing happened on a Texas ranch. The property was a vast holding devoted to cattle and to the controlled (and expensive) "harvest" of wildlife. Locked gates. Fences so high you needed an oxygen mask to climb over. Signs saying, "Trespassers will be shot. Survivors will be shot again." That sort of thing.

Anyway, a colony of raccoon set up to work the corn feeders positioned to attract white-tailed deer and wild turkey so that the rich sports from Dallas/Fort Worth could shoot from the comfort of nearby blinds. The ranch foreman called a friend and he called me. Several nights later, after a series of proclamations from the awesome maw of the ten-gauge autoloader I call MooseDick, the corn supply was saved.

How does one go about screaming in a raccoon? Not as easy as it might seem but not impossible. The raccoon nature causes them to mostly resist the standard distress screams. I am not saying they will not come to a rabbit distress because they sometimes will. But not dependably. The best sound I have found for 'coon is a sound that incorporates a 'coon kit distress holler. The effectiveness of that kit screaming seems to be enhanced when the piteous kit calls interact with the mean snarls of an enraged boar raccoon. I heard that cooperation the first time during a Texas hunt with wildlife professional Bill DelMonte of Nolan and vicinity.

Bill DelMonte makes his living doing biology work for the Texas Department of Wildlife & Recreation. His off-time, during one period, was spent recording a series of wildlife distress sounds, such sounds being marketed under the old Live Call label and later sold to the Johnny Stewart Company to be marketed under their label. The harmony achieved in his Raccoon Fight tape was and is the most effective 'coon calling sound I have heard.

Our first night among the 'coon caused us to drive night roads, senderos in Texas talk, to play the raccoon fight tape from the bed of the truck, legal in Texas law. We called 'coon close many times during a two-hour period, all coming close to the truck, all circling the truck, looking for a way up. Those who hope to use the Raccoon Fight Tape to call 'coon must have a device to cause the magnetic meanderings on the tape to turn to screams. I use and recommend the Johnny Stewart MS512, a compact cassette player powered by a 12-volt motorcycle battery (rechargeable). Nope, I do not own stock in the Johnny Stewart Company. I consider the MS-512 to be a reliable and sturdy player, available at moderate cost. Check advertisements in the already mentioned *Trapper & Predator Caller* to discover rock bottom pricing.

Successful 'coon calling, it seems to me, results when the hunter fully understands raccoon needs and raccoon nature. Read on to learn all I know (maybe more) on the raccoon. The raccoon is a heavy-bodied critter that might weigh forty pounds or more. An adult animal measures about three feet from nose to tip of tail. Body fur is coarse and will range from dark to a light and grizzled gray. The raccoon has a distinctive black facemask, a characteristic that has caused him to be called a woods bandit. The ten-inch tail is ringed with alternating bands of dirty white and black, provoking a second nickname, Old Ringtail.

The raccoon is prolific and has increased his range. The omnivorous 'coon moves into old and newly developed agricultural areas to make a home close to his groceries. Predator control projects in much of the intermountain West has caused the raccoon to prosper. A place is made for the raccoon when larger land predators are thinned.

The raccoon is adaptable. He is often found within the city limits of even the largest city. Some metropolitan landfills host a respectable raccoon population. Other raccoons, in metro and rural areas, are somewhat constant visitors to backyards-on the search for food.

The raccoon is not a fussy eater. Garbage dump 'coons might spend a lifetime eating the delicacies found in the dump. Waterway 'coons make their living catching and eating crawfish, minnows, frogs, and even snakes. Even though the food has just been retrieved from the water, the raccoon will sometimes wash it thoroughly before eating. That same raccoon will lose most of his fastidiousness when he finds a ripe piece of carrion on the bank. He will dive onto a rotting carp with a gusto that is a wonder to watch.

The raccoon, a true omnivore, will take fruits and vegetables when available. The 'coon fondness for corn, melons, and other produce is legendary. The raccoon might balance his vegetarian diet by eating eggs, and even those that lay the eggs. Eating sprees can turn his stocky body into a lard barrel. That stored fat will see the raccoon through the cold weather of winter.

The raccoon is an intermittent hibernator, not a hibernator in the true sense of the word. The raccoon will become less active or inactive during cold weather when food is scarce and will maintain cozy groupings in the hollows of trees and other natural openings. If the weather warms slightly the 'coon might come out to forage. The raccoon is likely to stay active year-round in the temperate climates.

Raccoons breed in midwinter, usually February and March. In warm climates they may breed year-round. The three to six young may be born in the hollow of a tree or in a rock crevice in a rock jumble. The kits show about two months after breeding. Male raccoons, being polygamous, do a lot of traveling during the breeding season. The female is a good mother, sometimes tending the kits for almost a full year, until she is ready to breed again.

All raccoon are skilled swimmers. And all can climb a tree as well as any animal can. The tree climbing might involve a search for food (persimmons and such) or might be because the 'coon needs a sanctuary. Even so, an adult boar 'coon has few natural enemies. Some weigh fifty pounds and are full of fight. Most large predators would prefer a supper less cranky.

The raccoon pelt is a staple of the fur industry. Prices fluctuate, just as the price paid for all fur fluctuates. Raccoon pelts prime about November and remain prime through February in much of the raccoon range. Raccoon meat is dark and moist. Depression babies born in the hardwood hills of the Missouri Ozarks gummed the tasty 'coon meat before the first tooth appeared. I speak from experience.

Raccoon are not often found far away from water. Tracks can easily be found in the mud at water's edge. Rear raccoon tracks are about three to four inches long and somewhat resemble a human foot. The rear is narrow and the front wide. Toe marks are not always present.

Raccoon are intermittent hibernators, choosing hollow trees, caves and spaces within rock jumbles.

'Coon droppings vary as diet varies. Look for crawfish shells or vegetable matter in the scat. Some areas of high raccoon population will show well defined trails leading from the feeding grounds to the bed grounds. As mentioned earlier in this chapter, a Raccoon Fight tape played through a battery powered caller is most effective. I like to scout my raccoon calling locations during daylight to get a better concept of the lay of the land. If I am not totally familiar with the area I may mark stand locations using plastic pennants.

Make the 'coon hunt during the dark. The raccoon I have met have been almost totally nocturnal. Daylight, even crepuscular calls, will have low response. Park your vehicle away from the calling stand and walk in the final two or three hundred yards. Will the raccoon be alarmed because of the vehicle? Maybe yes maybe no. Other critters that might respond most certainly will be alarmed. I set the battery-powered caller close to my sit-down and turn to low volume. If nothing shows in the first two or three minutes I turn the caller into a blaster, moving the volume knob extra loud.

Keep the beam of the finding light moving. A fast-moving raccoon might gallop too close when you swing slowly. Make an effort to flash the light high when there are trees close by. The raccoon I have met will sometimes climb a nearby tree to enjoy a better look. When eyes are located, on the ground or in the tree, reduce the call volume, verify the target, and prepare for the shot.

What kind of gun does a good job on raccoon? The Mag- 10, mentioned earlier, can be dandy when loaded with copper plated BBs. A three-inch twelve, loaded the same way, does dandy also. Riflemen will want to consider the .22 WRFM (shooting hollow points) or the .22 Hornet. Both do a deadly job on close range raccoon. The .222, loaded to somewhat slow velocity, can be effective. Larger calibers, obviously, will do as well but might kill the critter deader than need be.

Callers who live near lakes, rivers, marshes, and backwaters might consider using a boat to patrol the banks, calling about each third of a mile. I prefer to stay about fifty feet out. Work the scanning light so as much of the bank as possible becomes illuminated. Much of the time the critter appears as a flash of eyes in the brushy shoreline. Shooting at such requires your reflexes to be quick. 'Coon calling, when it comes right down to basics, is not that tough. Work the night shift, just as they do. Set up close to raccoon habitat. Choose a setup that makes it easy for the raccoon to get to you and easy for you to get to the raccoon. Play or blow a sound that is interesting to the raccoon. After that it is a matter of practice.

Called 'coon will sometimes highpoint to scan for danger.

chapter 39

Calling Red Fox

It was nine in the morning when I made the setup. Constant clouds covered the sun, causing a dismal aspect to come to my part of the Iliamna Barren Grounds in Alaska. More dismal than ordinary. Those same clouds provoked a gentle rain and a miserable wind. The same miserable wind that had blown without relief for the past week. I snugged my big, wet body to the west (I think it was west, it can be difficult to know on the barren grounds) of an insignificant willow thicket and made a last minute check of the muzzleloader. The cap was on the recessed and inline nipple. The plastic cup covered afforded a degree of moisture protection. Plastic wrap covered the bore and covered the front of the telescope sight. Minutes before I had poked in the powder and the lead. "If the grizzly comes," I muttered to myself as I ungloved to reach for the TallyHo, "I hope this miserable wet bastard goes bang."

Ten minutes into the screaming, a flowing flash of red came at the lope from the south (I think it was south), from the Iliamni Lake side. Not a grizz, not even close. The customer was one of those big and beautiful Alaska reds, coming at the gallop. I let that dog fox come close, licked the call slobbers from my lips, and raised the Knight Rifle. A semi-second later the trigger released and the bolt flew forward. The cap did not go bang and the powder did not go BANG. Only a depressing click as wet bolt smashed wet cap. I cocked and did it again. Another click. Several clicks later Gary "Slammer" Hull came at the charge from the far side of the willows, bringing the back-up gun, an A-Bolt Browning in .25-06. What did the red think of all of this? Curious. The fox considered it all to be damn odd. The critter sat 40 yards out to do a scratch. The 117-grain Sierra took him amidships during mid-scratch. I had called and killed my first Alaska red, killed him a lot deader than necessary. I collected the big pieces and we trudged off, looking for another.

The red fox ranges Alaska, parts of Canada, and nearly all of the continental United States. The coastal regions of some southeastern states have no reds. Nor does some of the West and much of the Southwest. A redless gap can be found in the Great Plains. As compensation, sort of, reds can be found in good numbers in much of the U.S. and that range is increasing even as we communicate.

The red fox found in much of the United States is likely a mutant. Our

Metal reeded calls containing a cottontail reed work well on reds.

native red Vulpes fulva (tawny fox) was not widely distributed in much of the East during pioneer times. Our English progenitors, lonesome for the foxhunts held among the rolling hills of home, sicced the beagles and the bassets onto the somewhat plentiful gray fox. Not much fun at all. The gray had a habit of holing up and a worse habit of climbing a tree to look down smugly at the hounds. The limeys sent home for a transplant. A few months later a load of reds arrived. Vulpes vulpes. The good kind.

The refugees looked around, got friendly with the local reds, and more or less thrived. The red found in much of the East and Midwest is a product of that friendship, probably. Just as all black bears are not black, all red foxes are not red. The few reds found in the northeast corner of Arizona, as an example, have fur that is blonde, somewhat the color of a blonde cocker spaniel. That sandy fox (tawny?) is less red than the red accent found on some of the grays.

Some red fox further confuse as they mutate. Some red fox are silver and some are black. One color variation has the typical reddish color but has a dark cross over the shoulders and down the back. All of the assorted colors can be found in a single litter but seldom are.

The typical red can range up to fifteen pounds when fully mature. The average weight is less, maybe as low as ten or eleven pounds. The coat is true fur, not hair as is the case with the gray fox, and is full and fine, rich reddish underfur protected by long guard hair. The body is a couple of feet long. The tail adds another foot of length, is bushy and is almost always white tipped. Throat, neck, and chest are also white and the feet are black accented. The red aspect, in totality, is grand.

The price paid for red fox pelts, as is the case with all other raw fur, cycles, responds to the twin masters of fashion and supply. Red fox fur has excellent insulation qualities. A red can bed when the temperature is so low it has to warm up to get damn cold. The red will find a hole when he can, maybe dig into the snow when he cannot, curl into a ball with that handsome tail around his nose, and stay somewhat warm. Maybe not toasty but sure in hell warm enough to stay alive. The red will stay holed during the blizzard and during the baddest part of a storm, coming out to hunt when weather improves.

The red is an opportunistic feeder. He eats when he can and what he can. Favored foods are mice and voles and any other rodent he can catch and kill. A hungry red can hear a mouse wearing Reeboks at fifty yards. That red will pause to pose with a foot aloft until he has zeroed to the target, maybe deciding

This handsome red surrendered to an enticement blown through a TallyHo. "Slammer" with Gerry.

The Barren Grounds Red was extra large and extra hungry.

direction of travel. That done, the red will leap and pounce, sometimes pinning the creeper in a mat of grass or leaves. Fox in agricultural areas (a favored habitat) regularly feed on rats, rabbits, birds (ground nesters like the bobwhite quail, the ringneck pheasant, waterfowl, and the wild turkey are particular targets), and even eggs and poultry. As is the case with other foxes, actually with all members of the wild dog family, the red owns a stomach that can find nourishment in fruits and vegetables as well as meat. A true omnivore.

Carrion can taste good to a red. I have seen hide and bones from young antelope and deer decorating the front porch of a red fox den. Nope, it is not likely the red made the kill, even though such has been documented. The scraps, much of the time, have been collected from kills effected by bigger dogs.

The vixen reds come into heat once each year (monestrous) and that estrus occurs during late January, maybe a little before or after. The males commonly fight for the right to shake the sugar tree and that fight can be exciting. The males stand nose-to-nose with feet interlocked, striving mightily to show dominance. They leap and cavort with full tails flowing. When dominance has been established, the loser skulks away and the winner leaves with the girl.

It is likely red fox pair somewhat permanently. The male and the female share denning duties. When the kids are old enough to make it on their own, the adults may go their separate ways to lead their own lives until the mating urges returns. Some biologists feel the same two fox will get together the following year, if both are still around.

The red fox found within northeastern Arizona habitat, a short grass prairie. Held by Bill Rice.

A red fox den might be established in an enlarged badger or woodchuck hole. If none such is available, the red will dig one, maybe selecting a site in the roots of a tree or under a substantial rock. Multiple tunnels commonly lead to the den, providing escape routes and ventilation. The mainly used tunnel is likely to face the east in colder climates so that the rising sun will warm somewhat.

Many reds have alternate dens, moving the kids to a new site when the parents perceive a threat. Working as a team the male and female can vacate suddenly, carrying the protesting pups in their mouth.

The red fox litter can be substantial. Dens containing ten pups have been documented. The average is lower, probably a half dozen or so. Pups are furred but blind at birth. Red fox milk is rich, much more rich than milk from a cow. Pups nurse frequently. The rich milk is supplemented by an equally rich regurgitated meat. The vixen is likely to bring bits of fur and feathers so that the pups might be amused as they learn a bit of the real world. Later, when the pups are ready, a live mouse or vole will be brought. Red fox pups learn the art of killing early on. The pups hunt with the adults when about two months old, starting on grasshoppers and such and then graduating to big game: mice, voles and other fox delicacies. When the pups are about five months old, when the frost hits, they are invited to get the hell gone, and they do. If the area around the den has a good food supply the young fox might not go far from home. If times are hard the young might travel a substantial distance looking for a piece of ground that offers survival advantage.

A biological study done at the University of Wisconsin documented an interesting dispersal. A young red fox, captured and tagged near Madison, was shot by a hunter near Montgomery County, Indiana, nine months later. The distance traveled? A straight-line measure of 250 miles. A littermate, tagged at the same time, was recaptured a year later, a few hundred yards from the original capture site. Go figure.

During dispersal can be a dandy time to scream at the red. There are more red fox to be called than at any other time of the year. The young of the year are out and about, a hungry gang of teenagers desperate to survive. Generally low hunting and poor survival skills cause them to eagerly cooperate. Look for dispersal in October, or thereabouts.

Fox are territorial. No surprise there. Most critters are so. The size of the red fox territory will be determined by prey density and food availability. A red might make a living on a few hundred acres if plenty of groceries are available. Areas less endowed might cause the fox to claim and protect a territory of five square miles. A Minnesota study showed an average territory of two square miles. That same study showed that collared animals did not often visit the neighbors.

Red fox, like all dogs, mark territory with urine and scat and will vocalize to warn off other fox. A fox that visits will be attacked. What causes the red fox to be such a grump? They have to be. They are not just fighting for their territory; they are fighting for their life. Red fox droppings are often seen along fence borders, farm roads, and paths. The scat is dog-like and is between coyote scat and gray fox scat in size. All such eat about the same kind of groceries, however, and absolute identification can be difficult. Scat found without a supporting track can remain a mystery.

The red fox track is somewhat distinctive. It is dog-like in configuration, is smaller than a coyote track, and larger than the track left by a gray fox. Front feet are larger than the rear. Prints made by a walking fox will appear in a nearly straight line. Prints left on firm ground will likely show as a partial, maybe only toes and a part of the pad.

Some fox dens will be found near elevated land features. A North Dakota biologist found red fox dens on mounds and hillocks scattered in overgrazed ground, maybe in hayed or otherwise idle land. That same study established that the reds there did not hibernate.

Reds are mainly nocturnal. I say so even though reds are at times seen hunting during daylight, most often during dead winter when food from night hunts is not enough. Winter fox will sometimes curl atop a high point (a hill, a hummock, a hay bale, a rockpile, all such) to sun and survey. Hunters who know this will drive farm roads and glass those high points. A located fox is stalked to within rifle range, or screamed to rifle range.

Reds can be a tough call, particularly during daylight. Daytime activity can cause the fox to just say no to the best-articulated scream. Night calling is most effective in most of the red fox range.

It is critical to scout night calling areas during daylight to get a feel for the land and to learn of hazards that might be a concomitant to shooting. Plan your setup so that you know the direction of likely approach. If the wind is more or less constant, consider that also. Use skunk musk as a masker. More information on night calls can be found in the chapter on night calling. A day visit will allow the opportunity to shake and howdy with the landowner. Midnight, as previously noted, is a poor time to go door knocking.

Day or night you are likely to have the best luck when calling to reds during the hungry months of January and February. The red has used up his fat reserve by then. The fox has to hunt or hunger. That hunger can cause him to respond to a screaming, even though he may stay suspicious.

Calling the weather, as mentioned in that chapter, can cause the red to cooperate. The red will be out and hunting as a storm front arrives and will be hungry and hunting when the storm leaves. The day before the storm and the day after can be dandy if such is not plagued by strong wind. I have also had luck calling on cloudy days. Such unsettled weather can cause the red to be nervous maybe restless is a better word-and they will interrupt their routine to travel and hunt during daylight. Foggy days are also good. The fog helps to hide the hunter. The fox feels hidden also and shows an unusual confidence.

The fog can cause the screaming to be subdued. Reduce the amount of distance between stands to compensate. Calling foggy nights can be frustrating. The fog disperses the beam of the light causing it to be difficult to see eyes.

The red fox I have met have not come to the call showing the eagerness seen in a gray or in a naive coyote. A red is wary by nature and his suspicion will increase each time he is fooled by a screaming. His keen nose can cause him to become alarmed, maybe before you sight him. Some red fox will circle to get downwind, to take a taste of the wind. Watch wind direction. Scream to the upwind when you can. When you cannot, scream to a crosswind. Use skunk musk as a masker.

The red fox is mainly a mouser. Calls that imitate the distress cry of a mouse or a bird, any non-threatening little critter, can be particularly effective. I like the sound made by the close-in callers for the first calls. I sometimes lip squeak to start the stand, hoping to suck in customers that might be close. If you use a battery-powered caller, consider using a tape containing the distress scream of a baby cottontail or one of the bird distress tapes. I have had good luck using the flicker (sometimes labeled as the Yellowhammer Woodpecker) distress on reds. Play either at medium volume. I scream to reds for between ten and fifteen minutes, just as I do to other dogs. Do I say no red fox will come after that time? I do not say so at all. I say, instead, it is unlikely you will see a lot of action after that amount of time. It is sometimes better, the way I see it, to pack up the junk and travel to a fresh setup where the odds of response will increase.

Reds become call shy after a bad experience or two. They must do so if they are to survive, but even an educated fox can be called. Try a different sound on these Ph.D. fox. If most in your area blow a TallyHo, go to a Crit'RCall, or vice versa. Switching to a battery-powered caller can make sense. The variety of sounds available can be mind-boggling. Please remember one fact. The paranoid red is a real wimp. Play a gray fox distress or a coyote pup distress, even a coyote howl, and you are not likely to fetch in a red. The metal reed calls sound similar, at least to my ear, no matter the mouth. The scream from a plastic reed call can change as the mouth changes and as the position of the same mouth moves a bit to titillate the plastic. The red fox range is widespread and there are a lot of reds within. The screamer who keeps on hunting, those that understand the red nature and tailor the technique to respond, are in for a lot of calling excitement.

A properly tanned pelt can trigger memories of happy hunts.

chapter 40

The Uncalled and the Unexpected

I consider the predator call to be misnamed. Sure, a call that imitates the distress scream of a prey animal will cause predators such as coyote, bobcat, fox, lion, bear, and too many others to mention, to come close. That same distress scream can cause other animals, a bunch of them not the least bit predatory, to come equally close. I have had songbirds come to nearly perch on my hat brim as they made the effort to seek out the source of bird distress sounds. Jackrabbits have come like grapes, in bunches, to investigate sounds that simulated the distress scream of a jackrabbit. I have had deer, elk, antelope, javelina, cattle, and horses come close to investigate a screaming. On one stand I called in a hippie. You want the truth? About anything with ears might respond to a properly sounded distress scream.

Why do non-predators come to a screaming when logic suggests they should run the other way? Don't know. Those who have responded have not shared their thinking. I speculate that some prey animals come to defend. The critters might lope in believing a son, daughter, or other relative might be in jeopardy. They respond, perhaps, hoping to effect a rescue. I offer a couple of examples to support this speculation.

Blair used a screech owl tape to cause this acorn woodpecker to come close.

This yellow shafted flicker responded to a bird distress tape.

Larry and I set up within the greasewood bordering a mesquite lined wash to do a screaming for coyote. A coyote came, trotted close, and received a .54 caliber Maxiball between the eyes. We kept on calling as we almost always do after the shot. Minutes later a crashing of brush announced the arrival of a heavy-bodied animal. A doe deer bounded into view, and boy, was she mad. Her ears were laid flat to her neck to show hostility. The body language that showed hostility doubled when she came upon the carcass of the coyote. Every hair stood at attention. She snorted and reared, bringing her front feet down to within inches of the coyote's head. That doe was a hundred pounds of ugly, each ounce of that ugly hating that poor dead coyote. Larry had to laugh and when he did I did. The doe retreated at an indignant trot. As she left a second deer, a half grown immature, trotted down the wash to join momma.

Another call caused a sounder of javelina to spook and disperse. Some, including several very young javelina, made a hard run away from the setup, obviously hoping to get as far away from the screaming as possible. Four of the gang did not run away. They came straight to the screams at a charge, making no attempt to be neighborly. The salt-and-pepper hair of their backs was at attention, causing them to look twice as big as their 35-pound size. And that was not enough. Tusks clacked dangerously and all of that was decorated with the most ferocious grunting. The foursome, obviously, hoped to intimidate the

A hungry pair of golden eagles ambushed a great horned owl and plucked it bald.

screamer, and they did. I sat tight and sat quiet until the outraged peccaries tired of being tough and trotted off to rejoin the sounder.

The hunter who understands the full potential of the screamer can use that knowledge to good advantage. Bird photographers and those who simply like to see birds at close range can play a screech owl distress tape to cause about every kind of songbird to come close. That same sound, played during the dark, can cause great horned owls to swoop to brush the cap brim with a wing tip, and at times, to light upon the limb of a nearby snag. Such visits offer excitement and offer the opportunity to capture somewhat shy wildlife on film.

The fawn distress scream can be a dandy way to call deer to the camera or to the gun. My experience has convinced me doe are the most common respondent. I say that even though I have used the fawn bleat to call buck deer. Screaming to deer can be an effective hunting technique when hunting during the rut. The screaming that brought the Child Molester Buck to the muzzleloader illustrates the point.

Larry and I had worked the alluvial ridges on the north side of the Harcuvar Range for two days. On each of those days I had used the fawn distress scream to bring a buck close. The first day the buck was a small-horned four-point that came to about 250 yards, then hung up to begin a nervous stomping and snorting. The distance was beyond comfortable range for the black powder gun. Also, I was not that interested. I walked one way and the buck walked the opposite.

The second day the buck was big, mighty big, probably more than 250 pounds on the hoof and carrying a grand four-point rack (Western count) that was dandy, maybe an honest 34" spread. I screamed the big buck, and his harem of does, to within fifty yards of Larry O. Trouble was, no clear shot was offered. A palo verde, a mesquite, or one of the does was always between. No shot. Larry and I returned to the area the next day, hoping for a second chance. I was set up on the lip of a desert bowl when I settled in to make a screaming. I blew as I almost always blow for deer. I placed the TallyHo to the corner of my mouth and exhaled out air to sound a series of somewhat long moans, doing my best to imitate a fawn in distress.

The four-point came a few minutes into the call, bringing along a pair of young does, jail bait. All three ran close, to about thirty yards, providing an excellent opportunity. The Child Molester weighed a bit over 200 pounds when field dressed. Using the distress scream to bring javelina close to the camera, the bow or the gun increases success.

Those who know javelina best know the main range of the pig-like critter is within Arizona, parts of New Mexico, Texas, and Old Mexico. Javelina run in herds (called sounders) and each adult member of that herd is committed to the integrity of the herd. That commitment causes a response when a danger is perceived. A threat causes adult members of the sounder to scatter. Immature javelina, those too little to keep up, freeze, hoping to become obscure or invisible. The adults will almost always halt the escape when they hear a distress scream that might be from one of the young. Some, I call them the enforcers, return to make the rescue.

Can it be dangerous to scream at javelina? I think not, although some might not agree. A calling companion who shared a close experience of the javelina kind most surely would disagree. It happened this way.

I took Fred to the high desert for a coyote screaming, the first time for him. A tusk clacking sounder of javelina showed at one stand and Fred showed a total lack of control when he shouted a warning, leaped to his feet, and took off down canyon at a brisk pace. Trouble was, down canyon was the way the pigs decided to go. Convinced the slavering horde was after him, Fred plowed through mesquite, cat claw, and at

Hawks, falcons, eagles and owls commonly come to bird and rabbit distress screams.

The raccoon-like coati mundi will come to the call within the right kind of country.

least one Teddy Bear Cholla. He would have been better to surrender to the pigs. I had one hell of a time running him down.

The ringtail cat, actually the cacomistile, is a nocturnal predator somewhat common to certain parts of the southwestern U.S., Mexico, and Central America. The ringtail cat is not a cat at all, but one of the three members of a family that includes raccoon and coatimundi. The ringtail is a sleek and slender animal about two feet long, half of that being tail. The body fur is short and gray brown grading to a cream on the belly. The tail is decorated with alternating bands of black and white. A big bull ringtail will weigh less than three pounds. Ringtail are night hunters and day sleepers. Do not expect to call many during the day. Do a screaming during the dark, in ringtail habitat, however, and the action can be dandy. I have my best luck calling within an area where scat or tracks show ringtail presence, using a non-threatening bird distress sound. As is the case with most night hunters, the ringtail has oversize eyes that illuminate like a pair of miniature moons when hit by the light. I have not found the little furbearers to be light shy, having used the flash on a camera to take more than one exposure before the cat-like critter leaves.

Birds of every sort will come to a proper screaming. Songbirds and owls have been mentioned. Hawks, eagles, ravens, and crows come about as well. I can't count the number of redtails I have called close during a screaming directed at other critters. I called seven Harris hawks during one stand one winter, at a time when these communal hunters were passing. Golden and bald eagles have responded. It can be difficult to make a screaming and not attract a raven or a crow in certain areas. All lend interest to the screaming. All can provide photo opportunities to those who are so inclined.

About every kind of game animal from bull buffalo to bighorn sheep has come to a screaming. I used the distress scream on one hunt to harvest a decent buck antelope. I had glassed the fifteen-inch buck on the fringe of a juniper push. A deliberate stalk caused me to be within about a half mile of his position when I blundered into a group of does. Knowing I would spook the does and they would spook the buck as they fled, I holed up. Knowing the antelope were in the rut, knowing the herd of does almost surely had a buck close by, I whipped out the predator call and started a screaming. The buck, nervous because he thought one of his sweeties was in anguish, came at a hop I call the rutting strut, a hopping that cause the four feet to bunch and to hit the ground together. Each time the feet hit, the buck sounded an explosive grunt. Even though he was not a buck to write home to mother about, I took the shot. The horns were fifteen-and-a-half inches and massive with decent paddles. I crouched to begin the dirty work. Halfway through a grunt caused me to look. A second buck antelope, likely the one I had stalked originally, watched from a hundred yards out.

Domestic and feral dogs will sometimes come to the screaming. Free-running dogs show regularly in country where an abundant population is present. The vast span of the Navajo Indian Reservation, lands that occupy about a fourth of the state of Arizona and then slops over into parts of New Mexico, Colorado, and Utah, is one such. Feral and free-running dogs are a problem there, so much so that tribal authorities have placed free-running dogs at risk, causing them to be a legal target to any screamer who buys the moderately priced small game hunting license.

A screamer never knows what to expect when he or she sets out to squeeze the rabbit. Nothing may come. The next screaming might cause a curious deer to come close. A call a quarter of a mile away might bring in a mountain lion or a bear. The suspense created, the not knowing what might show, creates an excitement that keeps us screaming.

chapter 41

Alibis and Other Lies

I do not often write about politics and politicians as I find thinking about such almost always causes a case of the vapors.

Being a former flatfoot I have perfected a system that lets me know when a politician is lying. I look to see if his or her mouth is moving.

To their credit, however, the least bad of the politicians I have met have practiced until they can look you in the eye, tell a whale of a whopper, look sincere and convince you they may have participated in the banana game but such was not technically dastardly and depraved.

This spin-man-ship, the way I see it, was perfected by the democrats within the Clinton administration and fine tuned by the republicans within the George W. Bush administration.

Careful consideration has caused me to believe this creative alibi-ing (sic) has an application within the sport of predator calling. I pondered up this wisdom shortly after a mishap witnessed by a Fish & Game guy named Ray Parent.

Ray called as I suffered my way through yet another episode of Laverne and Shirley, a welcomed interruption as Lennie and Squiggie were about to do their thang. "Whatcha doing?", Ray inquired. "Um, Ah, watching a National Geographic Special dealing with the evils of digging for oil upon the caribou range in Alaska," I answered just as Squiggie let loose with his insanely obnoxious giggle and as the laugh track nearly busted a gut in appreciation. Knowing how much my wife enjoyed watching and hearing Laverne, Shirley, Lennie, Squiggie and even Carmine, Ray pretended not to notice.

"I am noticing a fawn survival problem among the antelope herds within game management unit ten," Ray said soberly. "Gangs of coyote are gobbling the fawns before they hit the ground. You wanna join me tomorrow to do a bit of coyote control?" I said yes and headed for the bedroom, telling Annie I was obligated to an early up and unfortunately could not enjoy the remainder of her favorite program.

The dawn stand yielded up a sneaker who came back door and paused to peer from eighty yards out. I butt scooted to square with the target. Licked frost and slobber-sickles from my beard and sent a 52-grain copper coated chunk of lead toward the almost dead coyote necessaries. The coyote was too dumb to

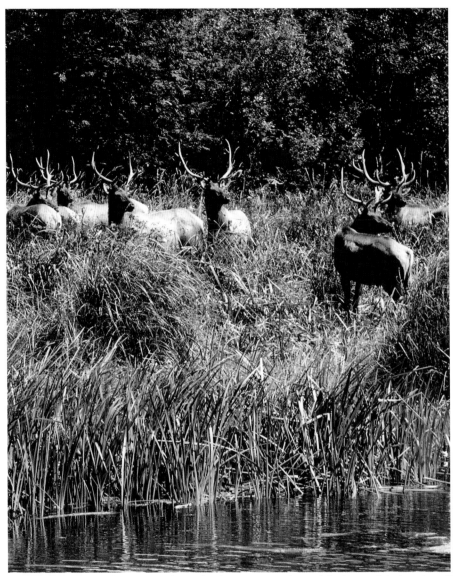

Young bull elk are much like young male people. Get a group together and the lying and the bragging will start.

know he had been killed. He headed for home and Mother with enthusiasm. I watched forlornly as Ray shouldered his .222 magnum and completed an impressive head shot on the running coyote at about two hundred yards.

At a subsequent set ups I screamed three single coyote within sure kill range. Unfortunately a series of middling mess ups caused sure kill range to change to sure miss range and the three musketeers departed, probably laughing their hairy butts off.

Finally I called a handsome silver belly so close I could smell the antelope on his breath. Big booger loafed by at an estimated ten yards, looking to be as big as a bull buffalo through the six power optics. I knew I could not miss. I did miss and the coyote left the county. "Howenhell can a shooter miss a big coyote at a pathetic eight yards?" Ray inquired rhetorically. I was almost certain it was a pathetic ten yards but did not deign to quibble. I had no easily available excuse for the eight yard miss (I continue to be convinced it was closer to ten yards) or for any of the other misses made that day.

Reluctantly, I allowed the warden to talk me into a sight-in at a hundred yard distant square of Charmin. The three shot grouping was Camp Perry quality. I vowed I would never again allow myself to be caught with my alibis down.

To my way of thinking every predator caller has to have been a rookie screamer at the start. Every rookie, I believe, makes dumb mistakes. Hell, it is a part of the job description. Are you ready for a truth? Even though it has been a while since I have considered myself to be a rookie I continue to make dumb mistakes. Not as many as I did during the prime of my rookie-hood, hopefully, but enough to cause me to continue kicking rocks and mumbling drat and dern-a-mitey with a depressing regularity. Having said so, let me also say that rookies and non-rookies alike sadly ignore an important aspect of screamer persona. I refer to the poorly understood technique of alibi-ing ones way out of a mess-up and not have a plethora of coyote poop decorating the credentials.

Permit me to offer an experience involving my-own-self and a high profile hunter, a hunter whose name will not be spoken (actually, written) but whose name would be quickly recognized by almost all who read this chapter. Here is a clue. His initials are GK. Still don't get it? Oh, all right! It was Gordy Krahn. OK?

Gordy was editor of *Trapper & Predator Caller* at the time and had traveled west to hang out with one of his masthead writers. We met at Sky Harbor Airport within Phoenix Arizona and immediately headed even more west to the burg of Wicken and beyond.

The desert was overly generous during the first day of screaming. We were mainly hunting creosote (greasewood) flats that bordered a mesquite choked drainage, knowing that coyote and other such would likely lay up within the shade of the mesquite to be cool and be safe, maybe munch on a mesquite bean or two and maybe munch on other mesquite bean munchers. The close nature of the terrain caused me to ask MooseDick (my ten gauge autoloader) to tag along and do a bit of wet work as opportunity permitted. Gordy (Little Booger) Krahn carried a scope sighted bolt action in .243 caliber, not the best tool, the way I see it, for wet work that is up close and personal when the gunner hopes to salvage and sell the fur.

As noted, a hell of a lot of coyote and maybe more came enthusiastically to the first day screams. Wishing to be a good host, maybe hoping to brown nose the boss a bit, I kept MooseDick under control and allowed Gordy the opportunity to off a few coyote. Unfortunately he did not. Little Booger missed sure kill close coyote with monotonous regularity. Frustrated, the usually even tempered booger muttered out a shucks and a dern and accused the airline baggage handlers of tossing his gun case about, all such causing the sight to shift.

Was the sight off? Don't know. Remembering my experience with Ray Parent I did not suggest a sight-in. I do know Gordo's kill ratio increased dramatically when we moved to more open country.

I thought then, and think now, that Gordo's alibi of imperfect sights was somewhat average. A careful pondering, it seems to me, could have created an alibi continuing more pizzazz.

I showed considerably more imagination during yet another hunt with Ray Parent. Ray and I had been friends for the longest time, since Ray was a rookie game and fish guy stationed at the pissant town of Seligman, Arizona and I was a road sergeant for the Arizona Highway Patrol within District Three at the Mohave County headquarters, in bigger pissant of a town called Kingman.

The cold weather screaming took place within a short grass prairie interrupted by shagbark juniper and sage. The kind of country where a coyote could live long and prosper.

I had done middling well at screaming and middling well at killing customers. During the last action of the day I fumbled the ball. An eager yodeler loped fifty yards close and paused broadside to decide if he was going to have supper or be supper. I believed it to be necessary to shift slightly to square with the target and the coyote turned paranoid. Body language told me the 'yote was a semi-second away from full flight. I hurried the shot, shooting at an awkward angle. The missed shot caused the coyote to make a Code Three gallop for the county line and caused Ray to smirk knowingly. "I am betting you have a really creative alibi ready to explain the miss, he speculated. "I missed a-purpose," I lied sincerely. "Just as the sear was ready to release the firing pin I noticed the narrow head on that coyote and decided she was a Mother. Knowing that today was Mothers Day, I moved off target and spared the life of that mother". "Heck fire", Ray blurted, "today is sure in heck not Mothers Day." "It's not?" says I, looking surprised. "Reckon I messed up again."

Appearing to be a hunter with a poor mind for dates, I figured, was better than being a hunter with a retarded trigger finger.

The alibi used during the Mommas Day hunt was creative but not nearly as much as the one I developed for the Plea from God hunt. Reverend Bill and I were screaming our way through sagebrush flats and push-downs upon the Seven Ranch when a coyote galloped out of thick sage and posed broadside a football field away. The angle of approach was awkward and I was forced to perform a sitting lean to the right, a difficult move for a right shouldered shooter. I snugged my right cheek to the Monte Carlo stock of the Sako and began the routine. Breathe s-l-o-w-l-y, draw a last deep breath, exhale partly, hold- hold-hold, begin a slow and steady squeeze upon the three pound trigger, say the words Coyote, you are one dead sumbitch. Bang! Fire and a fifty-two grain copper coated chunk of lead left the bore of the .22-250 at an estimated 3750 feet per second. Not knowing he had become dead the coyote performed a graceful and acrobatic leap around and disappeared into the sage.

"I declare, Brother Blair," Reverend Bill observed. "I do believe you missed that coyote. Those who believe you to be the best rifle shot within the entire State of Arizona and the most of New Mexico are obviously in error". Stifling a blasphemy I endeavored to appear pious. "Preacher," I said solemnly, "I did all I could do to kill that coyote and would have killed that coyote if God had kept his mouth shut. Unfortunately, just before the Sako went BANG God spoke to me. "Gerry," He (or She) said, trying to be friendly, "even though I know that many and maybe most coyote are miserable sumbitches who murder many of my defenseless creatures, sometimes eating such as they pathetically bleat for mercy, that coyote you are about to kill is a favorite of mine. I care for that coyote. I would consider it to be a personal favor if you would let this one live. Not wishing to provoke the Big Guy into doing the lightning bolt thing I moved off target at the last instant and scored a Maggies Drawers."

I do not intend to relate the circumstances of every creative alibi (knowing such would demand a book that weighed at least as much as a well endowed boar Alaskan brown bear) I feel it to be proper to add Uno mas, Mexican for one more, an occasion also involving a shot that landed considerably outside of the X-ring.

I was screaming a short grass (at times a no grass) prairie surrounded by a plethora of stringbark junipers when the pissant appeared at the far edge, maybe a third of a mile away. I scrunched my big butt an inch further into the duff. George Oakey and I watched and waited as the pissant metamorphosed into a coyote, an XXL male coming at a gallop. I was particularly anxious as I sat between Oak's .243 and the customer. It was obvious I would almost surely be the shooter.

I fired the first shot when the coyote was thirty five yards out. Hindsight tells me I should have waited another ten yards or so as the 3" load of copper plated BB's knocked the coyote down for only a half a handful of seconds. I fired the second shot when the coyote was up and running wobbly legged broadside. The coyote staggered, turned away and loped for the county line. The third shot was at the coyote butt at a distance of about sixty yards, marginal range for a three inch twelve.

"What happened," George smirked curiously. "As you know, George," I answered, "I gave up tobacco not long ago. That nickel cigar you smoked at lunch caused the craving to return. I was tolerating a bad case of the cigarette shakes when I tried to kill that coyote." Even though the incident took place a couple of dozen years ago my friend George Oakey has not smoked a cigar within by presence since.

Remember when I said uno mas? I have reconsidered. The alibi that follows is the absolute set-in-concrete, scouts honor uno mas. Maybe.

Vernon LaDuke and I were doing a screaming among fifty year old push-downs that bordered Cedar Flats, maybe a quarter of a mile north of the dirt road (Arizona freeway) that began near Camp Verde, crossed the flats, and continued on to hell and beyond. A timed fifteen minutes of screams produced no sighting but did produce an obnoxious and persistent motor mouth howler who tagged a howl to every scream. When it became obvious that motor mouth was all talk and no walk Duke and I un-hid, walked to the truck, and was headed home when I sighted the howler letting loose with one more howl. I eased to a stop, dismounted on the off side, stepped off the road and squeezed off a shot, hoping to take the coyote during mid-howl.

Even the somewhat gentle jump of the .22-250 caused the Sako to move off target. When I looked back the coyote was gone. Shooting off hand at a couple of hundred yards has never been my specialty and I was not optimistic. Even so, my step-dad and I walked out and made a deliberate search. "I cannot believe you would miss a shot like that," Duke observed. "Duke," I explained, "when I was thirteen years old and repeating the third grade I had a teacher I really liked. Miss Merkle carried a few extra pounds but had a really good heart. She seemed to enjoy rubbing the back of my neck when she thought I might be stressed. I came to love Miss Merkle even though she had a face that looked a lot like one of the Bill Countess English bulldogs. Duke, just before I pulled the trigger I noticed the coyote had a face a lot like that bulldog and I was reminded of Miss Merkle. The emotion of the moment caused me to miss that shot."

Duke and I were wandering about as I alibied and as the alibi ended Duke stumbled upon the carcass of a fresh dead coyote that looked a lot like the howler. Shot precisely through the lungs. Dead in his tracks. What did I do? What could I do? I continue to work on that one.

It is important, the way I see it, to mention that all neophyte callers make mistakes. All middling callers make mistakes. Sadly, even high profile callers make mistakes. All of us, it seems to me, need a way to retain a slather of dignity and retain a certain amount of stature. Creative alibiing does the job for me (some of the time) and is likely to do the job for you.

chapter 42

Skinning

Fur care begins with the shooting, continues during the retrieve, the transportation, the skinning, the repairs, the washing, stretching, and manicuring. "WHOA," you say. "Seems to me there is a lot more to precise fur handling than is obvious." You are exactly right, I answer. Read on to learn techniques that can cause the pelts you handle to look good on the wall and at the taxidermist, pelts that will bring out the generous nature of the most squinty-eyed fur-buyer.

Enlightened fur handling starts before the shot. I say so even though I know critters coming to the call must be "harvested" (God, how I hate that word) and know that such harvesting can be imprecise and somewhat destructive. Even so, the screamer has options when it comes time to do the wet work. One option, favored by some, involves the use of the moose gun, the elk gun, or

Gordy Krahn uses a choke chain or skinning gambrel as a skinning aid.

the bear gun. And they light into the customer with the enthusiasm usually reserved for the charging and close-range grizzly. SHOOT THAT SUCKER, and if he wriggles, shoot him again.

Honesty causes me to say such technique will almost always cause death, often a very messy death. The corpse, sad to say, is killed deader than need be. The collecting of the big pieces from the various zip codes can be time-consuming and depressing. You want my advice? Read the chapter dealing with caliber selection, read, and heed.

Shooting the precise caliber needed to cause the critter to become only moderately dead can be dandy when shot placement is precise. An imprecise hit with a precisely correct caliber, sad to say, can also cause the wet work to turn nasty. Later in this chapter I will describe a wonderful technique that can cause a holey hide to become nearly pristine. That technique is called sewing.

Screamers who hope to "harvest" the pelt (and that includes about all of us) will benefit if they address pre-skinning concerns. Critters shot with a high velocity centerfire, some of the time, will show an insignificant entry wound and no exit. No blood. "HOO BOY," some will say, "I did good on that 'un!!!" Such is not always the case. The entry wound, following the nature of warm flesh, is puckered. That pucker will almost surely unpucker as body temperature decreases. What happens then? Blood, brother, and lots of it. I carry paper towels in the pocket or the day pack and use such and a stick to poke in a plug.

The trip to the vehicle should show respect for the critter corpse. Resist the temptation to drag. The draggings I have seen (and participated in) have never caused an improvement to the critter hide. Some draggings have caused damage; broken hair, the collection of grass and sticks, and soiling by dirt or mud. Those who do not skin in the field should protect the carcass during transport. Protect from what? Dust, rain, snow, sun, grease, oil, and all such. Protect the carcass also from pee and poop that is likely to ooze from the pooter and pee-er as the sphincters relax. All such soiling are easily prevented but not easily corrected.

The timing of the skinning can be important. I have skinned hot critters, lukewarm critters, cold critters, and a few times, (shudder) frozen solid critters. Those experiences have provoked a strong opinion. The longer a skinning is delayed, the tougher the job. You want that put another way? Hot skinning a coyote might take ten minutes. That same coyote will demand two or three times as long when cold.

Skinning technique can vary as the experience and personality of the skinners vary. Even so, certain constants endure, particularly so when the skinning involves one of the most commonly called land predators coyote, fox, and bobcat. I find it most convenient to hang the animal during skinning. I say so even though I know skinners, some mighty good ones, who do not. Legendary

Dragging a coyote allows a photo op but can degrade the fur.

caller Murry Burnham of Marble Falls, Texas, can skin a grounded coyote fast and easy. Others, Larry Gates being one, start the skinning on the ground and transfer to the hang after the hind legs are exposed. Me? I hang from the get-go.

Those of us who are hangers need some sort of suspension device to cause the carcass to be at a convenient height. Something sturdy, a device that will resist the muscular manipulations common to my style of skinning. The best suspender I have found is a choke chain, available at the pet supply sections in discount department stores. I use one end of the choker to suspend a hind foot and attach the opposite end to a stout limb.

Skinning begins with knife selection. I skin using a sharp knife. The sharper the better. Knowing that most of the skinning will be done using the first half-inch of the blade, I choose a knife that is lightweight. Comfortable. A knife that does not unnecessarily tire the hand and wrist during the skinning of multiples.

There are two techniques used during the skinning of most furbearers, open and cased. Most critters, those destined for the fur trade, will be case-skinned. Open skinning is mostly reserved for those animal pelts to be used as rug mounts. Some fatsos, badger, beaver and that sort, will be open-skinned also. Case skinning, simply described, is a skinning that causes the pelt to be separated from the carcass at the rear legs and at the tail. The pelt is then pulled and cut away from the carcass, a bit like grabbing the top of a tube sock and pulling it from off the leg and the foot. Simple? Maybe. Read on to learn tips that cause the technique to be less traumatic.

I use the pointed blade of the knife to make a cut on the inside of each hind leg, extending from the crotch to the foot. Look for the color line that will always be visible, the place where the belly fur meets the back fur. Slip the point of the knife inside the fur, making the cutting from the inside out. Make the cut along that line. Cut a ring around each hind foot to release the fur, then use the fingers (and the knife when necessary) to strip the fur away from the hind legs down to the base of the tail. Use finger strength and maybe a bit of knife work to part the tail fur from the tailbone. You will be able to expose about two or three inches of the tailbone. Use a tail stripper (available from advertisers in *Trapper & Predator Caller* magazine), a pair of sticks, or a couple of big nails to facilitate the further stripping of the tail. Place the selected device to top and bottom of the exposed tailbone, at the place where the fur starts, and use strength and strong language to strip the tail completely free.

Place your fingers on the leather and use strength to pull the hide away from the flesh until you reach the front shoulders. Some hides strip easily and some strip reluctantly. The hides of hot critters strip most easily. If resistance is encountered, use the knife, returning to the pull as soon as practical. One caution, use finesse instead of brute strength when you encounter the wound caused by the bullet. Too much enthusiasm can cause a further tearing.

Freeing the pelt from the front shoulders can be tricky. I use a length of steel rod, maybe a big screwdriver or a no longer needed sharpening steel from the kitchen knife set, to intrude between the front of the shoulder, at its joining with the chest. Pressure applied to the rod can cause some of the front leg hide to strip away. Hand and finger pressure can further strip the legs. How much front leg fur is enough? I strip down to the elbow, make a cut around the elbow, and pull the leg through. Muscle power can cause the skin to strip down to the start of the neck after the front legs are released. The hide at the neck becomes tight and it is almost always necessary to use the knife. Do so with caution. The big arteries, the carotids, are close to the surface. Cutting into one will cause bleeding, usually a lot of bleeding.

The fox, it should be mentioned, is particularly small-necked. The hide will almost always hang up at the head. It will be necessary to cut and pull until the neck hide enlarges enough to pull over the head. Pull and cut the hide to the ear butts, using your fingers to locate such, and cut to release the ear butts from the meat of the skull. Continue to cut to the eyes and use the knife to

A tree limb or a fence post can raise a carcass to a comfortable height.

skin out each eye. The membrane stays with the skin. Skin on down to the lips and beyond, leaving the dark membrane with the skin. Finally, at the nose, cut the hide so that the nose stays attached to the pelt. Case skinning has been completed. If done in the field, turn the hide leather side in, hair side out. Use the knife to make a cut from tail butt to tail tip, exposing the leather. Doing so lets the tail leather be exposed to the air so it will dry properly. Those who leave the tail uncut risk inside decay, causing the hair of the tail to slip. Start at the nose and roll the pelt to a compact bundle, then store in a ZipLoc® gallon-size freezer bag. Why a freezer bag? If I do not intend to handle the fur immediately I can place it as is in the freezer to be handled some other time.

Skinning open, although seldom done on fur to be sold, fur intended to be tanned to serve as a wall hanger, or fur headed for a new life as a taxidermy mount, is done about the same as case (or tube) skinning. Hang the unskinned carcass and use the knife to make a cut at the color line on the inside of the rear legs, extending the cut from crotch to ankle, just as you would do with case skinning. Strip the tail away from the tailbone, just as you would do when case skinning. Now take the point of the knife and make a cut that extends from the crotch cut to the chin. Make another cut that extends from the inside ankle of each front foot to the center cut on the chest. Pull with the fingers, using the knife when needed, to remove the skin. Finally, make the tail cut described during the case skinning instruction.

Open-skinned pelts can be placed within the ZipLocs to be refrigerated or frozen. Fold the pelt, leather to leather, so that the pelt is halved long ways. Now make the roll. Some buyers will be willing to buy fur from un-skinned carcasses. Others will buy skinned fur that is not handled (buying green). In each case the price paid will be less than the price paid for fully-handled fur. The next chapter will cover the techniques of fur cleaning, fur repair, stretching, drying, and grooming.

Well handled fur looks good to the buyer and looks good on the wall. (Mark Middleton Photo).

chapter 43

Fur Handling

Fur handling is a series of simple steps that cause the green pelt to turn into a stretched and dried pelt of uncommon beauty. The term "stretching" is somewhat of a misnomer. Pelts are not stretched in the true sense of the word. They are, instead, tautened on a wood or wire stretcher so that the air dries the leather, permitting storage until the fur is sent to the tannery. Much of the time, intermediate steps are necessary before the pelt is ready for the stretcher.

Some pelts will be soiled. Blood, mud, or fecal material may have contaminated the fur. A part of the time those contaminants can be mostly brushed away when the pelt has dried. Other times the soiling will be so severe it is necessary to wash the pelt prior to handling. Some fur handlers, the purists, wash every pelt to make it look as good as can be. Why would an unsoiled pelt need washing? Coyote, fox, and bobcat do not often bathe. Try never. The pelts from wild critters almost always have natural oils to cause the fur to be somewhat waterproof. That natural oil will cooperate with dust and dirt to cause a dingy aspect to the fur. Washing takes out the grease and

Bobcat and most other predators are case skinned.

takes out the dust. A properly washed pelt presents a bright aspect, looking as good as can be.

Pelt washing takes a bit of time but is not difficult. Use a pail or sink full of lukewarm water flavored with a bit of liquid detergent. Turn the unhandled pelt hair side out and slosh that pelt around in the water until most of the contaminants transfer from pelt to water. Empty the pail, refill with more water, no detergent and repeat. Continue until the water stays clean.

Hold the wet pelt by the nose and use the other hand to strip water as you move the hand down, following the lay of the hair, to the tail. Repeat until excess water has been removed. Place the still wet pelt hair side out on a wood or wire stretcher frame and place it in a somewhat warm and dry place. When the hair has dried it is time to attend to other aspects.

Some pelts, as mentioned earlier, have holes in need of repair. Those that have been shot with a shotgun loaded with copper-plated BB's, or anything smaller, are not likely to need repair. Even though there may be a lot of holes, all small, such is not likely to alarm the fur buyer. Larger holes, those made by high velocity centerfires, almost always need a stitch or two. Maybe more. Do the stitching with a needle having a somewhat large throat.

I have used waxed fishing line and have used monofilament line. Waxed dental floss also works. Turn the pelt leather side out and use the knife to trim away bits of fat, leather and bloodshot meat. Pinch the tear together and use the needle and thread to single stitch, pushing through the leather only, avoiding the hair. Tie off each stitch using a square knot. Repeat, stitching every quarter inch or so, until the wound is closed.

Most hides need fleshing before being dried. The fleshing does take off bits of flesh left by the skinning but mostly takes off plates of muscle and fat. A fleshing knife and fleshing board, both available from advertisers in *Trapper & Predator Caller*, make the job easy. Place the pelt leather side out on the fleshing beam and then use the fleshing knife, held at an angle, to scrape the leather. Do not over-flesh. Doing so can harm the hair roots and cause hair loss.

Some pelts will contain burrs, pitch, and hair mats. Remove all such before starting the fleshing. If left, the fleshing knife will hang up there to cause a tear, provoking unnecessary repair. Hides that have been sewn can be fleshed, but must be fleshed carefully so that the knife does not cause a tear. Some areas, the ear butts for example, will not accommodate the fleshing knife. Use a knife to cut meat, muscle, and fat away. Is it a good idea to salt the ear butts and the leather of the tail? Absolutely not. Salting causes water to gather rather than leave. Something in the salt messes up the tanning operation. Do a good job of fleshing and no salt is needed.

Stretching can be done using wood or wire. Even though I am convinced fur stretched on wood has a better look, I am equally convinced the fur buyer does not have a preference. I use wire most often because it is faster to do so. Position the pelt cased on the wood stretcher (hair side in) and pull taut, using brads or small nails to attach the pelt to the stretcher at the hips, or using the clamps provided on the wire stretcher. Place the stretched fur in a moderately warm place to dry. How long does it take the leather of a pelt to crust? Don't know. Crusting will depend on temperature and humidity. Crusting might take an hour or two or might take a day or two. I suggest you experiment to learn crusting time where you live.

When the leather has crusted, maybe being eighty or ninety percent dry, remove it from the stretcher and turn the pelt so that the hair is out. This turning is most easily accomplished by turning the nose back into the mouth and pushing the head as far into the opening as reasonable. Push a pole, maybe the handle from a broom, into the opening to catch the nose. Stand the pole on a solid surface. Turn the hips so that the hair side is out and pull until the fur is completely turned.

What do you do if you mess up and let the leather get too dry to turn? Use a wet rag or wet paper toweling to slightly moisten the leather. Watch the drying closely (it will not take long) and make the turn when the time is right. Return the pelt to the stretcher, hair side out, and store upright, in a cool dry place, until the leather is completely dried. The dried fur can now be removed from the stretcher for storage. Before doing so, use a wire brush (I use a poodle brush) to comb and fluff the fur. Some fur handlers use air pressure from a compressor to do the job. Do not ignore the hair or fur on the tail.

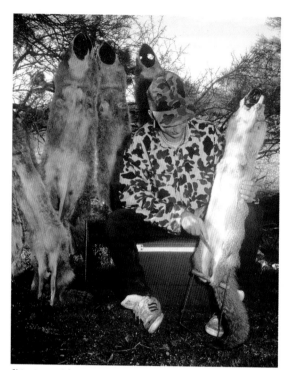

Skinning and fur handling during the hunt can be time consuming and takes time away from the hunt. Some hunters skin at night and freeze the fur.

Parts of the carcass can be salvaged, as a personal trophy or as a cash crop. If you call and handle a lot of predators, think about collecting the urine and the glands. The most desirable glands, the anal glands, are those located to the right and the left of the pooter. Others are located between the muscles of the hips and below the ears. Each is kidney bean shaped and is of a nasty gray color. Urine and glands can be sold to trappers or sometimes sold to a trapper supplier.

Skulls are also salable, the price determined by rarity. Some callers clean the skull and retain such as a trophy of the hunt. Some (I am one) have an extensive skull collection. Some are natural while others have painted-on decoration. How can a skull be cleaned? There are those about who provide a skull cleaning service. Skulls Unlimited, P.O. Box 6741, Moore, Oklahoma 73149 is one. Owner Jay Villemarette has been a trapper and caller. He cleans using dermestid beetle (carrion beetle) colonies, no boiling to weaken the bone. Cleaned skulls are handsome.

Those who wish to clean their own skulls (actually the skulls of called and killed predators) can do so. Cut the skull away from the vertebra. Use the knife to cut out the tongue and as much of the meat and muscle easily available. Place the skull in enough water to cover, adding a cup full of laundry soap and boil for about a half hour. Shut off the heat and leave the skull in the water until it cools. Use a section of clothes hangar wire to get into the brain cavity (through the vertebra hole) and mush up the cooked brains. Use air pressure or water pressure to remove the brains. Use a stiff bristle brush to clean away residual meat.

Predators can host an amazing variety of vermin. I shot a female coyote on one hunt that carried enough fleas to pull a wagon. Some fur handlers have advised leaving the pelt out overnight to allow the fleas the opportunity to abandon. This has not worked for me. The fleas I have come in contact with prefer warm fur to cold ground. I have hung hides out in sub-zero temperature for days and found fleas when I made an inspection. I have placed pelts within plastic bags and placed those plastic bags in the freezer. Some fleas, almost always, survive. What to do? Carry a 30-gallon trash bag on the hunt. Place the carcass of the customer within, spray a few squirts of a strong flea killer within, and tie shut. An hour or so of such can cause the healthiest flea to call in sick, maybe turn belly up, or to become too sick to worry about jumping on a screamer.

A couple of other precautions can help. Cut the tops from a holey pair of tube socks and carry those in a ZipLoc® liberally dosed with flea powder. Pull the tubes over the wrists at the start of the skinning. Use a spray insecticide, specific to the flea, to spray the feet and legs of a hung critter before starting the skinning. Finally, wear gloves to discourage fleas and to inhibit the transfer of critter blood to a cut on the human hand. Not heavy gloves. Wear the thin rubbers used by surgeons, almost always available at the pharmacy. Practice safe skinning.

Why worry about something as small as a flea? Because they are blood sucking little boogers that deserve to be hated, mostly. And too, the wrong kind of flea can transmit the dreaded bubonic plague or Hanta virus. Such can't always be treated, even if diagnosed early. The fleas that have given me trouble made the transfer as I posed for photos. Having a coyote, a fox, or a bobcat on the shoulder can cause an eye-catching photo. Trouble is, a bunch of fleas can transfer from the cooling carcass to my mostly warm one.

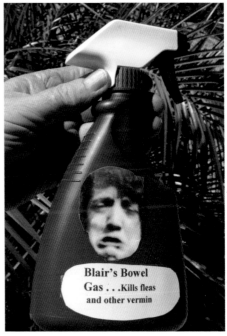

Fur handling is a skill that appears to be complicated but is actually not. Each step is simple and the simple series can cause a raw pelt to turn into a thing of beauty, for the wall or for the trade. Either way, the right kind of fur handler will take pride in his or her handiwork. That finished fur makes a statement about the standards of the handler.

Blair's Bowel Gas . . .Kills fleas and other vermin

A trash bag and a potent adios flea spray can cause creepy crawlies to desist and die.

chapter 44

Marketing

Some fur hunters do not sell the fur they collect. Some have the pelts tanned to serve as hunt trophies. Others send the fur to a furrier to have coats and jackets, maybe even hats and mittens, made for personal use. Others do sell. They sell the fur each time the buyer comes to town, or save the fur and sell it as a collection at season's end. This payday can be used to offset hunting expenses or can be used to buy the new fur gun or the battery-powered caller.

The amount of the check will be determined by geography, market conditions, the number of fur in the collection, and the skill of the fur handler. The condition of the individual pelts can have a major influence on the price paid. The fur buyer looks at a number of circumstances as he grades the fur to determine a fair price. What circumstances? The size of the pelt is one. Pelts from large and extra large animals bring a better price than do pelts from average or under-size animals. The lushness of the fur, both underfur and guard hair, can affect price. Pelts taken during the coldest part of the year almost always bring a better price than do pelts taken early in the season.

The buyer also checks to see if the pelt is prime. That word describes fur that is taken during the winter months when cold weather causes the fur to thicken and causes the leather to thin and become creamy. Prime refers to the condition of the leather. Unprime fur causes the leather to show a gray color, called blue in the trade. The grader also looks at fur or hair color. Most furbearers show color variation. That variation can be greatest when habitat conditions change but can be present in a common habitat. Bobcat from the West can be dandy, showing a desirable blue color to the back and a snow-white belly covered with stark spots. The fur from bobcat taken near the California coast, or from parts of the South and the East, will show a muddy body color with minimal fur on the belly. The price paid for each can vary substantially.

At certain times of the year the hide may be prime, but the hair or fur degrades to cause the price to drop. Some animals rub the hip area in the spring to rid themselves of the thick winter coat. This rubbing is most noticeable on coyote and fox. As summer causes warming temperature, the guard hair on some furbearers begins to curl, creating a condition called singeing, a second condition that can cause price to plummet.

The market condition is a circumstance that is beyond the seller's control. The fur market can be influenced by fashion, the amount of hold-over fur (pelts in storage from the previous season), and by the amount of a particular fur that is available to the market. Some sellers hesitate to sell early in the season, figuring the market price is indefinite. Such hold the fur to season's end, hoping for the best price then. Selling early can be a gamble. So can selling late. If I knew all there was to know about the fur market I would likely be rich, or at least richer, and wouldn't have to write for a living.

A second circumstance within the seller's control is the amount of care devoted to fur handling. Well-handled fur will always bring a better price.

The fur taker has three general options when it comes time to sell. Option number one involves the country buyer, a person in the community who buys and sells fur for a living, or as a concomitant to another business, perhaps a trapping supply house or a sporting goods store. Maybe both. Other country buyers travel regular routes during the fur season, stopping at announced locations to grade and make an offer on fur collections. A country buyer must offer a fair price if he or she is to stay in business. His or her reputation as one who offers a fair price or as one who takes advantage can influence business longevity.

The country buyer, sometimes a trapper or a screamer himself, knows local conditions and knows local fur. He has time, usually, to offer good advice on ways to improve fur-handling skills. Some will buy fur on the carcass or "green" fur, fur that is skinned but not handled.

One further advantage comes to the screamer who sells locally. He or she can have the fur graded and has the opportunity to discuss grading technique with the buyer. The offer can be considered and accepted or rejected. Selling to a fur house is a second option. The seller packages the collection and sends it off to the fur house. It is wise to call or write the fur house ahead of time, to learn conditions of acceptance and shipping regulations. Most of the fur houses grade the collection, call or mail an offer, then hold the collection for a certain time (maybe ten days) to give the seller the opportunity to accept or reject. Rejection of the offer causes the fur to be shipped back to the seller, at the seller's expense.

The last fur selling option is the fur auction, selling the fur collection through a consignment house. Auctions are organized by groups and individuals who receive and market the fur in a warehouse sort of setting. Some state trapping associations sponsor auctions. Fur can be delivered personally or can be shipped. Employees arrange the fur into logical lots and sometimes groom the fur a bit to disguise transportation evidence. The auction sponsors charge a percentage of the bid price as a commission.

Multiple buyers walk the floor to inspect and grade the lots. If inclined to bid, the buyer marks his or her bid on a sheet. The advantage of competition causes the offer to be generally fair. Sellers are offered protection through the minimum bid mechanism. Each lot of fur (a lot of fur is fur from the same species or same subspecies and same seller, sometimes of similar grading) has a space where the seller can mark the minimum price they will accept. If no offer meets or exceeds that minimum the fur is not sold. The seller pays a flat fee to the auction house and gets the fur back.

My experience causes me to believe the local buyer (when fair) is the best buyer for the small collection. That country buyer usually markets the fur he has purchased through one of the auction houses, increasing paid price by about twenty percent to make his profit. That same experience causes me to think mid-season (January) is the time to sell. There is not often a lot of new fur on the market during early season sales; much of the material offered is stale stuff, hold-over fur. Buyers do not dig deep for such. Season prices have stabilized by mid-season. Fresh fur hits the market. Much of that fur comes from the prime fur time of winter. End of season sales can be good or can be bad. I have seen years when prices peak at the last sale of the season. Some buyers have delayed buying, hoping for a better price, and now must scurry to find enough fur to satisfy their contract commitments. Screamers who feel the price offered is unfair have the option of holding the fur through the summer to place it on the market during the next season. In climates that enjoy mild summer temperatures the fur can be hung in a cool and well ventilated area. Hot summers can be hard on fur. It is better to freeze the handled or green fur to retain a degree of freshness.

Complicated market conditions can cause prices that are puzzling. Those market conditions will sometimes conspire to take much of the profit out of fur selling. No market condition, fortunately, can take the fun out of the screaming.

Appendices

Mouth Calls:
Arizona Predator Calls
1634 W. Charleston Avenue
Phoenix AZ 85023

Beastmasters
2635 Bamboo Drive
Lake Havasu City, AZ 86403

Burnham Brothers
www.burnhambrothers.com

Cedar Hill Game Call Co.
Jerry Antley
238 Vic Allen Road
Downsville, LA 71234

Crit'RCall
Rocky Mountain Wildlife Products
P.O. Box 999
LaPorte CO 80535
www.critrcall.com

Dan Thompson Predator Calls
P.O. Box 624
Rawlins, WY 82301

E.L.K. INC
P.O. Box 85
Gardiner, MT 59030
www.elkinc.com

Heck's Horny Predator Calls
Rocky Mountain Fur Company
14950 Hwy 20-26
Caldwell ID 83607
www.rockymtnfireworksandfur.com

Hunter Burnham Calls
www.burnhamcalls.com

Knight&Hale Game Calls
www.knightandhale.com

Lohmans (Circe Calls)
www.kolpin.com

Porath Game Calls
P.O. Box 96
Milan, MI 48160
www.AllPredatorCalls.com

Primos Hunting Calls
www.primos.com

Rhino Calls
6115 W. Mescal Street
Glendale, AZ 85304
www.rhinocalls.com

Scott Kramer, Custom Maker
Ridgeville, IN
www.brushwolfpredatorcalls.com

Steve Barbour
1106 N. Avenue L
Haskell, TX 79521
www.sbarbour@westex.net

THO Calls
62 Parker Street
Manchester, NH 03102
www.thogamecalls.com

Tony Tebbe Game Calls
4117 Forestview Ct., NE
Cedar Rapids. IA 52411
www.CustomPredatorCalls.com

Varmint Caller
www.varmintcaller.com

Zepp's Predator Calls
1574 N. Via Dorado
Tucson AZ 85715
email: Zepp's@cox.net

Battery Powered Callers:
Burnham Brothers
P.O. Box 427
Menard, Texas 76859
www.burnhambrothers.com

Cass Creek
www.casscreek.com

DSE Outdoor Products
Box 30, Indian Valley, VA 24105
www.dse-outdoors.com

Extreme Dimension Wildlife Calls
(Phantom Pro Series Digital)
P.O. Box 220
Hampden, Maine 04444
www.PhantomCalls.com

FoxPro Systems
609 W. Fourth St.
Lewistown, PA 17044
www.GoFoxPro.com

GameTraks
P.O. Box 363
Sturtevant, WI 53177
www.gametraks.com

Johnny Stewart-Hunter's Specialties
600 HuntingtonCt. NE
Cedar Rapids, IA 524402
www.hunterspec.com

Lohmans, Flambeau Outdoors
www.flambeauoutdoors.com

Minaska Outdoors
3120 N. 33rd Street
Lincoln, NE 68504
www.Minaskaoutdoors.com

Western Rivers Predation
1582 N. Broad St.
Lexington TN 38351

Decoys:
Custom Robotic Wildlife Inc
www.wildlifedecoys.com

DSE Outdoor Products
Box 30
Indian Valley, VA 24105
www.dsepotdoors.com

Edge Expedite
www.edgeexpedite.com

Flambeau Outdoors
www.flambeauoutdoors.com

FoxPro Systems
609 W. Fourth Street
Lewistown, PA 17044
www.gofoxpro.com

Mojo Outdoors
www.mojooutdoors.com

OutFoxed Product
www.outfoxedproducts.com
Renzo's Decoys
www.renzosdecoys.com

Western Rivers
1582 Broad Street
Lexington TN 38351
www.westernrivers.com

Websites:
PredatorMasters
www.predatormaster.com

HuntMasters
www.huntmastersbbs.com

Fins and Furs Outdoors
www.finsandfur.net

Recommended Viewing:
Masters' Secrets to Predator Calling
Gerry Blair hunts the hunters
Beastmasters
2635 Bamboo Drive
Lake Havasu City AZ 86403

Hunting the Hunters
Rocky Mountain Wildlife Products
P. O. Box 990
LaPorte CO 80535

Coyote Behavior
(Awarded Gold Ribbon by IF&V)
Gone with the Wind
Interview with a Coyote
(Kid's Hunting Video).
Outdoor Bear Adventures CCSI Coyote
Down (Kid's Hunting Video)

Jay Nistetter-Rhino Calls Media
Solutions
6115 W Mescal Street
Glendale, AZ 85304
www.rhinocalls.com

Predator Hunting in the East
Part 1: Back to Basics
404 Little Solida Road
South Point, Ohio 45680
www.keescalls.com

Predator Calling Clubs:
(Courtesy of Paul Wait, Editor, *Trapper &*
Predator Caller Magazine)

ARIZONA
Arizona Predator Callers
Box 1172
Mesa AZ 85211
president@azpredatorcallers.com

Phoenix Varmint Callers
Box 87153
Phoenix AZ 85080
PVCI@sportsmancommunity.com
or visit www.pvci.org

Southern Arizona Wildlife Callers
Box 78273
Tucson AZ 85703
membership@soazwildlifecallers,org

CALIFORNIA
California Predators Club
president@californiapredatorsclub.com

Riverside Varmint Callers
1desert@sbcglobal.net

Bakersfield Predator Hunters Club
www.californiavarmintcallers.
combakersfield.htm

High Desert Predator Callers
www.thevarmintcallers.com/meeting.htm

Predator Callers of Orange County
donjamroz@cox.net

IDAHO
Gem State Predator Hunters
ravenarrl@aol.com

KANSAS
Kansas Fur Harvesters Association
24685 Lyon Road, Chanute, KS 66720

NEBRASKA
Nebraska Fur Harvesters Association
Box 251
Valentine, NE 69201

NEVADA
Great Basin Predator Callers
Box 1686
Elko, NV 89803

NEW MEXICO
New Mexico Predator Callers Association
Danny Batastini
Box 296
Carrizoozo, NM 88301

NEW YORK
Bark At The Moon Coyote Club
www.bucksnorthuntingworld.com

NORTH DAKOTA
North Dakota Fur Hunters and Trappers
Association
tischrc@ndak.net

OKLAHOMA
First Oklahoma Trapper and Predator
Callers Association
83 Spring Creek Way
Locust Grove, OK 74352

PENNSYLVANIA
Pennsylvania Predator Hunters
Association
nitehunter1@comcast.net

Pennsylvania Trappers Association
billdee@epix.net

TEXAS
Texas Trappers and Fur Hunters
Association
Rt 2 Box1000
San Agustine, TX 75972

Texas Predator Posse
http://texaspredatorposse.ipbhost.com

WISCONSIN
shurkmans@hotmail.com or
www.wisconsinvarminters.com

NATIONAL
Coyote Club
coyotesforever@aol.com

Recommended reading:
Calling East & West
Gerry Blair
2635 Bamboo Drive
Lake Havasu City, AZ 86403

Trapper & Predator Caller Magazine
Krause Publications
700 East State Street
Iola, WI 54990

Varmint Hunter Magazine
P.O. Box 759,
Pierre, SD 57501

Predator Extreme
P.O. Box 698
Birmingham, AL 35201

Predator Hunting
700 East State Street
Iola WI 54990

Predator Calls: The First Fifty Years
Jay Nistetter
6115 Mescal Street
Glendale AZ 85304